BULLIED

In this examination of the ubiquitous practice of bullying among youth, compelling first-person stories vividly convey the lived experience of peer torment and how it impacted the lives of five diverse young women. Author Keith Berry's own autoethnographic narratives and analysis add important relational communication, methodological, and ethical dimensions to their accounts. The personal stories create an opening to understand how this form of physical and verbal violence shapes identities, relationships, communication, and the construction of meaning among a variety of youth. The layered narrative

- describes the practices constituting bullying and how youth work to cope with peer torment and its aftermath, largely focusing on identity construction and well-being;
- addresses contemporary cyberbullying as well as other forms of relational aggression in many social contexts across race, gender, and sexual orientations;
- is written in a compelling way to be accessible to students in communication, education, psychology, social welfare, and other fields.

Keith Berry is Associate Professor in the Department of Communication at the University of South Florida and past Chair of the National Communication Association's (NCA's) Ethnography Division. He currently serves as Co-Chair of NCA's Anti-Bullying Task Force.

WRITING LIVES
Ethnographic Narratives
Series Editors: Arthur P. Bochner and Carolyn Ellis
University of South Florida

Writing Lives: Ethnographic Narratives publishes narrative representations of qualitative research projects. The series editors seek manuscripts that blur the boundaries between humanities and social sciences. We encourage novel and evocative forms of expressing concrete lived experience, including autoethnographic, literary, poetic, artistic, visual, performative, critical, multi-voiced, conversational, and co-constructed representations. We are interested in ethnographic narratives that depict local stories; employ literary modes of scene setting, dialogue, character development, and unfolding action; and include the author's critical reflections on the research and writing process, such as research ethics, alternative modes of inquiry and representation, reflexivity, and evocative storytelling. Proposals and manuscripts should be directed to abochner@usf.edu or cellis@usf.edu.

Volumes in this series:

BULLIED

Tales of Torment, Identity, and Youth

Keith Berry

Routledge
Taylor & Francis Group

NEW YORK AND LONDON

First published 2016
by Routledge
711 Third Avenue, New York, NY 10017

and by Routledge
2 Park Square, Milton Park, Abingdon, Oxon, OX14 4RN

Routledge is an imprint of the Taylor & Francis Group, an informa business

Library of Congress Cataloging-in-Publication Data
A catalog record for this book has been requested

ISBN: 978-1-62958-250-4 (hbk)
ISBN: 978-1-62958-251-1 (pbk)
ISBN: 978-1-315-55874-5 (ebk)

Typeset in Bembo
by Saxon Graphics Ltd, Derby

CONTENTS

PREFACE

In this book I use autoethnography and personal narrative to examine youth bullying and identity from a relational communication perspective. In particular, I focus on symbolically negotiated interactions, relationships, and identities produced in bullying performances. The basis for this book is a research study I conducted in conjunction with the students enrolled in a past interpersonal communication course. There are four central elements to the book. I share stories of my experiences teaching the class and mentoring students concerning their bullying stories. I convey and analyze five compelling stories of bullying written by students, all of which come from women. Joining their stories are five "reflexive interludes," which include stories of bullying from my youth. Each interlude also includes a "methodological dilemma," where I explore practical questions that relate to conducting this research.

Examining bullying through the frameworks of story, relational communication, and identity entails engaging multifaceted, complex, and uncertain issues. Four main assumptions underlie the argument I make in this book:

1. Bullying is a real, disturbing, and menacing problem of contemporary lived experience.
2. Interactions, relationships, and the symbolic construction of meaning comprise the heart of the problem. Thus, bullying is a decidedly communicative phenomenon.
3. The harm perpetrated in bullying involves injury to victims' identity/ies, and often their bodies. Bullying questions, evaluates, and makes a spectacle out of the "others" who are its victims, which drives feelings of injury and dis-ease.
4. Autoethnography and personal narrative offer a unique and valuable entry point for understanding bullying from the perspective of those who experienced the problem first hand and lived to tell their stories.

The purpose of this book is to provide a reflexive space of personal stories that invites meaningful contact with how bullying informs and governs lives. By attending to candid and emotional detail, these stories speak to the ways in which bullying ensnarls and distresses victims. This book is at once a report on research and a collaborative class journey. The students and I revisit experiences, attempting to come to terms with how we understand bullying today, and how others might meaningfully engage the problem through story.

The activities of bullying and bullying research take many forms and speak to myriad conceptual issues. Stories from the five women, along with my own, that are featured in this book show the ways bullying occurs and the harm/s and overall impact of being bullied, particularly with respect to identity negotiation and well-being. The stories invite readers to experience the most salient issues informing our bullying, such as: being "different," depression, self-harming practices (e.g., cutting and suicidal ideation), rumination, avoidance, isolation, "toughness," change, friendship, trust, betrayal, queering identity, cyberbullying, family bullies, embodiment, and sexual assault. Given my autoethnographic and personal narrative approach, stories and storytelling also serve as a prominent issue or "character" in this book.

I see each of the five participants' stories as a distinct account. Each may also be read with, or in contrast to, the other stories, which include my own. My stories were not written to play off of, or respond to, their stories.

While the narrative- and communicative-based approaches in this book will uncover a wide range of conceptual issues, the aim and scope of the book keep me from examining particular issues at length. The present work is not intended, for instance, to study:

- "causes" of bullying, even though some of the stories point to and ask readers to think about such issues.
- biological factors that inform the constitution of identities within bullying, even though biology does matter.
- structural and institutional issues related to bullying, including choices made by school systems, administrators, teachers, and counselors to intervene in bullying, even though some of the stories and analyses give just cause for such inquiry.
- what bullying says about girls, young women, women in general, per se, even though this book is pervasively gendered and feminist.
- intergenerational issues concerning practices and effects of bullying, even though a look at participants' and my stories side by side will make available a portrait of youth similarly and differently negotiating bullying.

Each of the above issues merits future research.

This book unfolds with each chapter sharing one student's story. In the first half of the chapter, I convey her story. The second half of each chapter is my analysis of that story. In each analysis I explore: 1) the story in terms of communication and the constitution of identity and 2) specific thematic issues presented by the story. These analyses are organized around aspects of each participant's life that preceded their accounts of bullying, the experience of living amidst bullying, and the aftermath of bullying. A "reflexive interlude" and "methodological dilemma" appear after each of the five main chapters. I share the ways I work to reconcile the dilemmas in Chapter 7. I describe salient issues concerning the teaching and research processes that led to this book in the Appendix.

Working on this book has immersed me in a research and writing process unlike any other I have experienced. I have been in close contact with pain and suffering—others' and my own—staying close to these stories, and their attendant feelings, for two years. Consequently, I have kept certain people in heart and mind throughout the process as a means of sustenance and inspiration—people whose lives have been affected, and sometimes ended, by bullying, as well as those who have a vested interest in learning about bullying and creating meaningful change. I have written this book for and with:

- youth who have committed suicide as a result of being bullied. I wish you had received the care and the peace of mind you deserved, before it was too late. May your search for ways to feel better never be in vain.
- youth who continue to be bullied. You are likely hurting, and may doubt that who you are, just as you are, is good enough. I write convinced you are enough and you are loved.
- youth who bully others. You also have a story. Although I do not focus on bullies' stories in the book, you deserve to tell yours. We will learn your story.
- parents, friends and family, teachers, administrators, and other school staff. May these stories resonate with ones you have witnessed, draw to your attention to new ones, and enable you to respond well.
- people who were bullied in their youth. I hope these stories do justice to the experiences of bullying, and offer you unique ways to heal from the pain and suffering you endured.
- students, teachers, and researchers who study and educate on issues of bullying. I want this book to contribute to class discussions and debates, and future research on bullying, in ways that help you to help others understand and intervene well to bullying.

I dream that many people will read and benefit from this book, and will mindfully engage in dialogue on bullying. At the same time, if the book helps only one person, then all of the effort, and the challenges that have comprised my journey, will have been worth it.

Writing this book has most certainly helped me.

ACKNOWLEDGMENTS

Countless people have supported me as I wrote this book. Some folks have been especially influential.

Thanks Iman, Jessi, Jezebel, Lauren, and Ena for letting me engage with your stories. May they change lives. Thanks to all of the students in my two fall 2013 interpersonal communication classes at the University of South Florida whose powerful discussions and stories about bullying stressed to me the importance of this book.

Arthur P. Bochner and Carolyn Ellis, my editors in the Writing Lives series. Art, your editorial feedback and insight was precise, caring, and wise. Carolyn, your ideas, encouragement, and overall support throughout this process have been invaluable. The editorial support and friendship from both of you has been powerful and unending; the book would not be what it is today without your care.

Mitch Allen, Publisher, Left Coast Press, your support of this book has been instrumental. I cannot thank you enough.

To my faculty colleagues in the Department of Communication at the University of South Florida, and to the staff and graduate students in the Department. I am thrilled to be part of this community.

My best friends and fellow academics, Tony E. Adams and Jay Brower. Thanks for reviewing many pages of this book, and for your never-ending love—and our ongoing shtick and laughs. Tony, your leadership on behalf of autoethnography never ceases to amaze me. Thank you for always being that guy who's sitting at the Starbucks around the corner from the hospital, in case I needed you. There will never be another Charles and Sparks. Jay, DB, thanks for being family, and for your epic support as I climbed out of the "pits of hell" back in the day, even as others "tried to pull me back in." You personify friendship, and what it means to advocate justice in research, teaching, and as applied to people's everyday lives.

Catherine M. Gillotti ("Gilly" in Chapter 1), my "chosen sister," thanks for introducing me to the discipline of Communication and to conscientious communication research and teaching. You are amazing, as was your feedback on the book.

Chris Patti, for your mindful and timely review of key chapters of this book.

Thanks to my family for their ongoing support. Mom and Dad, your love and encouragement enabled me to survive and flourish throughout my life, and have made this book possible. I hope my work here makes you proud. Thanks to my sister, Kathleen, and her husband, Kevin, and my nieces Addison, Morgan, and Peyton Steffey. It has been amazing to have you along for the ride. Kathleen—you were right, I was up for this new and bigger challenge! Thanks also to my brother, Kevin, and my nephews Kyle, Alec, and Sean Berry, as well as to my brother's new and expanded family Margaret, Megan, Brenna, and Ginger ("Coco Channel") Murphy. Last but not least, thanks to other members of my extended family, especially my aunts, Ellen and Maureen Berry, and my uncle Bob Berry. My youth would not have been as good as it was without your love.

Lenore Langsdorf, my major professor back in graduate school, for teaching me phenomenology, a life-changing way of looking at lived experience, especially self-understanding and the constitution of subjectivity. That mentoring and friendship continues today to provide me (and others) with a fundamental ground through which to work, creating the conditions which make possible the ways in which I perform as teacher and researcher.

To Joan Kaywell, Director of the SCATTER program in the College of Education at the University of South Florida, and to the SCATTER students who served as research assistants in an earlier stage of this research project.

To Brent Notbohm and Cheri Henderson, your support from a distance, and sometimes from the bliss of your tent in the Boundary Waters, has meant the world to me. I miss you both. Thanks also to Dante Morelli, Stefan Pagnucci and family, and Matthew Arthur for your friendship.

To numerous other endeared colleagues and friends, from today and my youth: Lynette Adams, Stephanie Adams, Ahmet Atay, Jay Baglia, Sister Barabara Mary, Christie Beck, Derek Bolen, Robin Boylorn, Jane Campbell and Theresa Carilli, Lynda Carter (aka "Wonder Woman"), Devika Chawla, Ms. Cheek, Jennifer Christensen, Robin P. Clair, Wren Colker, Renee Cowan, John Marc Cuellar, Sara Amira de la Garza, Norman Denzin, Marcelo Diversi, Shirley Drew, Laura Ellingson, Deanna Fassett, Sandra Faulkner, Elissa Foster, Larry Frey, Wendy Gak, Patricia Geist-Martin, Craig Gingrich-Philbrook, Cindy Graham, Jonny Gray, Rachel Griffin, Rona T. Halualani, Karen Hand-Harper, Tina Harris, Ms. Hasz, Jason Held, Andrew Herrmann, Ms. Hinkey, Joyce Hocker, Nathan Hodges, Stacy Holman Jones, Kathy Hytten, Ms. Jaynes, Steve Johns, Christine Kiesinger, Bob Kriezek, Peggy, Floyd, Chad, and Kent Lareau, Patricia Levy, Kurt Lindemann, Mrs. Linderman, Karen Lovaas, Cathy Maes and the community at Pach's Place in Tampa, FL, Melanie Mills, Claudio Moreira,

Jerry Moreno, W. Benjamin Myers, Scott Myers, Cheryl Nicholas, Ephraim Nikoi, Blake Paxton, Sandy Pensoneau-Conway, Ronald J. Pelias, Benjamin Plante, Joni Plante, Christopher Poulos, Kevin Prendergast, David Purnell, Kourtney Quinn and my friends at City Dog in Tampa, Tasha Rennels, Matthew Rennels, Rhoda Robinson, Leslie Rossman, Simon Rousset, Desiree Rowe, Steve Ryder, Lynne Skrbina, Chad Skrbina, Robert Smith, Patty Sotirin, Lisa Spinazola, Alex Strait, Nathan Stucky, Shelby Swafford, Lisa Tillmann, Satoshi Toyosaki, Sarah J. Tracy, Jillian Tullis, Paaige Turner, Gina Warren Abston, and Jennifer Whalen.

To my late friend and collaborator, John T. Warren. I have thought about you across every step of writing this book. I miss you every day.

Last but certainly not least, to the many teachers and staff in my elementary, middle, and high school who worked tirelessly on the behalf of students, and likely for too little pay: you are amazing. Thank you for all that you have done. To the girls and women in my life, my platonic loves who allowed me to be more at peace and happy in your presence, I have not forgotten how special you are.

1

BULLYING

A Narrative Opening to a Relational Problem

"Here we go!" I say.

"Another new semester is here!" Gilly responds. "I'm excited to meet with my health communication class. What about you?"

"I'm teaching interpersonal communication and am really looking forward to working with these students. I have special plans for the semester."

On the first day of the fall semester, Gilly (Catherine Gillotti) and I, both professors of communication but at different universities, are engaging in our ritual call of support and enthusiasm.

"That's right. Remind me again about your plans?"

"The class takes an applied approach to studying interpersonal communication— as it relates to the societal problem of bullying. For their final project, I'm asking each student to use autoethnography and personal narrative to convey stories of bullying and identity from their youth. We'll be working on their stories throughout the semester."

"That sounds great ... and intense."

"Thanks. While I am excited, I am also nervous about how writing their stories will affect the students. The assignment asks them to confront their pasts in personal ways. Some will be revisiting a period that was difficult for them. They'll be reminded of the stigma and shame associated with bullying."

"I understand. Thankfully I had no issues with bullying, and never witnessed bullying. That might seem strange, but the nuns at my school kept students in line!" We both laugh.

"Maybe you were one of the lucky ones who escaped bullying."

"Maybe so."

"I'm trying to imagine the accounts they will write. Although some students may have written stories before for other courses, I suspect most will be new to using autoethnography. A lot goes into telling personal stories, especially those that explore pain and suffering."

"I know it will be a great class for the students *and* you. This theme relates to your book research, right?"

"Yes, once the semester is finished, I hope many of the students will participate in my research, which means letting me include their work in the book I'm going to write on bullying."

"I bet you'll receive a positive response. Sharing their stories gives students a chance to do something good with what they are learning."

"Thanks, I hope so. The class and this topic are personal for me. For some reason, bullying has this hold on me. It's powerful, but I don't yet know why. I'll be including stories of being bullied from my youth in the book too. I want to understand them better."

"I'm not surprised given your enthusiasm for reflexivity and autoethnography," she says.

"Yes! I have already been working on my stories, and exploring memories from thirty-five years ago has been a challenging experience."

"I am thrilled you are writing this book on bullying. I cannot think of many other problems more influential in young persons' interpersonal lives. It's become an epidemic."

"True. Just when I think more people have a good handle on the imprint bullying leaves on young bodies and beings, I hear of yet another person being harmed, or harming themselves, and sometimes gravely. It's…" I sigh.

"Senseless and terrible," Gilly finishes my thought.

"Nowadays when I learn of a new case of bullying, I feel this ache in the pit of my stomach."

"I do too. And a majority of the bullying that happens doesn't even make the news. There is much more of it going on than we know. I'm wondering, though, do you think people are now *more* aware of the harms of bullying?"

"Yes, but simply *knowing of* bullying, or how bad it is, isn't enough."

"Right, *knowing of* is important, but that doesn't mean people understand or stay tuned into the problem."

"Here's the pattern I see: the latest case of bullying appears on the Internet or television, or we hear stories at the office or when talking with friends or family. Then there's some impassioned response, which helps to create public attention. Only then it seems as though we quickly move on to the next big story of the moment. I worry that public and personal attention concerning bullying is fleeting and superficial. More people are aware *that* bullying is a problem, but they don't necessarily understand *how* it works, or the hold it has on participants, especially victims"

Gilly sighs. "Nope…"

"More people are listening, and want to do something meaningful in response to bullying. Frankly, I don't think there has ever been a more opportune time than now to examine bullying in up close and personal ways; to intimately understand how bullying occurs, how victims try to cope, and the aftermath of this violence."

"Sounds like you're ready for class … and the book!"

"You know, I struggled in my youth, but I lived to tell my story. Many others have struggled, and many are still hurting today. Their stories are waiting to be told. I want my book to offer a creative opening in the conversation about what bullying entails and what we can do about it. Stories offer such an opening." Gilly's cell reception becomes spotty, which tells me she is now at her campus and looking for a spot in the parking garage. "I *am* ready. Thank you for your support."

"Of course…"

"Wait, I just realized we talked so much about my stuff you haven't told me about what you'll be doing in health communication!"

"No worries, I'll tell you about it next time. Have a great first day."

"You, too."

First Encounter

"Interpersonal communication? Yes, you're in the correct room. Welcome, come on in!"

It is about ten minutes before class begins. I am standing near the door to my classroom, greeting students as they enter the room.

"Hello, find a seat…" I say to more students, all new faces to me, as they arrive to the room. I feel excited and a little nervous.

As the start of class draws closer, I feel the usual warm rush of adrenaline creep across my body, which is already heated from another scorching and humid Tampa day. I begin to make my way from the doorway to the left of the podium at the front middle of the room. I try to avoid the "center" of the classroom as much as possible when teaching, hoping to stress for students that class is about "us" and not only "me." I want them to know the dialogue we will create together and the unique lived experience and stories they bring to the classroom are our priority. Each time another student enters, I feel the heat and humidity from outside clash with the heavily air-conditioned climate inside, a battle that— similar to the relational issues concerning bullying the students and I will explore this semester—often leaves us tarrying back and forth between hot and cold, pain and comfort, sadness and happiness, and working to feel better about the space in between.

"Hello … come on in, it's cooler in here!" I am scanning the room, smiling as I make eye contact with many of the students. Many of them are doing the same. We are new to each other, at least for now. Noticing it is time to start, I grab my notes and begin.

"Okay … hello!" I say.

"Hello," several students mirror back to me.

"Welcome to SPC 3301—a course in which we'll study interpersonal communication, a way of communicating that significantly shapes *every* person's life. My name is Keith Berry. I teach in the Department of Communication. I'm happy to see you.

"This semester we'll be studying interpersonal communication by looking at the societal problem of bullying, specifically how bullying occurs among youth and the ways it affects their identity. By that I mean how youth understand themselves. I know the topic will provide us with lots of ways to learn about interpersonal communication and bullying." Noticing a young man suddenly raise his hand, I ask, "Yes?"

He responds, "Will we have to confess to the class how we were bullies in school?!" Several students chuckle.

"You will only share what you wish, but 'confess' is an intriguing word choice," I respond. "Your lived experience with bullying—however it is you relate to the problem—will matter greatly in this class." He leans back in his seat, as several other students nod their heads and perk up in response to my last statement.

"This is a dialogue-based course, so I'd like us to get right into an introductory discussion on how bullying has been a part of your interpersonal lives. Don't worry, we'll have plenty of time to review the syllabus later. Right now I'd like to take a brief survey."

One student jokingly asks, "Will this be on the test?"

I reply with a smile, and say, "For what it's worth, we will not have conventional exams in this course." Sighs of relief cut across the room. "However, you'll have plenty to do, and I suspect your final project will test you." A couple students snicker.

"Prompt one: Raise your hand if you ever saw someone be bullied in your youth."

"What do you consider youth?" a student in the front row asks.

"That's an important question. While there are many ways to define the term, we'll use it to mean school-aged youth—persons who are in elementary, middle, or high school." The student seems to accept the distinction, so I continue. "So, who saw someone bullied?"

All twenty-five students in the class raise their hands right away. I ask them to simply notice and remember this unanimous response.

"Next, raise your hand if *you* were bullied." All but two students raise their hands.

Several students begin to comment to me, or others around them. "Oh it was nasty." "Terrible stuff how badly I was bullied." I again note for them the abundance of hands.

"Finally, raise your hand if you've ever bullied someone else." I see at least half of the students raise their hands. Some nervously giggle, others look deadly serious.

"Thanks for participating. So, what do these responses make you think about bullying?"

A young man sitting at the front of the room and wearing a USF Athletics t-shirt quickly raises his hand and says, "I'm not surprised. Bullying was *all over the place* in my high school."

I reply, "Good, and thanks for getting us started. Others?"

A woman in the front row raises her hand and leans forward. "I agree with him, the results did not surprise me. I'm Ena, by the way. Bullying was widespread in my school. I also want to mention the survey makes me feel sad … and angry."

"Are you comfortable talking about why it makes you feel this way?"

"Yes, I am comfortable. It's horrible so many people in here have been bullied, and everyone in here has seen bullying. Too many young people don't realize, or care about, how much communication affects others' lives. Bullying changes people. I've lived it—it's bad!"

Another male student appears to be frustrated and jumps into the discussion. "Look, while I agree with a lot of these ideas, I also believe bullying is a lot more complicated than a lot of people think. People generalize that *bullies are horrible people* and *victims are innocent little angels*. But are all of them? Are they always? I am concerned with how we try to stop bullying. I don't feel many people are willing to be honest about the problem."

"I appreciate these perspectives, and, yes, bullying is a complicated, not simple, issue."

"Can I say something?" another young woman asks.

"Of course, let's hear from you and then we'll take a quick break."

"I agree that sometimes people oversimplify bullying. I also believe bullying is terribly violent and kids underestimate the power of communication, like Ena was saying. Oh, I'm Lauren."

"Hi, Lauren, I'm glad you're here. Keep going."

"While I believe most adults might be doing the best they can, I don't think they realize how their responses are sometimes unhelpful. Young people hear things like 'Honey, don't pay attention to people who don't treat you well' and 'Baby, you know who you are, others don't matter' or the infamous 'Sticks and stones may break my bones, but words will never hurt me.' I know they're trying to help, but here's the truth from my youth: It was often hard not to pay attention to others, unless I wanted to be a social recluse; I *was* often confident about myself back then, but that didn't stop me from being bullied badly; and finally, while that nursery rhyme is cute, I am living proof that 'words' can hurt even the strongest kid!"

Several students applaud Lauren, while two men and a woman in front snap their fingers in the air in support of her. "Well put," I say.

"Was that too much?" Lauren asks.

"No, it was *perfect*, as was this first discussion. I love the passion in here. Something tells me we're in store for a powerful class."

Lots of smiles fill students' faces.

"Keep these ideas in mind during break. First, I cannot imagine having a thorough conversation about bullying without taking seriously how communication relates to the problem. Second, I often hear others talk about how difficult it is to respond to bullying in helpful ways. I have struggled in the past with deciding what I can do to help. Yet, preparing for this class has led me to the answer: we will write personal narratives, or stories, about what bullying was like in our youth."

"Personal stories about our bullying, eh?" a student sitting right in front of me says with a smile. Others look intrigued, and some are wide eyed and seem surprised or nervous.

"Yes, your final project will ask you to write a personal narrative in which you convey the bullying you experienced in your youth. This gives you something to think about: what's *your* story of bullying?! I'll share more about the project in a couple weeks. Have a nice break."

As I walk to get a soda from the machine, I think about our introductory discussion. Listening to students share details of their experiences puts a more human perspective on bullying; it makes the problem feel more "real," and the need for a response more urgent. I am also impressed by the specificity with which students spoke, and no less on the first night of class after summer break. Bullying clearly matters to many of them.

Bullying Imperatives

Multiple aspects of lived experience inform the stories people live, tell, and understand. This makes discerning "beginnings" complex. To attempt to identify only one beginning seems futile (Schrag, 2003). "All starting points are contingent. One could always choose another beginning" (Schrag, 1997, p. 2). In this way, my book is inspired by at least four starting points. I call these "bullying imperatives": *relational being, statistical, cultural and everyday interaction,* and *mindful.*[1] These imperatives are interrelated and open-ended factors that make the work of this book necessary and important.

Relational Being

The *relational being* imperative speaks to the formative relationship between communication, identity, and bullying. Communication is "a symbolic process whereby reality is produced, maintained, repaired, and transformed" (Carey, 1989, p. 17); that is, it is a social practice in which persons form, continue or perpetuate, mend, and make anew human understanding. The relational communication perspective I use in the book assumes communication is a jointly accomplished process in which people use linguistic and embodied messages to symbolically co-create, share, use, and interpret meaning within interaction and relationships. In this sense, communicators are interdependent beings who exhibit and draw upon their mutual influence. As Gergen (2009) writes, "We are always already emerging from relationship; we cannot step out of relationship; even in our most private moments we are never alone" (p. xv). In addition, relational communication is situated; persons make sense of interaction and relationships within the distinct cultural contexts in which they are enacted and made meaningful. Such relating is always performed from the unique vantage point of persons' lived experience, and in ways that are both apparent and dwell outside conversation partners' immediate awareness. In these ways, deploying a relational communication perspective entails looking at communication in complex and dynamic ways, keeping ourselves open to learn from its messiness, even as we stand in awe of the systematic and resourceful ways it makes life with others possible.

This imperative assumes that communication and identity are intrinsically connected. The concept of "identity" is subject to considerable debate. At the very least, identity generally refers to who persons understand themselves and others to be. I take a relational approach to understanding bullying and youth identity. This perspective works in contrast to biological and traditionally psychological positions that treat identity as an "internal" phenomenon— something that dwells "inside" persons and awaits expression (see Carbaugh, 1996). While biology is relevant to identity, I focus mainly on how identity is made *within* interaction, or *between* conversation partners. I look at the ways identity is constructed (i.e., made, formed, created) within interactions and relationships. The messages enacted, including *how* they are enacted (linguistically and embodied, just for starters), create the cultural conditions that make possible, and often necessary, distinct performances of selves. The use of "selves" here is important, insofar as identity is rarely, if ever, a matter of "one self." Instead, persons are a culmination of multiple, and sometimes contradictory, selves, whether or not we are aware of this multiplicity. Further, the social construction of identity is a *constitutive process* (Berry 2005; Gergen, 2009, 1991; Heidegger, 1996/1953; Langsdorf, 2002; Schrag, 2003, 1997), meaning persons emerge from the lived experience of communication making and remaking themselves over time. Thus, identities are conditioned by the twists and turns of communication, and subject to change.[2]

A closer inspection of identity suggests that who people are or become is often a matter not only of formation but also of *negotiation* (see Bardhan & Orbe, 2012; Berry, 2007, 2012; Durham, 2014; Jackson, 2002). Identity negotiation is a contested process informed, and sometimes governed, by social constraints (e.g., issues of power). People negotiate who they are with and for others. As a result, how one performs is rarely, if ever, only a matter of who one might understand her/himself to be. Instead it often entails being others' versions of ourselves.

Dwelling at the heart of identity negotiation is the desire to avoid stigma. Stigmatized persons embody disfavored or "spoiled" identities; who they are, or who others understand them to be, falls outside of what the "mainstream" of society deems "normal" and "acceptable" (Goffman, 1963). Persons "ascribe" or assign such identities to others, yet, one may also "avow," or assign them to oneself. More specifically, to stigmatize is to "other" persons, judging and shaming, and thereby isolating and excluding them as a result of their "objectionable" qualities. Stigmatizing creates conditions of duress under which "others" must cope in the face of persecution. How does one cope in the face of such persecution? Persons might attempt to "pass," or hide their unfavorable identity (Yoshino, 2007). For instance, many Lesbian, Gay, and Bisexual (LGB) persons have often attempted to conceal their sexual orientation by passing as heterosexual. Persons may also attempt to "cover" the disfavored characteristic they embody to avoid or lessen persecution. They perform in ways that attempt to make the stigmatized qualities less visible or less obtrusive to/for others. Here LGB are "out" to others, yet they downplay that aspect of their identity, for instance, by not being affectionate in public.

In short, the intrinsic and dynamic connection between relating and being necessitates the careful examination of bullying and identity. Youth who participate in bullying are immersed in communicative performances that negotiate the ways in which they come to understand their and others' identities, and their worlds generally. Bullying is more than "just words" or "innocent" play, as folk wisdom sometimes suggests. It is a process through which one's personhood is symbolically shaped and reshaped. For victims this process often entails heartbreaking consequences.

Statistical Imperative

The *statistical imperative* speaks to the prevalence of bullying. Consider, for example:

- Approximately 30% of youth males and females, especially those in sixth through eighth grade, report moderate or frequent participation in bullying, whether as a bully (13%), victim (11%), or both (6%) (Nansel, Overpeck, Pilla, Ruan, Simons-Morton, & Scheidt, 2001; see also Juvonen, Graham, & Schuster, 2003).
- In contrast, Glover, Gough, Johnson and Cartwright (2010) contend that between 40% and 80% of youth are bullied, and 7% of youth experience more severe bullying.
- One in three American school children between grades 6 through 10 are affected by bullying (The Bully Project, 2013). Six out of ten teenagers say they witness bullying in school once a day. Some 64% of children who were bullied did not report it. Some 10% of students who drop out of school do so as a result of repeated bullying. Nearly 70% of students think schools respond poorly to bullying.

Also, the level of schooling matters. For instance, Neiman and Hill (2011) has demonstrated the rate of violent incidents as well as the rate of reported bullying was higher in middle school than in primary schools or high schools. Generally, while statistics on the frequency of bullying vary from study to study, research suggests that in different ways, and to varying degrees, bullying continues to be a significant problem with which youth must contend.

The prevalence of bullying has also been studied specifically in terms of hostile school climates. Kosciw, Greytak, Palmer, and Boesen's (2014) national study with the Gay, Lesbian and Straight Education Network (GLSEN) surveyed 7,898 students between the ages of 13 and 21, and demonstrated additional and distressing conditions of bullying. For instance:

- Some 56% of students felt unsafe at school due to sexual orientation, and 38% due to their gender expression, leading many to miss school and skip attending school events and activities.
- A total of 71% of LGBT (Lesbian, Gay, Bisexual, Transgender) students heard "gay" used in a derogatory way, and 65% heard other homophobic comments.
- Some 56% experienced negative remarks about gender expression.
- Over 51% had received homophobic and negative remarks about gender expression from teachers and school staff.
- While 74% of students were verbally harassed in the past year due to their sexual orientation, and 55% because of their gender expression, a significant number of students were physically harassed in the last year (74% LGBT, 36% due to gender expression).
- A majority of students reported experiencing policies that discriminated against them based on sexual orientation and gender expression (e.g., being disciplined for public displays of affection by LGBT, attending a school dance with someone of the same sex).
- Climate issues significantly affect transgendered students: 42% reported being prevented from using their preferred names; 59% were made to use only the bathroom or locker room of their legal sex; and 32% were prevented from "inappropriate" clothes based on their legal sex.

These are a few of the worrisome results from the acclaimed GLSEN study. They emphasize the destructive climates in which some youth, especially those who perform difference in terms of gender and sexuality, must survive. Keep in mind that the statistics presented above relate only to *reported* bullying. Youth who have been harmed, or who harm others, but who have not come forward out of fear of judgment, shame, or punishment are not included in these data.

Though bullying continues to rattle young people's lives, some popular press writers and researchers have questioned bullying's prevalence, for instance, by speaking to "myths of bullying" (Cloud, 2012) and cyberbullying as an "overrated phenomenon" (Olweus, 2012). The U.S. Department of Education's National Center for Education Statistics recently reported the first decline in rates of bullying in the United States since they began documenting the problem in 2005 (Sisaye, 2015), suggesting that anti-bullying efforts may be having a positive effect. Still, bullying is a significant problem that needs our attention, if progress is to continue.

Cultural and Everyday Interaction Imperative

The *cultural and everyday interaction imperative* concerns the ways in which bullying is a cultural issue intrinsically related to everyday life.[3] Bullying is a prominent issue across a diverse number of contexts in U.S. cultural life today. At the time of this writing, a Google search of the term "bullying" resulted in approximately 78 million entries; 77 million entries for "school bullying"; and 43 million entries for "bullying youth." Yet, such attention to the issue is not surprising. Whether appearing as "breaking news" on cable news stations, "liked" and "shared" posts on Facebook or Twitter, or anti-bullying policies instituted by schools, stories of the latest tragic episode of bullying, its consequences, and calls to reform the problem, abound. Significant events in popular culture and politics have further helped to bring the problem into public consciousness, including: anti-bullying organizations (The Bully Project); television programs (*GLEE*) and documentaries (*Bully*); internationally popular musical performers (Lady Gaga's "Monster Ball Tour" and her "Born this Way Foundation"); and first of their kind governmental events and initiatives (President Obama's "White House Conference on Bullying Prevention" in 2011 and the web resource Stopbullying.gov).

In a recent "Ted Talk," former White House intern Monica Lewinsky described the brutal cyberbullying—perhaps the first of its kind—through which she suffered after her sexual encounters with then President Clinton went public. Almost 5 million people have viewed Lewinsky's talk in the first five months after its posting. Also, the cultural emphasis on bullying is made more evident by the overwhelming public response to the June 2012 bullying of "Karen (Klein) the Bus Monitor." Klein, a senior citizen, was viciously bullied by student passengers on a school bus in which she served as a monitor. After a video of her attack went viral, she received over $700,000 in donations to a "vacation fund" set up for her. Klein has since established the "Karen Klein Anti-Bullying Association." These are just a scant few of the numerous and prominent examples of the cultural experience of bullying to date.

Bullying has become an issue *du jour* in everyday social interaction. I am speaking here of everyday relating *about* bullying. When I tell others I am writing a book on bullying, they tell me how they feel the book is "so important" or "much needed." Then they typically disclose (without prompting by me) their bullying experiences. Their responses frequently come in the form of specific, detailed, and personal stories. For instance, a friend tells me, "I still remember what it felt like to be bullied today, and I am 60 years old!" My teenage nephew Alec tells me, "I think girls have the hardest time … their bullying is vicious!" My six-year-old niece Addison tells me she hopes that her new eye glasses, the first pair she's ever worn, don't get her bullied when she wears them to school for the first time. "The scars I have from being bullied…" a woman begins to share with me at a Weight Watchers meeting, but she cannot finish because she gets too emotional. "Keith, this is vital work you're doing here, people can be so cruel," a massage therapist, Alex, tells me repeatedly as we discuss my book research across numerous sessions. He follows up with me, checking on the progress of my book each session. Other people will send me links or newspaper clippings with stories about recent bullying, and poems and quotations about youth enduring and surviving bullying. Indeed, more people are talking with me about bullying, and I suspect I am not alone in this experience.

This book responds to the considerable cultural and interpersonal attention given to bullying. Many persons are engaged with the problem, and many identify with its participants, especially the victims. However, knowing-of does not necessarily mean the problem is understood and felt. I often observe people talking about bullying by using unsupported generalizations,[4] such as about who bullies and victims are and what bullying entails, and by "psychologizing," or attempting to read the minds and hearts of youth who participate in bullying. Seeking to avoid simplistic reasoning, I write this book to situate and further ground this complicated problem. I want readers to live with the stories and storytellers (Frank, 1995)—to experience them not just with thought but with their bodies and feelings.

Mindful Imperative

A final factor motivates me to write this book: the *mindful imperative*. Rooted in Buddhism (see Batchelor, 1997; Chödrön, 2002; Hanh, 1975) and psychology (see Langer, 1989), mindfulness is a diversely understood concept and practice relevant to communication (Burgoon, Berger, & Waldron, 2000). It is also a constructive way to demonstrate competence in interpersonal conflict (Canary, Lakey, & Sillars, 2013) and intercultural communication (Wiseman, 2002). I use the term to mean the deliberate practice of being aware and living in the present moment, being open and paying attention to all the present moment offers, and doing so with gentleness, patience, non-judgment, and even humor. Being mindful involves working to openly engage with pain and suffering as universal conditions of human life, and relating to people as fundamentally interconnected beings who shape each other's lives in loving and harmful ways. In these ways, communicating with mindfulness helps people not only perform competently, but also more ethically and compassionately.[5]

The mindful imperative informs the book because of the harm associated with bullying. I assume all persons deserve to live in peace and free from violence. Bullying undermines and works against this ethic. Youth who bully others perform in ways that oppress victims physically and psychologically (Farrington, 1993), and, in so doing, as I detail below, take advantage of and hurt vulnerable beings. These ways of relating would seem to be the antithesis of mindfulness, as they effectively advocate cruelty and violence, rather than care, respect, and love, or at the very least a tolerance for one's conversation partners. Thus, this book is important because communication merits more mindful, not mindless, ways of relating.[6]

Going Deeper Three Weeks Later

The students and I have spent the last three weeks focusing on foundations of interpersonal communication and identity, such as the axioms of communication,[7] and the role of culture, perception, and identity in communication. In today's class, I want the students to think about bullying more reflexively.

"Today I'd like us to dig deeper into bullying," I say to the class. "I want to learn more about how *you* understand and talk about the problem."

"You want to hear our voices, you're saying?" a young woman says from the back of the room. Her name is Iman, and I've been impressed by the things she's had to say so far in class discussions.

"Exactly, I believe your voices are among the most important resources for combatting bullying today."

"Okay, I get it."

"So, it's time to continue our bullying dialogue. I am about to read you two prompts. After hearing each, I want you to write down the one word or short phrase that fills in the blank, or represents what you believe about bullying. We'll go around the room and share all our responses; therefore, you want to choose something you're willing to share. Pick words or phrases that are personal and powerful to you. Here's the twist, you can give your answer, but you cannot explain it. After we share all of them, I'll invite you to ask each other questions."

The students move to get out their notebooks and pens. Some of them look intrigued and excited. Others moan and grumble about having to write things down. They'd probably rather answer them on their technological devices.

"Okay, let's begin," I say, giving the prompts from memory. "'The best word I'd use to describe bullies is (blank).'" I give them a minute to think and write. "Here's the second: 'Bullying is (blank).'"

I give them a minute or two to think again, and repeat the prompt for a few students. I'm eager to see how they see bullies and bullying.

"So, let's hear your responses to the first prompt, bullies are…" As we go around the room the students share interesting responses, including "wrong," "jealous," "hurt," "angry," "afraid," "desperate," "beneficial," "frightening," and "worthy of a beating." The responses centering on hurt and anger are repeated numerous times.

"I've got to know why bullies are 'worthy of a beating'," a student says out loud, to which another student echoes, "Yeah, what's that mean?"

"I said that," a male student responds from the back of the room, "because that's how I was brought up. No one should treat other people in hurtful ways. But if you do, then you need to get taken down. I know it sounds bad, but I'm being honest." Students nod in agreement.

"Thank you for your honesty," I say. "One of the curious things about what you've shared is that the perspective advocates a violent response to violence." He nods confidently in agreement. We spend a few minutes talking about the power of family and cultural values. Not wanting to spend too much time on any one response, I move us on to another point.

"Many of you gave responses that suggest bullies are people who are working through difficult emotional issues of their own. Who wants to speak to that perspective and help us understand what you mean?"

"I will," a woman said from the front row. "People hurt others because they themselves are hurt."

"I agree—they're scared of something, or maybe of someone," another student shares.

"That's an interesting perspective, and it's also a popular one in regard to bullying. Although I'm sure these psychological issues and questions will come up again, I want to focus more on *how* bullying happens within communication and the ways in which people who bully and have been bullied talk about the impact it has had on their lives."

A woman sitting upfront leans over to the woman sitting to her right and asks, "So, will you tell us why you believe bullies are 'frightening'? It's Jessi, right?"

"Yes, there was a time when I bullied others." As Jessi speaks there's a tremble to her voice, and her neck is turning red. "I no longer bully people, but I was a bully once and probably hurt people. Sometimes I am scared to think about who I was and how I treated other people."

"Thanks for your honesty," I say. "I'm glad you can now look at that time differently. It's important for us to hear your story." She smiles as she starts to doodle in her notebook.

"I sense from your contributions that many of you have strong and personal opinions about bullying. Now let's move on to the next prompt."

"Can we wait for just one second?" a student interrupts, as she turns to a person sitting by the door. "I've got to ask you: how are bullies *beneficial* to communication?"

The woman replies, "Because if it hadn't been for being bullied, I wouldn't be who I am today. The hurt I endured taught me so much about myself." Students fill the classroom with "ahhhss" and "oooohs."

"Excellent point," I add. "Bullying is often talked about in negative ways, and I understand that, because it is so often harmful. Is that all that bullying is, though? Are there other layers of meaning to bullying? Please keep these questions in mind."

Bullying Research Literature: An Expansive Tale

Bullying is a prominent area of research across a diverse number of academic disciplines, with interests spanning from children's early educational experiences to adult lives. For instance, a growing number of scholars have studied workplace bullying (see, for instance, Lutgen-Sandvik, Tracy, & Alberts, 2007). In this book, I focus solely on bullying among youth as an international phenomenon (Jimerson, Swearer, & Espelage, 2010; Smith, Morita, Junger-Tas, Olweus, Catalano, & Slee,

1999) that has been studied for the past four decades (Hymel & Swearer, 2015). Also commonly referred to as "peer bullying" or "school bullying," scholars have examined this problem to learn how bullying is performed, its consequences on youths' lives, and the ways researchers and practitioners can intervene.

In the following review, I explore the history of bullying research, definitional issues, bullying's participants, bullying's impact, cyberbullying, and connections between sexual violence, homophobia, and bullying. I then describe how this book joins this scholarly tale.

Waves of Bullying Inquiry

The earliest public interest in bullying often is linked to the 1857 novel by Thomas Hughes, *Tom Brown's Schooldays* (Rigby, 2001). The novel portrayed violence committed against English children at Rugby School, garnering significant public concern for the welfare of young people. More recently, research on bullying has emerged through a series of "waves" (Smith, 2011). The first wave (1970s–1988) is associated with Heinemann's (1972) observational research on group aggression, or "mobbing," among peers at school in Sweden. Olweus's (1973) research on mobbing in Scandinavian schools extended Heinemann's work by examining how bullying occurs, its frequency, and its long-term impact (see Olweus, 1993). He argued that aggression is not just performed in groups but didactically, or interpersonally. In the second wave (1988–mid-1990s), researchers began to establish a program of inquiry on bullying that extended beyond Scandinavia to include researchers in England, Canada, and the United States. The conceptualization of "bullying" evolved to include indirect and relational bullying (see below). Between the 1990s and 2004, the third wave, there was an established international program of bullying research, which entailed increased studies and publications on bullying with scholars from many countries. This wave focused more deeply on the nature of bullying, such as who participated in the aggression and how. The fourth wave (2004–present) has shown a significant departure from the historical focus on face-to-face (hereafter: traditional) bullying and a heightened interest in cyberbullying.

Defining and Locating Bullying

Although the concept of "bullying" resists a single definition (Harachi, Catalano, & Hawkins, 1999), researchers commonly agree upon certain attributes. Olweus (2010) writes, "A student is being bullied or victimized when he or she is exposed, repeatedly and over time, to negative actions on the part of one or more other students" (p. 11). Bullying is understood to be intentional behavior and involves a power imbalance (real or perceived) between aggressors and victims; that is, bullies often deliberately seek to cause harm to their victims, and "the student who is exposed to negative actions has difficulty defending himself or herself" (p. 11; see also Alsaker & Gutzwiller-Helfenfinger, 2010). Victims may be unable to defend themselves physically, emotionally, and/or relationally (e.g., youth who bully others may have the advantage of larger social groups or cliques, or be dominant physically). Olweus further writes:

> *We say a student is being bullied when another student, or several other students,* say mean and hurtful things or make fun of him or her or call him or her mean and hurtful names; completely ignore or exclude him or her from their group of friends or leave him or her out of things on purpose; hit, kick, push, shove around, or lock him or her inside a room; tell lies or spread false rumors about him or her or send mean notes and try to make other students dislike him or her; and other hurtful things like that.
>
> (p. 12, emphasis in original)

When these conditions persist over time, they constitute bullying. Recurring teasing performed "in a mean and hurtful way" (p. 12) is bullying; yet, this teasing, however unpleasant, is not bullying when performed playfully, or when there is no power imbalance (Nansel et al., 2001).[8]

At least two additional factors shape bullying. First, bullying is common in groups where youth cannot likely escape (e.g., school, locker rooms) (Kosciw et al., 2014; Smith et al., 1999). Second, bullying often takes place in locations and at times where and when adult oversight is less likely (Farrington, 1993). Thus, bullying is "unseen" and more "successful," since victims' ability to defend themselves or be assisted by adults is impaired.

The above conceptualization points to the ways in which bullying informs and is informed by interaction and relationships (see O'Connell, Pepler, & Craig, 1999; Pörhölä, Karhunen, & Rainivaara, 2006). Bullying cannot happen without communicators and communication. Youth who participate in bullying are engaged with a *systematic process*, or interrelated phases that may or may not have identifiable starting or ending points. They use and interpret *messages*, direct (physical or verbal attacks) and indirect (gossip, social exclusion), that have a primary audience (its victims), and often secondary *audiences* (peers of the bullies or victims). The *conversation partners* have an existing interpersonal relationship (friendships, school peers), though sometimes they are strangers. Further, bullying entails *goals* (harm, defend, attack, cope, humiliate, self-protection) that participants may or may not acknowledge, discuss, or understand and are shaped by social constraints, such as power dynamics. Bullying is a mode of interpersonal conflict (Wilmot & Hocker, 2011), in general, and a subset of aggression, in particular (Smorti, Menesini, & Smith, 2003).

Indeed, bullying is a relational problem involving communicators who perform different identities and roles. Research generally operates with the categories of "bullies" (aggressors), "victims" (the victimized), "bully-victims" (victims who bully others as a consequence of being bullied), and "bystanders" (witnesses to the bullying, e.g., friends, teachers, family). Bystanders who speak up against bullying are identified in some anti-bullying campaigns as "upstanders" (The Bully Project, 2015). Salmivalli, Lagerspetz, Björkqvist, Österman, and Kaukiainen (1996) conceptualizes bullying as a dynamic *group* process that entails specific roles. They add the categories of "reinforcer" (of the bully), "assistant" (of the bully), and "defender" (of the victim). Salmivalli (1999) contends peer groups contribute to both bullying and remedying the problem.[9]

Who Bullies and Is Bullied

Researchers have investigated bullying in terms of *age* and *sex/gender* of its participants. Youth who bully are commonly seven to sixteen years old. While their bullying tends to decrease as they get older, these youth often find themselves in trouble with the law later as adults (Olweus, 1993). In terms of sex/gender, research has shown differences between how bullying is performed by boys and girls. Boys have been known to participate in bullying more frequently than girls (Olweus, 1993) and are often understood to be more aggressive (Coie & Dodge, 1998). However, over the last two decades research has focused on the ways in which girls perform bullying through a distinct mode of aggression commonly referred to as "relational aggression." As Crick and Bigbee (1998) write:

> Relational aggression harms others through hurtful manipulation of their peer relationships or friendships (e.g., retaliating against a peer by purposefully excluding her from one's social group), whereas overt aggression harms others through physical damage or the threat of such damage (e.g., threatening to beat up a peer unless she complies with a request).
>
> (p. 337)

Relational aggression, also known as "indirect victimization," involves telling lies or spreading rumors about victims and/or bullying through the withdrawal of friendships (Crick & Bigbee, 1998). Often considered a subtler form of bullying, relational aggression can be more difficult to identify. Nevertheless, this mode of bullying is typically enacted by girls, and comprises a majority of the bullying experienced by girls today.

While there is no one type of youth who is bullied or who bullies others, research has suggested shared characteristics for both of these social locations (Cook, Williams, Guerra, Kim, & Sadek, 2010). On the one hand, youth who are bullied are prone to suffer from personal issues (including anxiety and insecurity), are frequently guarded, sensitive, and soft spoken, are susceptible to deep emotional responses and withdrawal, have low self-esteem and self-images, and may feel isolated at school and be without significant friends (Olweus, 1993). These young people often became the targets of bullying because they do not conform to "mainstream" norms and values (Davis, Randall, Ambrose, & Orand, 2015; Thornberg & Knutsen, 2011).

On the other hand, youth who bully others tend to exhibit dominant and assertive personalities, have a positive orientation to violence, are known for being impulsive and needing to dominate others, have little empathy with their victims, and, contrary to popular belief, show little anxiety and insecurity, and do not lack self-esteem (Olweus, 1993). In addition, they are inclined to victimize others out of a need for dominance and power, because they enjoy others' harm and suffering, and/or because they want things from the victims (money, cigarettes, beer, etc.). Research further suggests they victimize others as a result of inner flaws and to improve their social status (Thornberg & Knutsen, 2011).

Why youth bully or are bullied remains something of a mystery (Rivers & Duncan, 2013). This book focuses primarily on how bullying happens and its impact. I approach any issues concerning the "whys" of bullying in terms of conditions that make bullying possible and consequential. As I mentioned in the Preface, I am more interested in "risk factors" than in making claims about "causes" (Orpinas & Horne, 2006).

The Personal Imprint of Bullying

Scholars have brought significant attention to a range of damaging consequences that result from bullying. Bullying has been shown to undercut victims' capacity to trust others (Cowie, 2013), enhance feelings of loneliness and/or social isolation or marginalization (Cowie, 2013; Glover et al., 2010; Juvonen et al., 2003), and undermine victims' senses of self (Glover et al., 2010). Youth who are bullied are more prone to depression (Bond, Carlin, Thomas, Rubin, & Patton, 2001; Hawker & Boulton, 2000; Juvonen et al., 2003) and they suffer increased risks of self-harm, such as suicide and suicidal ideation (Bowes, Wolke, Joinson, Tanya Lareya, & Lewis, 2014; Rigby & Slee, 1999). Lines (2007) observed that "53% of participants reported having contemplated self-harm as a result of bullying at school, while 40% said they had attempted at least once, and 30% more than once" (p. 187). Also, bully-victims are prone to high levels of school and relationship problems (Juvonen et al., 2003).

Bullying also takes a toll on bullies. Youth who bully are prone to more serious violent behavior (Nansel et al., 2001), issues with mental health (Kumpulainen & Räsänen, 2000), school problems, conduct disorders, and substance use (Hinduja & Patchin, 2008), as well as issues with the law later in life (Olweus, 1993). Since bullying is rooted in aggression and the use of power over others, there is a greater chance bullies will not be able to develop prosocial relational skills that assist in developing healthy relationships (Cowie, 2013).

Bullying can also impact its observers. For instance, research has shown that witnessing bullying can create risks to mental health, which, incidentally, can exceed the level of risks associated with being bullied or bullying someone, whether or not these observers were victims of bullying themselves (Rivers, Poteat, Noret, & Ashurst, 2009). Additionally, Jeffrey, Miller, and Linn's (2001) research with bystanders, or "secondary victims" (p. 143), suggests that exposure to bullying leads youth to feel indifferent toward bullying, less sympathetic to the distress of victims, and less inclined to intercede on behalf of victims.

In sum, scholars have studied the nature of traditional bullying and its impact on youth with impressive depth and breadth. Bullying is a multifaceted process that intimately implicates its participants and creates conditions for significant and sometimes long-lasting (inter)personal harm. However, when bullying takes place using technology, "the new friend of the bully" (Rivers, 2011, pp. 15–16), the problem becomes more complicated. Understanding the practices and consequences of cyberbullying is especially relevant in today's socially networked, digitally involved world.

Cyberbullying

Over the past two decades, cyberbullying has precipitated a massive shift in bullying and bullying research. Also known as "cyber aggression" and "electronic aggression," cyberbullying is defined as "an aggressive, intentional act carried out by a group or individual, *using electronic forms of contact*, repeatedly and over time against a victim who cannot easily defend him or herself" (Smith, Mahdavi, Carvalho, Fisher, Russell, & Tippett, 2008, p. 376, emphasis in original). Research suggests approximately 24% of students have been cyberbullied and approximately 16% have cyberbullied others at some period in their life (Patchin & Hinduja, 2013). Youth who cyberbully are individuals or groups who use various technologies including social media, emails, websites, chatrooms, SMS/text messages, instant messaging, and mobile phones. In cyberbullying, "a bully can send or post hurtful, humiliating, or even threatening messages and content to a victim, to third parties, or to a public forum or environment that many other online participants visit" (Patchin & Hinduja, 2012, p. viii). This increased visibility, combined with an increased ability for the anonymity of bullies, makes it more difficult for victims to defend themselves and increases chances for humiliation and embarrassment. These characteristics set cyberbullying apart from traditional bullying. For instance, cyberbullying creates physical distance between aggressors and victims, can happen at any time during the day and week (as opposed to only, say, at school), allows cyberbullies to easily spread and duplicate derogatory materials from one location to another, and creates a context in which there is less chance for interpersonal feedback that might reveal to aggressors the impact of her/his actions (see Schultze-Krumbholz & Scheithauer, 2015).

Similar to traditional bullying, cyberbullying is informed by sex/gender. Both boys and girls participate in cyberbullying (Grigg, 2010). However, their role in this bullying tends to differ based on sex and gender. For instance, on the one hand, research suggests girls are more prone to being victims of cyberbullying

(Hinduja & Patchin, 2008). On the other hand, boys are more likely than girls to be aggressors in this "new playground" for bullying (Li, 2007).

Several additional factors inform cyberbullying. Similar to traditional bullying, cyberbullying often stems from relationship issues at school, such as ending of relationships, resentment, and prejudice (Hinduja & Patchin, 2008; Hoff & Mitchell, 2009), and cyberbullies are often traditional bullies (Smith et al., 2008). In addition, research has shown youth who cyberbully often target victims anonymously, enabling them to be/come someone different than who they are outside of this contexts, and, thus, face a decreased chance for sanctions for their behavior (Grigg, 2010; Kowalski & Limber, 2007; Schultze-Krumbholz & Scheithauer, 2015). Although anonymous, aggressors frequently share with others that they have cyberbullied (Slonje, Smith, & Frisén, 2012). In addition, cyberbullying has been known to involve the use of highly sexual and sexually aggressive content (Grigg, 2010), adding to the emotional vulnerability of bullying. Also, victims often do not disclose their experiences with being cyberbullied. Consequently, parents and other adults often don't know (soon enough) about the violence their children are enduring (Li, 2007; Slonje & Smith, 2008).

Clearly cyberbullying creates conditions for significant and personal impact on victims. Cyber victims are prone to emotional and psychological distress, including depression, anxiety, and paranoia (Schultze-Krumbholz & Scheithauer, 2015). Research also suggests cyberbullying can lead to extreme outcomes, such as suicidal ideation (Hinduja & Patchin, 2010). Victims of cyberbullying, as well as traditional bullying, are more likely to experience suicidal ideation and attempt suicide than those who are not bullied (Hinduja & Patchin, 2010). Research suggests victims are more prone to these outcomes than aggressors. Additionally, youth who cyberbully may feel less remorse than traditional bullies (Slonje et al., 2012).

In review, cyberbullying exhibits many of the defining characteristics of traditional bullying (e.g., deliberate enactment of harm, repeated over time, power imbalance), yet is also unique (e.g., enacted electronically, the possibility of anonymous bullying, increased visibility of victims). Cyberbullying also presents distinct challenges in this more recent wave of bullying research. Indeed, the onset of newer and more sophisticated communication technologies presents novel ways of bullying and, thus, new complexities to reconcile. While technology is connecting people quicker than ever before, it is also creating the conditions for disconnection and harm (Turkle, 2011).

Bullying, Homophobia, and Sexual Violence

Recently scholars have brought into focus "homophobic bullying" (Rivers, 2011). This aggression involves "negative beliefs, attitudes, stereotypes, and behaviors toward gays and lesbians or those perceived to be gay and lesbian

(Espelage & Low, 2013, p. 172), and typically involves name calling and being ridiculed in front of others. Research has demonstrated that homophobic bullying permeates educational institutions and can lead youth to suffer from low self-esteem (Rivers, 2011). Such aggression is often interrelated to sex/gender and race. Pascoe's (2007) research suggests adolescent boys who berate other boys by calling them "faggots" may also, and perhaps more so, be attacking boys for being less "masculine." Forrow (2012) explores issues of social support, or a lack thereof, for gay/queer black men, and the ways in which prominent anti-bullying movements, such as the "It Gets Better" campaign, fail to represent how "[f]or young people who are experiencing poverty, racism, HIV, bad public schools, or violence within their homes, it may not 'just get better' by virtue of getting older" (p. 148). And Kimmel and Mahler (2003) contend that twenty-eight random school shootings that have plagued American schools since 1982 entailed youth committing horrific violence as a result of being viciously bullied and related threats to their manhood. In short, while many lesbian, gay, bisexual, queer, and transgender youth continue to face bullying in schools (Kosciw et al., 2014), there remains a paucity of research that integrates the areas of bullying and homophobia (Espelage & Low, 2013).

Researchers have recently begun to explore bullying as it relates to sexual violence and sexual harassment. Espelage and Low (2013) write, "The problem of sexual violence and harassment in adolescent interpersonal relationships is approaching pandemic proportions in part because the violence and the harassment have been normalized" (p. 169). Felix and Green (2010) propose: "sexual harassment is similar to bullying, in that it is a form of aggressive behavior in a relationship characterized by an imbalance of power; however the content of the interaction is sexualized or related to the gender of the victim" (p. 177).[10] Although sexual violence and harassment are significant problems for youth today, few studies consider bullying from this perspective (Espelage & Low, 2013).

This book and the stories that follow add to the research on bullying in several unique ways. Much of the studies on bullying are rooted in traditional, quantitative research. While beneficial in bringing attention to bullying and an essential foundation for understanding this subject, these studies are unable to offer the rich potential and complex, experiential nuances of a narrative and autoethnographic inquiry that centralizes personal stories of bullying and bullied beings and that investigates the problem in situated and intimate ways. In other words, bullying research to date lacks detailed and particular focus on the emotional lived experience of bullying that stories can provide. Also, while researchers commonly talk about bullying in social terms, and communication researchers have studied bullying,[11] we need more inquiry conducted from a communication perspective, particularly a relational communication approach that explores interaction, relationships, and identity negotiation. Further, research on peer bullying almost exclusively focuses on its relationship to school. While school is a potent and vital site, peer bullying occurs in multiple contexts (e.g., family) and its aggressors are not solely peers (Berry & Adams, 2016; Monks & Coyne, 2011). Overall, relational stories on bullying offer overdue and innovative ways for expanding what we know about and how we might respond to this problem.

Why Autoethnographic Stories

Autoethnography is a systematic approach to research and writing that uses evocative storytelling to examine lived experience in culture (Adams, Holman Jones, & Ellis, 2015; Bochner & Ellis, 2016; Holman Jones, Adams, & Ellis, 2013). Autoethnographers seek to convey self-conscious accounts, those that "matter, to us, to those we wrote about, and to those who found our pages," and that help render researchers "connected, relationally, politically" (Pelias, 2015). The approach involves autobiographical practices of introspection (Ellis, 1991) and reflexivity (see Berry, 2013b; Ellis, 2004), which is to say the inquiry is deeply and unapologetically rooted in the unique vantage point of researchers' lived experience with others.[12] Also, autoethnography advocates diversity in concept and form, and being a welcoming space in which researchers are able to examine issues often overlooked or ignored by traditional research, especially stories of hardship, pain, and suffering (Ellis & Bochner, 2000; Ellis, Adams, & Bochner, 2011). In these ways, autoethnography enables scholars to creatively enact one-of-a-kind research that emphasizes openness and vulnerability from both autoethnographers and readers.

Autoethnographic research is well suited to applied research (Berry, 2006; Berry & Patti, 2015), such as bullying. Autoethnographers examine pressing cultural and relational problems to help make lives better. Relatedly, scholars who use critical autoethnography use the approach to outwardly critique taken-for-granted cultural issues and realities (see Boylorn & Orbe, 2013; Madison, 2005), and/or to "queer" or trouble normative positions on culture (Holman Jones & Adams, 2010).[13] This potential to create cultural change is possible because of the communicative nature of autoethnographic stories (Berry & Patti, 2015). As Bochner (2012) writes:

> The truths of autoethnography exist between storyteller and story listener; they dwell in the listeners' or readers' engagement with the writers' struggle with adversity, the heartbreaking feelings of stigma and marginalization, the resistance to the authority to canonical discourses, the therapeutic desire to face up to the challenges of life and to emerge with greater self-knowledge, the opposition to the repression of the body, the difficulty of finding words to make bodily dysfunction meaningful, the desire for self-expression, and the urge to speak to and assist a community of fellow sufferers.
>
> (p. 161, emphasis in original; see also Bochner, 2014)

When crafted well, stories are rhetorical and speak to and rely on others. As Frank (1995) writes, "Storytelling is *for* an other just as much as it is for oneself. In the reciprocity that is storytelling, the teller offers herself as guide to the other's self-formation" (p. 17, emphasis in original).

Autoethnography also creates the conditions for researchers or storytellers to experience personal change in doing their work. Scholars have explored this potential in different ways, including epiphanies (Denzin, 1988), healing (DeSalvo, 1999), catharsis (Ellis, 2004), revision (Ellis, 2009), and personal transformation (Crawford, 1996). Much of my research has focused on the transformation of subjectivity, or the making and remaking of researchers' selves, that is possible from the identity negotiation that is inherent to autoethnography (Berry, 2013b). Across these different ways of talking about this issue dwells a shared and promising position: the introspective and reflexive practices of autoethnography make possible novel performances of selves for researchers, which were unavailable prior to this reflexive labor.

Stories have been used by researchers and popular press authors to explore and educate others about bullying. Scholarly work has focused on various contexts, including "coming out" (Adams, 2011; Fox, 2014; Rivers, 2011), intergenerational and multicultural conflict (Arroyo & Gómez, 2013), and masculinity in sports (Anderson, 2013). In addition, Bosacki, Marini, and Dane's (2006) arts-based approach shows the ways in which drawings and narratives, as well as open-ended questions, can uncover children's views of bullying, and Salas (2005) has advocated staged embodiment in theater as a constructive response to bullying.[14] Further, research has suggested stories and novels can help children learn about bullying and bullying prevention (see, for example, Cowie & Jennifer, 2008; Teglasi & Rothman, 2001).

Popular press books increasingly use personal stories to draw attention to bullying. For instance, Kurzweil's (2015) memoir takes readers across the world as he tries to find Cesar Augustus, his childhood bully. Solomon (2012) explores bullying as it is related to crime and the infamous school shootings at Columbine by Eric Harris and Dylan Klebold, which resulted from their being badly bullied at school. Columbine is widely identified as having launched public attention in the United States about bullying. In addition, books on bullying published for youth and/or parent audiences use short stories (see, for example, Kilpatrick, 2012; Savage & Miller, 2011). While researchers and popular writers have helped build what we know about bullying, no full-length book that uses autoethnography and personal narratives of victims to examine bullying and identity negotiation has yet to be published.[15]

Rigby, Smith, and Pepler (2004) write, "There is now a clear moral imperative on teachers and educators to act to reduce bullying in schools; and a moral imperative on researchers to try to give the most informed advice in this respect" (p. 1). Autoethnography and personal narrative create an instructive opening through which to pursue this goal. The stories I convey and examine in this book come from persons who have battled bullying "on the ground," and, thus, maintain intimate contact with the problem. The "informed advice" they provide is specific, detailed, intimate, and relevant to multiple audiences, including but not limited to researchers, teachers, educators, and parents. This book demonstrates how the process of rendering and sharing their stories creates a powerful opening for storytellers to better understand the violence they lived through and the persons they have become as a result.

Responding to bullying involves mindfully getting closer to, and staying with, the problem, even if being close to the pain and suffering is scary and unwanted. As the current state of research on bullying suggests, we need more research that shows how bullying happens and the ways it implicates and changes bodies and beings, reflexive stories that "grab us by the collar and demand that we listen and that we feel" (Bochner & Ellis, 2006, p. 120), and help us to understand the complicated social realities of bullying. As the bullying stories that follow show, autoethnography and personal narrative rise to this challenge.

Time to Write

"It's time to talk more about your bullying stories." I pass a stack of handouts to a student sitting upfront, who takes one and begins to circulate them around the room. It is the fourth week of the semester, time for the students to begin writing.

"As you know, for your final project each of you will formally write a story that shows how bullying was relevant to your life in your youth, and how it impacted you and others. Given our class emphasis is on interpersonal communication and identity, be sure to incorporate the interactions and relationships that comprised the bullying, and how bullying informed who the characters in your story understood themselves and others to be. Your story should be between eight and twelve typed, double spaced pages in length. No outside sources are required or encouraged. Overall, while each story will be unique, the goal for all of us is to write in creative, descriptive, and evocative ways. Let me pause here to answer any questions you may have."

"No outside research?" a student asks.

"No, instead simply focus on telling your story. Your experience is the research."

"I can handle that," a student from the back chimes. Several students chuckle.

"Can you talk a bit more about what you say here about *standpoint?*" asks Jezebel, a student who has quickly become a leader in the class.

"Sure, look at it this way: your standpoint is the social location, or the role you played, in bullying. Were you the bully? Victim? Bystander? Or? It is not uncommon to perform multiple standpoints, and your story can focus on more than one, if relevant to your experience." Jezebel nods her head, letting me know she gets it, and that I can move on with the discussion.

Another student asks, "On the handout you say it's okay to include middle school, but to focus mainly on high school. What if bullying was more intense during middle school?"

I pause for a second to collect my thoughts. "Interesting—when I first designed the project I figured high school was more prevalent. Was bullying more prevalent for you in middle school?" Several students nod in agreement, some emphatically.

"Okay, then it is important to tell those stories. Go for it."

"Can we focus on bullying in the family?" asks another student.

"If you had significant bullying in your family in your youth, then tell that story. After all, this is about your lived experience. What other questions do you have?"

No one speaks up. Some of the students look shell-shocked. They see that this assignment is going to require hard work and a unique type of intimacy. Many also look excited, like they are already working on stories in their heads.

"Okay, before we move on, I also want you to know I've loved the strong positions you've shared so far about bullying. Many of you have asked me privately how you can help with anti-bullying efforts. Here's one thing you can do—use your story as an inquiry into your own experience and understanding of bullying and as a chance to help others better understand bullying.

"Many of you have told me you believe you have a meaningful story to tell, but are nervous. Some of you are excited but still really nervous. That's okay and not surprising. I have a quotation for you that I'd like you to consider. Yoshino (2007) writes:

> We all have a story we must repeat until we get it right, a story whose conveniences must be corrected and whose simplifications must be seen through before we are done with it, or it is done with us. Each time I tell my story, I am released, yet there is also the story from which I yearn to be released.
>
> (p. 50)

His writing makes me think of your bullying stories. What if your energy, excitement, or nerves are, at least in part, signs that telling your story, and telling it in your own terms, is that important? What if it means that you want to make sure you 'get it right', to experience the feeling of being 'released'. It's possible, right?

"Here's what I know for sure: we'll work on telling your stories together. The process will be challenging, but I know you're up for the challenge. I cannot wait to see what you create!"

By the end of the semester most of the students produced stories that showed impressive accounts of life-shaping bullying. They used candid and evocative prose to demonstrate the harm and trauma enacted through bullying and the relevance of communication and identity to such violence. Overall, the quality of their stories confirmed my desire to dig deeper and to formally conduct this study.[16]

The remainder of this book is dedicated to conveying and exploring the five standout stories of bullying from the class, and my stories. The student accounts were written by Iman, Jessi, Jezebel, Lauren, and Ena and are presented in this order.[17] In the book's conclusion (Chapter 7), I return to stories from the classroom, on the last day of class for the semester. I also further examine issues of communication, identity negotiation, and the use of autoethnography and personal narrative in bullying research.

Notes

1 The idea of linking "imperatives" to bullying research is, in part, inspired from Martin and Nakayama's (2004) discussion of a number of imperatives that inform the study of intercultural communication.

2 In this book when I use "performance," "performing," etc. when describing and analyzing identity, I am invoking the constitutive sense of the term. Thus, performing self or identity is a creative, linguistic, and embodied process in which people collaborate in making and remaking identity/ies. I do not use performance in the common theatrical sense of the term, to mean "pretending" or "faking."

3 The cultural and social interaction levels of bullying are mutually informing social practices, meaning the cultural (macro) practices can be said to inform the interaction (micro) practices, and vice versa (see Schatzki, Knorr-Cetina, & Von Savigny, 2001).

4 Everyday discourse in media and relational communication about bullying often takes the form of "bloodless abstractions" (Schrag, 1994, p. 122), or positions that fail to take into account the lived experience of bullying, and the ways in which lived experience creates the most fertile ground on which to understand and respond to bullying.

5 Chödrön's (2002) orientation to mindfulness teaches that the practice of being compassionate is an act deserved of the other *and* one's self. Her perspective captured and stayed in my heart from the moment I first read it years ago, and has guided the ways in which I've worked with the students' and my stories. I included this passage from her on the course syllabus:

> When we talk of compassion, we usually mean working with those less fortunate than ourselves. Because we have better opportunities, a good education, and good health, we should be compassionate toward those poor people who don't have any of that. However, in working with the teachings on how to awaken compassion and in trying to help others, we might come to realize that compassionate action involves working with ourselves as much as working with others. Compassionate action is a practice, one of the most advanced. There's nothing more advanced than relating with others. There's nothing more advanced than communication—compassionate communication. (pp. 101–102)

6 I believe these imperatives should resonate in useful ways with readers rooted in various disciplinary, cultural, and personal backgrounds. Yet, I include them here also knowing all stories are "partial, partisan, and problematic" (Goodall, 2000, p. 55). That is, stories are incomplete, a matter of perspective, and subject to dialogue and debate. These reasons for studying bullying as I do in this book make the most sense to me at this time in our history with bullying and bullying research. Others will and should offer their reasons, perhaps some that are different than mine. I welcome them into this important conversation.

7 See Watzlawick, Bavelas, and Jackson (1967, pp. 48–51). For additional germinal research informing a relational communication perspective, see Blumer (1986), Mead (1934), and Brown and Levinson (1987).

8 The "intentional" aspect is emphasized across most bullying research, and this book also engages with bullying as a deliberate act. That said, relational communication, which bullying is, involves planned and unplanned expression and the making/sharing/interpreting/using of meaning. This calls us to stay open to acts of aggression

that may have been unconscious or unplanned, but nonetheless persons (especially victims) live these actions as bullying.

"Repeatedly, and over time" is also commonly used and endorsed as part of the definition of bullying. Most stories in the book demonstrate the harmful force of this repetition. However, I also assume aggression need not recur over a specific time period in order for persons to feel as though they have been bullied.

Further, the distinction between bullying and teasing based on whether or not an act is "playful" is noteworthy. Relationally, I assume both parties within an interaction that is potentially problematic need to agree on this condition/distinction. All stories in the book are rooted in the belief that none of the aggression shown is playful teasing.

9 Definitions are vital and risky. They provide pathways that help researchers to conduct meaningful inquiry, yet applying definitions also entails the risk of imposing terms and meanings onto others, who may for reasons of cultural distinctiveness or variation, not agree with this application. In this book I tentatively use the common term and definition of "bullying," because my five participants and I identify with and use the term.

10 For a helpful description of differences between sexual harassment and bullying, see Felix and Green (2010).

11 See, for example, Bishop Mills and Carwile (2009), Kowalski (2011), and Vogl-Bauer (2014).

12 "Reflexivity" is a contested theoretical concept and methodological practice (see Berry & Clair, 2011) that dwells firmly at the foundation of research that uses autoethnography. Amid the different definitions and approaches, sometimes the simplest view things say the most. Pelias (2004) captures reflexivity best when he writes: "It lives for maybe" (p. 12).

13 My use of "outwardly" is important. Many of the assumptions and practices that guide autoethnography locate the approach as "critical," whether or not autoethnographies explicitly reference the term.

14 See Leavy (2015) for a helpful account of the promise and vitality of arts-based research.

15 While this book is unique in these ways, it is also important to note that my book would not be possible in the same ways without Ellis (2004) and Fassett and Warren (2007).

16 The Appendix includes key aspects of my teaching and research process informing the book, as well as a diverse range of organizations that provide anti-bullying resources.

17 All names in the students' stories are pseudonyms chosen by the students.

2

CUTTING THROUGH

The Journey and Horror of Finding Self-Love

IMAN

Iman's vividly recalls her first day of psychotherapy:

> I remember it was one of the many days I took off from school because I did not feel well. My mother and I entered a depressing looking room—no bright color to be found, just a thousand shades of brown scattered across the room. A dark and gloomy room as this one was, you would have thought my mother and I had entered a funeral home.

The cold conditions of the therapist's office set the tone for what would continue to be a scary experience. Within the first few minutes of her session the therapist reported that "Iman suffers from severe depression," a statement that left Iman gasping for air and sobbing for the rest of the session: "I was terrified. Being told I had some illness was incredibly scary, because at the time I had no idea why I felt so bad." Iman, an African-American woman, only remembers going to one or two sessions; the attempt at getting help was counterproductive and did more harm than good.[1] In her story Iman names the therapist "Trigger," because she introduced the label of "severely depressed" that launched a period of depression that would last for more than seven years. Trigger made it necessary for Iman to try to understand why she felt sad and confused.

Hearing the diagnosis for the first time, Iman started experimenting with ways of coping:

> This was the day, the first day my body discovered how to completely shut down and "block out." My form of blocking out was quite simple: I blocked

out all outside noises that were around me. When I blocked out it was as if I was trapped in a glass room and could see everything around me, but could not say anything. When I blocked out I muted everything and anything that was around me, and I muted my thoughts as well. The actual words that Trigger spoke aren't important to my story. For after a short couple of minutes during the session I began to block out everything she said. After she told me how I would have to go to a special high school because I had already missed too much class because of my depression, I zoned out completely from her voice. This was my first day of blocking out, and unfortunately it was not my last.

Iman left Trigger's office that day without an understanding of her "problem." She only knew she felt different. Those feelings led her to doubt and dislike herself and to not know who she was. What a precarious position: living with a dis-ease that she felt but could not describe.

At first, blocking out seemed to work. Iman writes, "For once I didn't have to think so much. You would think that relaxing and not thinking about things would be good. But this wasn't my experience." Instead of beginning to understand what troubled her, and to feel more comfortable and at peace, she began a month-long period during which she lived in deep seclusion: "I distanced myself from the world, my family and friends, I even isolated myself from my own thoughts." Trigger had intensified the uncertainty and sadness Iman felt. How could she feel better? Why would others not leave her alone?

While Iman remembers middle school as a time of innocence, when kids seemed to learn and play in ways that showed their acceptance of each other, high school was entirely different. As she writes, "High school is when I started putting all the pieces together, when my nightmare began." Because she always had lived in white communities, most of Iman's friends were white. However, the lack of non-white friends mattered very little to her: "As a child you see no color, color was never an issue to me … until I grew up and finally opened my eyes in high school to see the judgmental, color-obsessed world we live in." Entering high school she immersed herself into frightening new situations and relationships in which race mattered.

Much of Iman's youth was comprised of others ridiculing and harassing her based on her being a black person. In the process of writing her story, she realized these pressures were part of her life well before high school:

> Most of my harassment started in middle school. I was constantly picked on for being a "white black girl," or for talking "too white." When the ridiculing first started I thought nothing of it, until it got to the point where I started noticing that kids of my own race started rejecting me. I was been picked on for not being "black enough." I wasn't accepted in the black community, and I never felt welcomed among a group of black people. Being bullied by kids of my own race, a group of people with whom I should share commonalties and bonds, was so confusing.

Her blackness, or insufficient blackness, presented challenges with which she needed to grapple. Others demanded that she be someone she was not, even though she did not demand the same from them. She felt bullied for simply trying to be herself, a demand which baffled Iman and prompted her to reflect on the consequences of how people handle bullying:

> Going through the stages of a youth, bullying is swept under the rug. As a child you don't want to admit people don't like you. You grow up thinking everyone should get along. Not being accepted by an overwhelming number of people made me feel uncomfortable in a way where I developed several different insecurities, which isn't surprising, because I have doubted myself throughout much of my life.

She lived in doubt and discomfort, vulnerable to and around others, and feeling defenseless, because she never learned how to defend herself.

Iman's problems were confounded by the ridicule she felt from members of her own family. As she writes, "My family is close and dear to my heart. But they played a significant role in my bullying and depression. I would get bullied at school, then I would come home and hear some of the same comments." Much of the ridicule occurred at larger family events, socials or "get-togethers." These gatherings were supposed to be about family members coming together and eating, laughing, bonding, and catching up on the good things that were going on in their lives. Yet she regularly felt like a target of harassment, bullying that typically went unnoticed by everyone except Iman:

> I don't think there was anything "off limits" when it came to bullying me. From my voice, to the clothes I wore, to the majority of white friends I had. I was constantly being picked on for just being who I was. They were always on me, commenting on what I did or didn't wear, or what I did or didn't do, and always in ways that critiqued me for "acting white." It felt like they wanted to make sure I didn't forget I was black.

Understandably these family experiences created a lasting imprint: "Throughout my whole life, I have never been comfortable in my own skin." Their bullying made Iman feel like she was doing something wrong and that she did not belong. Also, she was rarely comfortable when communicating with others, only when she was alone and could not be critiqued.

She was at ease, however, when she spent time with close friends, whom she could guarantee would accept her. Iman continued to seek support, yet found little help from others, including from those people who were supposed to love her as she was, fully and unconditionally—her family.

One of Iman's most powerful memories of bullying occurred in gym class. It involved a young girl, who also identified as African American, whom she named

"Destroyer," because that is what she constantly tried to do: ruin gym class and "destroy" Iman. She describes her bully as someone who "wasn't the best looking girl." Iman was tall but slim, while Destroyer was shorter and bigger physically, that is, "big boned." These differences mattered to her in regards to the bullying: "Often bigger people feel more comfortable picking on someone smaller than them, so I guess that's why she picked me as her victim." She could not fathom any deeper reasons for Destroyer's bullying. In fact, she did not know much about her bully, only that they shared the same locker room for gym, that all students needed to report to the locker room before and after gym, and that in that space Destroyer could strike at any time.

It was imperative for Iman to remain vigilant to her surroundings, which became an indelible part of her memory of high school:

> I can recall everyday walking into the locker room hoping she didn't approach me or say anything to me; I constantly had to look over my shoulder to make sure I was aware of my surroundings. I needed to be aware and ready for her.

This vigilance was her means of protecting herself from more confrontations with Destroyer:

> She always stared at, and taunted, me, trying to get me to react. I always tried to not give in. As I did with others, I tried my normal trick of blocking out, shutting out the constant name calling and harassment. I tried to ignore Destroyer, but it didn't always work. Across the locker room she would constantly shout at me these off-the-wall things, like asking me "Why am I so 'bougie'?" or "Why do I talk like a 'white girl'?" The intimidation was constant. There wasn't a day that went by when she had something nice to say to me. She yelled at me whatever she could think of that was negative and hurtful.

Such prolonged intimidation and the hyper-vigilance it required to stay okay shocked Iman: "Every day in that locker room felt surreal to me. It's as if I wasn't there. I was in such disbelief that in my junior year of high school someone would have the audacity to bully and harass me." She thought bullying was something that happened to younger people, not to juniors and seniors, and certainly not to her.

Destroyer became a regular part of Iman's life for the next several months, and the taunts and name calling escalated. Iman kept up her regular practice of "taking it," ignoring her, and just letting Destroyer continue to bully her. However, eventually a different action was needed, because her current way of coping wasn't helping. She had reached her limit:

> One day I remember we were all walking in … or maybe it was out … of the locker room and Destroyer opened her mouth and started her usual

heckling. I lost it. I was fed up with her harassing me. I don't even remember what I said. I just remember lashing out at her, and finally speaking up for myself. I also remember the shocked look on her face. As usual Destroyer has some slick bullshit to say, and before she could begin her usual five-minute long rant, I stopped her in her tracks, and yelled in the most sarcastic tone possible, "Do you feel better about yourself now!?" She continued to rant on how I was a "white girl," and how I "wasn't about to do anything physical against her." She was right, I wasn't about to do anything to her, unless she threw the first punch.

The argument broke up before the situation could escalate any further, or before the gym teachers would overhear the altercation and need to intervene. It was over for now. Yet her dis-ease continued to grow, and she was incredulous over her bully's choices:

> You would think after I finally stood up for myself she would have backed down, but she didn't! A couple of days later Destroyer and her friends came to my lacrosse practice and threatened me. I remember it well. My team and I were doing simple passing drills, when all of a sudden I saw them appear. My team practiced in an open area, so often you would see people pass by the field. Yet it was sort of creepy to see her show up at my practice. The fact that she knew I played lacrosse and where I practiced was beyond weird and even stalker-ish. I was in total shock; I did nothing to deserve such negative attention from this girl!

Iman does not remember how the bullying ended, however, she mentions that eventually she had taken enough, and reported Destroyer to the school administration. Soon after, the bullying and Destroyer faded out of her life.

Although Destroyer had released Iman from her hold, her fears of being threatened everyday of her life continued. Bullying had harmed her life in lasting ways. She felt a need to brace herself for harm that occurred, and reoccurred, at school and home. She longed to find ways to live happily as a "severely depressed person" whose identity was so displeasing to everyone but her.

Iman recalls the last year or so of high school being especially bad. She became isolated, only hanging out with a few people. She continued to cope by blocking out all that was negative, quickly dismissing any painful ideas or memories from her thinking the moment they appeared:

> I had no time for nonsense, and I forever had a guard up against people, never letting in anyone. This is how I coped, for holding on to all of the pain I have endured in my life was honestly too heavy for me to hold. Holding on to all of the pain is what kept my depression alive and deepening. Blocking out the majority of ridiculing and bullying was my coping method.

Bullying had changed her, and she was aware of the change: "Not fitting in, I turned into a cold person in high school." Iman was different, and because of the ineffectiveness of the blocking out strategy, she lacked ways to feel better. Consequently, she continued to lack the support and feelings of comfort she so desperately needed and deserved. Her journey to feel better continued.

With no answers in sight, Iman turned to serious thoughts of harming herself:

> There were nights when I'd be in my room, lying on my bed, and in a constant battle with myself on why my life was worth living. No one accepted me. No one liked me, and because of that, I didn't like myself. Even if people around me were smiling, they still would make a negative comment about my not fitting in, or not being good enough. The negative energy I endured over the years made me hate myself. I was never good enough for anything, or anyone, so my life didn't seem to me to be of much value. There were several nights when I cried myself to sleep with thoughts of committing suicide. I cried because I knew I shouldn't want to take my life, yet the thoughts constantly running through my mind told me suicide was the only option. I could not identify my purpose for living. Was I here for others' comical relief?

Iman considered suicide for several years. They began after she was diagnosed by Trigger, and she links them directly to her having been bullied. She would debate with herself over whether or not to end her life. Yet, that option never won the debate; to her, suicide was too extreme of an option. Still, she needed a way to ease her pain, and decided to resort to other drastic measures.

Iman remembers her first night of "cutting" clearly and with precise detail:

> I looked all over the house for the right blade, and I knew right where to look: my dad works on houses, and so he had all sorts of blades and construction tools. While looking for his tools I stumbled across a very sharp paper opener, or maybe it was an envelope opener—I'm not sure the correct terminology for the device. The blade was sharp, and so after that night, the opener became my tool of relief. My stomach was the spot on my body where I chose to cut. I wanted an area where no one could see any marks, unless I showed them.

The painful act of cutting allowed her to feel better:

> It's weird to think that self-inflicting pain can be an escape from the pain that you endure from your problems. However, it was my escape. Though I was hurting myself I didn't feel the pain. I felt the pain, but the pain felt like a release. Each time I cut myself I felt like the pain of hating myself took a pause for those brief moments.

Through those cuts she felt a sense of peace that alleviated—even if temporarily—her suffering. She felt a relief that was unavailable in her blocking out tactic. In her cutting, she felt a reprieve that worked for her when she was depressed:

> I think most people would say, "So what you were picked on, but you knew who you were ... you were black!" Others might say, "People will say all types of things, you just have to be strong." Though both of the statements might be true, they don't come close to explaining my pain. Every day I would walk around hating myself, not understanding why I wasn't good enough for certain people, wondering why people would constantly judge me, wondering why they were quick to put me down the moment they met me. It might be easy for those same people to say, "be yourself ... be confident, and don't listen to them," but when *even your own family* picks at these same painful wounds, and those actions are allowed to continue, what is a young person to think? I was a child who hated myself, and saw no other way out.

She lived exhaustingly as a child who needed to figure out adult-like problems. She felt lost and unhappy: "Children are supposed to be filled with joy and curiosity about the world. Instead I was in fear of the world."

Iman does not remember a specific moment when she started to feel better. By the time she turned eighteen, family members mostly had stopped bullying her. When they did subject her to criticism, she stopped taking it. "I was older and stronger," she writes. "When they'd dish it out, I simply began to talk back to their bullying, and eventually it stopped." In addition, the undercover cutting practices continued nightly, for a month. When it no longer was helping, she just stopped: "I was at a point where I was like, 'okay, Iman, you either are going to die, or you need to find a purpose.'" Thankfully she opted for the latter, and soon began to live in healthier ways. She has no more thoughts of suicide, and has not returned to cutting since that period in her youth.

Iman ends her story by reflecting on how bullying changed her, and the ways she now understands herself, and others:

> Bullying is a disgusting disease and should never be put on others, because it can inflict so much pain and hardship. I know this pain because I felt it. Yet, although for the majority of my youth I was depressed, and even might have lost myself, I can now say that these experiences have shaped me for the better. I have learned so much over the years from having to battle with such difficulties that I have recently turned all the negatives to positives. Being so hurt and alone as a kid has helped teach me how to love and care. I often look back at the times when I've been hurt, and think about how I would never wish that pain on another individual. My pain has helped me be a more compassionate person. It's kind of ironic when

you think about it; feeling so hurt and alone over the years has given me a hunger for love and affection. I have become a giving and compassionate person, and I seek people in my life who are similar in those ways.

Part of this shift is also a new way of taking care of, and loving, herself:

The fourteen-year-old, self-hating "white black girl" is now twenty-two years old, and a woman of self-love. After high school I entered college and started experiencing things for myself. I still suffer from constant thinking. But I don't let other voices be as influential in how I think and feel as they were before. My first year of college, I went to an all-black university, and there I found self-love. Attending a majority black college helped me embrace my black identity. For once I wasn't a minority, I was a majority. I am a *black* woman who has found her identity despite all the years in which I felt like it was being withheld from me. I am a *survior* of the bullying epidemic.

Today Iman is still searching for her purpose in life, unsure, and at times, anxious about what her next steps in life will be. Having lived through much struggle, she seeks a way to bring her warm presence to her professional life, in order to make a difference. She says she is pursuing this purpose in ways that feel more authentic in regards to who she is, as the proud black woman who has survived much, and now lives boldly, as herself.

ANALYZING IMAN'S STORY

Iman's story hinges on the poignant disclosure, "I have never been comfortable in my own skin." Her statement points to the harsh ways others bullied her within the dual contexts of family and school, and the visceral ways she experienced their violence.

Troubling "Trigger"

"Iman suffers from severe depression"—a statement made by her therapist that dwells at the heart of her story. Iman was only fourteen years old when "Trigger" diagnosed her as severely depressed, a condition she knew nothing about, except that it was bad. Although meant to be a way to begin treatment, Iman's diagnosis appeared only to exasperate her problems. She now had to deal with a new identity. At this point Iman was living through the frightening process of figuring out her newly ascribed identity of being a "depressed" and "ill" person. Her story reveals how she internalized Trigger's diagnosis. She felt like someone who was "broken" and "needing fixed," which confounded the struggles she already felt by being "different." Many youth her age already feel awkward and uncertain. It is part of the maturing process. But not everyone has to accommodate the label "severely depressed," which marked Iman as flawed.

The emphasis Iman places on mental illness provides an entry point for reflecting on a distinct mode of suffering within the bullying experience. She refers to herself as a "severely depressed person," and a "depressed fourteen year old" many additional times in a longer version of the story that she submitted for the class assignment. This identity marker suggests how difficult it can be to negotiate the label of "mental illness," especially for young people who also are living with bullying. Bullying is intense enough. The presence of a depression identity, though, adds layers of complexity, and intensity. For instance, should the identity of being "mentally ill" become known to others, the "ill" person may feel greater risk as a target for others who detect the already vulnerable, depressed person as prey for bullying. In these ways, Iman's emphasis on being bullied stresses the stigma she attached to living as "other."

Bullied (Black) Body

Iman's story accentuates the complex and varied ways bodies matter to bullying. Bodies are the portals through which people experience, and come to be in the world (Adams & Berry, 2013; Heidegger, 1996/1953; Leder, 1990). That is, we perform ourselves through our bodies—how we live, and who we understand ourselves, and others, to be, as well as the meaningfulness of our relational lives. The embodied nature of bullying is prominent in a diverse number of ways in Iman's account. For instance, Iman's body brings bullies into contact with her across a number of contexts (e.g., social functions with families, exchanges across intimidating locker room spaces), provides bullies with fodder for bullying communicative action (e.g., clothes and voices that look and sound "white," or at least not "black enough"), prompts introspection in regards to issues that are intrapersonal (e.g., self-evaluation as "broken") and relational (e.g., lack of acceptance and feelings of belonging), and serves as the vessels through which Iman's attempts to cope are performed (e.g., as the withdrawn and isolated self, rarely comfortable around most others, and cutting). In these ways, bodies are rich, resourceful, and difficult sites of negotiating encounters through which we orient, focus, introspect, and relate. *Bullied* bodies are the site of scrutiny, dismissal, and violence, often in stigmatizing ways. Yet, they are also the only bodies bullied people have. This is one of the things that makes Iman's never having felt comfortable in her own skin so distressing. It is the only skin she has, but others make her feel that how she lives within that skin is not enough. Even more troubling, Iman treated their disapproval as if it expressed the Truth of who she was.

Iman's story shines a light on the ways in which some raced bodies are preferred to others, pointing to fundamental issues of identity negotiation in the aftermath of bullying. Boylorn (2013a) describes similar pressures that stem from her growing up black and female in the rural southern United States. In her hometown of Sweetwater, North Carolina, being light-skinned black girls was better than being dark-skinned. Boylorn writes, "It hurt to be called black. Nobody ever said it but it was understood that there was something wonderful, better, and altogether beautiful about being the light, bright, damn near white version of black" (p. 86). Elsewhere, Boylorn (2013b) writes:

> [I]t was no secret that being dark-skinned was not preferable or privileged. On the playground, children would chant, "If you white, you all right, if you brown, get down, if you black, get back!" We didn't understand why race mattered but it was clear that it did, especially outside of our homes. We understood the dynamics of colorism at play, even tho we didn't have the language.
>
> (pp. 179–180)

Boylorn was the "pretty ole dark-skinned girl" (2013b, p. 179) and Iman was either "not black enough" or "too white." Both lived knowing the culturally established expectations for raced bodies, and moreover, that they fell short of the normative bar. In addition, both girls understood that the ways in which they lived in and through their bodies were inadequate, and, thus, that they, too, were never enough.

I initiated follow-up conversations with Iman to better understand how she felt about the impact of being bullied by family members. Iman spoke pointedly about how family members' treated her. She specifically focused on the contradictory messages inherent to her experience of being bullied. She explained:

> I did not make the choice to live in this neighborhood, but I certainly had to deal with the consequences. In bed late at night, unable to sleep because of my troubles, I would imagine saying to my family, "Look … I would have loved it if you had put me in a black school, or one with more black kids. But you didn't. You put me in this white area. How else did you expect me to act?"

Iman calls attention to the difficulties inherent to living within such contradictions. She grew up in a predominantly white neighborhood and identified closely with white friends and peers, people whom her family wanted her to get to know and befriend. But at school she was ridiculed for not being "black enough." As she explained, "I was dammed if I did and dammed if I didn't!" She had to endure a tenuous relational reality, one whose contradictions become clearer when we consider alternative ways Iman might have performed. For instance, how would others have perceived her had she performed "black" in ways that contradicted how those around her were performing? She might then have been ascribed a different identity, but one equally problematic and stigmatizing, such as "black girl in a white town," or even more questionable, "thug black girl … trying to be white." The contradictions leave no way out of the confusion and hurt yielded by bullying. She says, "I was doing the best I could with what I had available to me, but, yet again, the bullies wanted something different from me."

These tensions suggest youth and her family bullied Iman because they felt she was attempting to pass (Yoshino, 2007) as white and trying to hide her blackness. Her clothing, voice, and friends—these are the central tells, to family members and Destroyer, that she was trying to be someone she wasn't, and not who they knew and wanted her to be. Their bullying effectively marked what they deemed to be an identity breach: an egregious violation deserving of disapproval and sanctioning. Bullying worked as a demand for Iman to "reverse cover" (Yoshino, 2007)—that is, to perform as a more "authentic" black girl, one who was "less white" and "more black."

Iman did not feel like she was hiding anything, but simply being herself; however, her family saw things much differently. As she confirms, "It felt like they wanted to make sure I didn't forget I was black." On one level, there is good reason for family members to want Iman to perform her race body in a culturally relevant manner. They were, after all, immersed in a largely white area. They may have wanted her to acknowledge and maintain her cultural heritage, or try to protect herself from the violence and injustice of racism. Still, Iman felt they delivered this concern through critique and ridicule that hurt and further stigmatized her.

In Iman's case, bullying speaks to an underlying logic that seeks to create and maintain fixed racial categories, especially what it can mean to be, and to invoke, the social categories of "black" and "white" (Nakayama & Krizek, 1995; Warren, 2001). Black raced bodies that disrupt these set categories in their everyday performances (as family member, peer, community member) are subjected to scrutiny and discipline by both black and white persons; they are reminded never to forget who they "really are," to stop trying to pass and live more openly and authentically. White perceptions of what is "fitting," "appropriate," and "authentic" dominate. In this sense, "Whiteness [was] like air, everywhere all at once, even when you were not paying attention, and invisible" (Boylorn, 2013a, p. 21).

Numbing the Pain

Iman's coping tactic of "blocking out" points to a strategy of handling the pressures of bullying through withdrawal. She first implemented this strategy on the day of Trigger's diagnosis—"the first day my body discovered how to completely shut down"—and heavily relying on blocking out throughout high school. She withdrew because she was suffering and needed to feel better. As she writes, "I was trapped in a glass room and could see everything around me, but could not say anything. When I blocked out I muted everything and anything that was around me, and I muted my thoughts as well." In these ways, bullying rendered her physically present, but psychological and emotionally absent. Confronting her bullies, and communicating about the problems with others, or even reflecting on them, was simply too much for her to handle. Blocking out allowed her to "check out" from the pain and uncertainty, at least temporarily. She was "trapped" and disengaged, yet, also safe.

Iman's story calls attention to how the costs of bullying can become deeply personal and painful. On the one hand, being bullied on a regular basis made her into a perpetually numbed, or anesthetized, young girl. She became someone who did not have to think about, or feel, confusion and hurt; blocking out released her from needing to participate in more aware ways. This strategy, in effect, put those thoughts and feelings, and the task of dealing with her troubles more directly on reserve. On the other hand, the way she talks about being "isolated" and "guarded" also prevented her from participating in interactions that might have reminded her that being herself was both okay and important, how understandable it was for her to be suffering, given the circumstances, and how it might be helpful to think about her situation, and herself, differently. Numbed and secluded, she prevented others from reminding her of the positive aspects of her life, and how amazing she was—precisely as she was. She effectively was "on hold" within the tensions of her bullying experience, dwelling in between the lived experience of harm created through bullying and the possibilities for care that might have developed had she not blocked out but rather opened up to what others could do for her. But there were no others once she isolated herself![2]

There are at least two additional ways of understanding Iman's coping strategy. First, because a lot of her bullying came from family members, she might have felt that talking with others who were closest to her (i.e., the family members) was pointless and risky. Indeed, opening up may have raised even more questions, further complicating her coping. If family members were bullying her, maybe this is what family does? Maybe it is something she just needs to take, or suffer through? Second, Iman notes that she did not have time for this "nonsense" (being bullied and dealing fully with the bullying). Thus, although it entailed bottling up painful thoughts and feelings, blocking out became an efficient way to respond. Perhaps it was her way to exert some control within a relational process that felt uncontrollable.

Boylorn's (2013a) brief description of the way she used breathing to handle the cultural pressures she faced resonates with this reading of Iman's blocking out: "Holding my breath was rehearsed rebellion. I was younger than ten when I started breathing in without breathing out" (p. 74). Iman practiced numbing herself by blocking. She became good at it. It served as a way for her to "rebel," that is, to resist the pressures repeatedly created for her through bullying, but without having to confront the bullies, or the pain. But this technique was not a solution and could sustain her for only so long.

On the Indecisive Brink

Iman's inner turmoil over whether or not to commit suicide demonstrates the emotional toll that being bullied can take. Her story shows her continuing to be bullied on multiple fronts, and with no foreseeable resolution. As a result, she questions why she was living. She did not want a life exclusively lived in the service to more powerful others. She had become an especially anxious girl immersed in self-doubt and self-hate. The questions with which she was grappling had life-and-death consequences. In short, bullying took a drastic toll on Iman. Suicide was now an option. Surrounded by ridicule and rejection, Iman had reached the lowest moment in her narrative history of bullying.

Suicide became a viable "out," a final escape from the pain that was exhausting and isolating her. Yet, her experience was not uniquely hers. For instance, Boylorn (2013a) suffered from mental depression and was taken to a "white lady psychiatrist" for therapy (p. 89). Like Iman, Boylorn's therapy was ineffective for her and she envisioned suicide:

> By the sixth grade I developed a fascination with dying … I imagined my childhood death would be glorious. Instead of a nuisance or pitiful child I would be remembered as the "poor black girl with so much life left to life."
>
> (p. 89)

Iman did not envision suicide as "glorious," but as deadly serious. She needed a way to "fix" the problems created by a stigmatized identity and to no longer be stuck in a space in which she perceived limited possibilities for living differently and being truly safe and happy.

Iman's contemplation of suicide shows the contradictory conditions that some victims endure and sort through as they negotiate the aftermath of bullying. If Iman killed herself, the pain would go away, but she would be dead. As a result, the bullies would "win." However, if Iman rejected the option of suicide, the bullying would likely continue. Living at the mercy of bullies and depression was not the life she wanted. She wanted something more meaningful than a life of fear, sadness, and criticism. Although these difficult tensions pervaded Iman's decision making, they also helped to prevent a swift and tragic move to suicide.

Iman's story shows how confounding tensions dwell in the treacherous reasoning of victims of bullying. Bullying had taken her to the deepest limits of despair. Thankfully the inner debates revealed to her that there might still be some hope.

Cutting to the Point (of Relief)

Iman's story briefly conveys her choice to cut, an increasingly common mode of self-harm. According to Brown and Kimball (2013), self-harm entails "the intentional harming of one's body in order to reduce emotional pain and cope with overwhelming emotions" (p. 195; see Turner, 2002). Between 13 and 24% of high school students report inflicting harm against themselves (see also Laye-Gindhu & Schonert-Reichl, 2005; Muehlenkamp & Gutierrez, 2004, 2007).

There are a number of ways to perform self-harm, including "[c]utting, burning, punching oneself, banging one's head, pulling one's hair out, constantly scratching oneself, picking scabs or interfering with wound healing, and breaking bones" (Brown & Kimball, 2013, p. 195). Cutting entails making smaller and numerous cuts in select parts of the person's body. Cutters find relief through the process. Self-harm activities, such as cutting, serve to promote coping mechanisms, and often are enacted as "productive" alternatives to suicide insofar as they keep the person who is suffering alive.

Iman cut herself in ways that show how coping with being bullied requires some victims to perform as "secret apprenticeship" (Garfinkel, 1967). Needing to avoid being detected by others to avoid further stigmatization, she carefully managed her actions. Her story provides a vivid picture of how she secured the cutting device and determined where to make the cuts. As a reader, I envisioned her secretly creeping throughout the house, late at night when her parents are asleep, searching for the ideal blade. As she suggests, only a "very sharp" "tool of relief" would do. To further avoid detection she diligently and methodologically worked to cut her stomach, a spot she could hide from the view of others.[3]

Indeed, the secrecy with which Iman was living deepened with her cutting, and for good reasons. Keeping the secret allowed her to maintain the status quo mode of coping (i.e., blocking out and cutting), and put her in control of her own pain. She became the source of her own pain rather than the victim of someone else's "cutting." Furthermore, if she lost the secret, she would likely need to cope differently, more openly, for which she was not ready. Her parents would be appalled by her cutting, and would work to prevent the self-harm at all costs, which likely would limit the freedom and autonomy through which Iman would be able to cope and live. She would likely be forced to address her pain directly, and be asked to enter therapy again with Trigger. Moreover, if her cutting was detected, she effectively would be "outted" as a "cutter." Others would know that she was the type of person who handled her problems in a mutilating way. As a secret apprentice she was able to pass, or hide, the stigmatized identity of someone who self-harms and suffers from mental illness, a stigma that would likely perpetuate her feelings of "otherness."

Neither Iman's story nor my analysis advocate self-harm practices, such as cutting, as reasonable options for victims of bullying to relieve suffering. Still, cutting made it possible for Iman to avoid suicide and find a path on which to find some relief that "blocking out" failed to provide. Granted, the cutting was ironic, given that she suffered from the hurt of others, and as a way of feeling better opted to hurt herself. Indeed, by creating physical pain to alleviate emotional pain, she deepened her immersion in contradictions. Further, she was injuring her body, expanding her doubt and self-hatred. While the cutting didn't take away her stigmatized identity of "white/black girl," it did, in fact, help her to survive. Iman chose cutting to negotiate the stressors of coping with her stigmatized (black) identity. However, by sharing the story, Iman effectively avows herself as a "cutter," and as someone who suffers from severe mental illness. In doing so, she introduces an additional level of stigma to her story and identity.

Although Iman kept cutting secret, it was still a relational process. Her relation to others informed the performance. For instance, her parents bought the blade that enabled the cutting to occur; she felt the need to avoid detection, fearing how others would react; and ultimately she wanted to live in order to be with her family. Although not aware of the cutting, others were implicated by, or "in" each cut. As Schrag (2003) writes, "No 'I' is an island entire of itself; every subject is a piece of the continent of other subjects, a part of the main of intersubjectivity" (p. 125; see also p. 132). Thus, Iman's cutting makes sense and helps us understand the complexities of bullying as a relational process. Her story challenges us to acknowledge and account for the visible and hidden ways others inform, and sometimes govern, lives, and especially some of the most vulnerable relational partners.

Learned Compassion

Iman ends her story with a brief but beautiful expression of the time she spent at her all-black university, the turning point that made the beginning of her new life possible. She asks readers to consider the therapeutic power of experiencing an affirming community. At that school, she was able to readily identify with people like herself, and to participate and experiment with her identity in ways that felt more authentic. She was now less likely to be ridiculed by others and could begin to let go of how terribly she suffered. Her concession of still being a ruminator today confirms that she is human, vulnerable, and someone whose current ways of living are informed by her narrative history. She tells her story to remind us, and herself, how difficult her bullying was, how being bullied left an imprint on her.

Notes

1   Iman self-identifies using both "African American" and "black." Therefore, I use both in this book.

2   I do not mean to suggest that Iman, the victim, is to blame for these consequences related to her ways of coping. She was doing the best she could in the face of ongoing bullying and distress. Her being isolated in this way is a further indication of the severity of the issues that can result from being bullied.

3   The "secret apprenticeship" concept beautifully speaks to the interconnection between performing in social life and identity negotiation. The perspective could be applied to all stories in this book.

THE LITTLE PROFESSOR

Reflexive Interlude 1

Some thirty-five years since you first experienced bullying, you re-visit salient factors of your life and identity from back then; dimensions of "you" and your phenomenological lifeworld (everyday reality) that inform your experience with bullying and youth. You do so to bring clarity to memories that time's passing has rendered distant and foggy, and knowing how stories provide a fertile pathway for this reflexive work.[1]

Cultural Background

The 1970s and 1980s, the heart of your youth, and you are living within a television boom. You have an extensive list of favorite programs and are fascinated by the ways characters on these shows live through relational and identity problems. Rarely a day passes when you are not watching your favorite programs with family and friends, or by yourself. Your shows are laden with myopic portraits of conflict, sexuality, and masculinity that, to your younger self, are truthful, attractive, and without issue. For instance, you are drawn to the squeaky clean image of the blended family on *The Brady Bunch*, who *always* resolves complex conflict issues, including bullying, in neat and tidy ways, thirty minutes at a time; how on *Three's Company* the main character Jack pretends to be gay, so he could justify living with two female roommates to Mr. Roper, their homophobic landlord; and how actors Don Johnson and Phillip Michael Thomas ("Crockett" and "Tubbs") on the pop cultural phenomenon *Miami Vice* embody the quintessential image of the masculine ideal of this time—rugged toughness from head to toe, even though both characters are also often adorned with fashionable floral-print shirts.

The larger webs of culture in which you live tell certain stories about identity. You're a citizen of the United States, meaning you live in a nation largely shaped by Judeo-Christian values. While there are some persons who self-identify as being affiliated with other religions, or no religion whatsoever, Christianity dwells at the center of cultural life. Issues of same-sex attraction and love are usually talked about in public as aberrations, if they are even talked about at all. They are parts of uncomfortable plotlines on television dramas or comedies, and fodder for standup comediennes. In addition, your introduction to politics comes at a time when the president is Ronald Reagan, whom you adore because of his affable post-Hollywood, down home, joke-telling persona. You don't pay attention to the specifics about his conservative politics and their effects. Relatedly, you are growing up at the beginning of the AIDS epidemic, about which Reagan (like most politicians) remains silent for years. The sparse amount of television news coverage on the issue at this time alarms the public to the "gay cancer" spreading among "sick homosexuals." You do not understand what this means, but believe it regards "others," not you; indeed, AIDS pertains to and is caused by "immoral" others, whom you hear many people judge and shame, and whom you believe you should be judging and shaming.

Peer aggression is a common condition of lived experience in your youth, yet it is not a widely discussed cultural phenomenon that you hear talked about in terms of "bullying," per se. You hear adults describe and rationalize this aggression in certain ways as it pertains to boys, rationalizing it as a matter of "boys being boys," or a "natural part of growing up." You watch fathers on television tell their sons who are being bullied they need to defend themselves and fight back, and with even greater force than was exhibited by the aggressor, if they wish the bullying to end. You hear that from your own father and brother, but cannot ever imagine yourself being able, or wanting, to fight back. You are not tough. Rarely, if ever, do you hear about bullying committed by and against girls; you presume girls aren't and can't be bullies. Holistically, you are held within these influential cultural webs, which reveal and prioritize certain ways of living, all the while concealing and/or dismissing others. Still, you are too young to understand how they influence your identity.

You were born in Lansing, Illinois, a southern suburb of Chicago, by two loving "baby boomer" parents. Your mother is an elementary and middle school teacher there, a profession to which she proudly talks about as a "calling" and not just a "job." Mom is a passionate educator who is committed to educating from the heart, and specializes in teaching students from marginalized populations. Your father is a roofer who works tirelessly tarring industrial or flat roofs on buildings in the Chicagoland area. Sometimes he works on the roofs of skyscrapers downtown, which amazes you as a child. Your Dad is a staunch union advocate who is dedicated to his fellow roofers, and has sacrificed much to help provide for his family. You witness his sacrifice in the discoloration of his tar- and sun-burned skin on his face and arms, and by the long baths he takes to relieve his achy bones after getting home from work. Your parents model the importance of being disciplined and working hard. They show you how relating well with others matters, even when the ways in which others treat you contradicts such kindness.

You have great memories of walking to the local pool with your brother, sister, and neighborhood friends, spending many summer days swimming at the park district pool together. You fondly remember dance shows you and your sister used to perform to "Like a Virgin," the first hit from the new singer, Madonna, and to the sensational new video for Michael Jackson's latest song, "Thriller," on MTV. You are able to truly be yourself around your sister, which makes you happy.

Your parents are rearing you in a white, middle-class, Roman Catholic family of mixed Irish and German decent. These factors of your identity are important to the family, and they will come to be important to your identity as you age. All of your family and most of your close friends are white. While the innate privileges of your whiteness are not discussed, you learn from your parents about diversity and the importance of trying to treat all people, especially people of color, with love. Socioeconomically you are fortunate to always have a safe and comfortable place to live, food to eat, and many of the toys you desire. You do not realize the sacrifices your parents are making to allow you to live in these ways; indeed, you are lucky in ways that do not yet make sense to you. As a Catholic you attend mass on most Sundays, and your parents enroll you in Catechism classes. You are told to be devoted to Jesus Christ, God, and scripture, which, at the very least, involves being hyper-vigilant about the dangers of sin and the importance of forgiveness and reconciliation. Also, you are taught to honor your being Irish and German, and especially the Irish background. You love to hear stories about when Grandma and Grandpa Berry immigrated by boat to America in the early 1900s. They sojourned here to begin a family of their own in the United States, even though that meant leaving behind family, friends, and counties Kerry and Mayo respectively. You are prideful about their history, however, that pride is rarely enough to make you enjoy the bitter tasting corned beef and cabbage your family compels you to eat, or "at least try, honey" on every St. Patrick's Day.

Early Schooling, Dis-ease, and Bullying

You attend public elementary and middle schools. Since both schools are about a mile from where you live, you usually walk to and from school each day. Learning excites you, which teachers are quick to note. You flourish from their guidance, and work hard at being an ideal student. You are lucky to be learning from "teacher's teachers"; artists who help shape children into successful learners.

Your fourth grade teacher, Mrs. Linderman, is your favorite. She is a tall, pretty Greek woman in her thirties. You will do anything for her and feel like she will do the same for you. When you are working at your desk sometimes you look up to see if she's watching you. You hope she notices how hard you are working for her. Sometimes she is looking at you and smiling. You smile back and then, embarrassed, quickly jump back to work. In her class Mrs. Linderman gives you the nickname, "the little professor," a prophetic name that makes you happy. You don't think she usually gives nicknames to many students, so you must be special.

You love being the "little professor," an esteemed identity that sparks your love for creativity and living in unique and different ways. Not many kids after all are professors. Your professorial tools include a large inventory of paper (notebook, cardboard), pencils (colored or lead), markers (scented, permanent), and crayons (the largest box possible, with the built-in sharpener). Your most cherished possession is your five-color *Bic* ballpoint pen. Clicking from color to color in only a split second, this pen makes you feel inspired, smart, and in charge. Your imagination is perhaps your most trusted friend. Delving deeply into the imaginary allows you to see endless possibilities for doing what you want and being who you wish, one colorful stroke of the pen at a time.

Although you love school, you feel unsettled when you are there, and you are prone to getting headaches and upset stomachs. You try to keep news about not feeling well to yourself, because you hope it will pass and do not want to stand out to other students. Often you cannot name a specific ailment, so you simply tell your teachers you "just don't feel right." They send you to the school's nurse, Ms. Reese. When you arrive to her office she greats you with a concerned look, a deep but soft voice, and a loving hug. "Not feeling well again, Mr. Berry?" she says, gesturing to the seat by her desk. She often gives you a dose of Donnatal, your prescription stomach medicine that she keeps locked up in her cabinet. You despise its taste and sometimes wonder which is worse: your nervous stomach or the medicine. Although you do not understand why, it feels better to be in the quiet and away from the class. These escapes help to calm you.

Yet, sometimes neither the escape to Mrs. Reese, nor the medicine help you feel better. Then you turn to the only person you feel might help: Mom. Your mother teaches at your elementary school, and her classroom is only a couple of short hallways away. You periodically ask Mrs. Linderman if you can go see your mother, sometimes telling her that you just have to ask Mom a "quick question," and she gives you her permission every time. When you show up in Mom's class, often interrupting her teaching mid-sentence, she looks at you in a startled but knowing way. The two of you meet behind her desk, and she whispers, "Not feeling well again, honey?" You say, "No, I don't feel good. I just feel weird. I'm sorry, Mom." To which she quickly replies, "Sweetie, you should never apologize for how you feel—you will feel better soon. I know it." Just hearing her reassurance usually helps you, and is enough to carry you until the end of the school day. You take a peppermint candy from the secret supply she keeps in her desk drawer, and begin to make your way to the door, to return to class.

In fourth grade the "little professor" is bullied for the first time. One day you are rearranging the supplies on your desk during class when, all of a sudden, your hand hits your pencil case, which falls to the ground, spilling all of its contents onto the floor. Noticing what happened, Jim, your friend who is sitting immediately to your right, humorously says, "Oh, Keith, what did you do? Keither … you're such a *feifer*." Smiling and shaking your head at him, you go to pick up the pencils. Yet, as you bend your chubby body over to reach the ground, you feel your shirt fall to your shoulders, exposing your belly, and your pants and underwear fall down from your waist, exposing several inches of your butt crack. In response, two students sitting near you, bigger and tougher athletic kids who are not your friends, begin to laugh and point their fingers at you. They begin to loudly repeat, "Feifer … feifer … such a dumb, fat feifer!" Their actions get the attention of others, who then begin to laugh and point at you. You need help and begin to panic. *What do I do? They keep laughing and pointing. Who will help me? Mrs. Linderman is busy with other students. It is too late in the afternoon to go to the nurse's office. And Mom is at home sick today.* Feeling embarrassed for exposing yourself, and humiliated from their mocking, your face instantly turns bright crimson. The only thing you feel you can do is look down and stare at the piece of paper on which you are doodling. Luckily, a few minutes later you are saved by the bell, signaling it is time to go home.

Over the next three weeks they continue to bully you: when they pass you in the hallway, ask to borrow your pencil in class, or roll a pitch to you during kickball, they chant, "feeeeeeifer, feeeeeeifer, what a dumb, fat feifer." You say nothing and try to ignore them, most often walking away, or looking in the other direction. Yet, you still hear these mean words they chant and you sense that other people are looking at you. Their bullying makes you feel clumsy and stupid. "Don't be so clumsy like that," you tell yourself, or they'll continue to bully you. Eventually, Mrs. Lindeman notices their chanting in class and how you turn red and sink lower in the seat at your desk each time they say "feifer." So, one day after hearing it used in class again, she puts down her book and says, "Okay, I have an announcement. You *will stop* using 'feifer,' and I am serious." After this warning, you never hear anyone say it again in her presence, but boys continue to mock you from time to time, mainly at gym or at lunch.

Although their bullying eventually stopped, its impact on you lingered. When you see these boys, you think of how they treated you, and you fear they will try something. You attempt to avoid them at all costs, often waiting to enter the line at lunch until they have finished getting their lunches, ignoring them when they try to talk with you in class. Granted, others have been aggressive with you in the past, and you are already a nervous and awfully seriously little boy. However, this conflict marks the first time you are bullied, and their aggression has amplified the dis-ease you feel. When you close your eyes, you see your chubby belly and exposed butt crack on display to others, and you hear, and feel, your classmates pointing and laughing at you. *When will they come at me again? Why did I have to drop those pencils? What if I make other mistakes in the future? Why do I have to have so many types of pencils in that bag? Next time I won't be so foolish. I'll be smarter and more careful. I know better. I must do better.*

At the end of the fourth grade you write your first story, titled "Who Me?" It is not for a school assignment; you just feel compelled to write it. You spend many days thinking about the story. You begin to create sketches of your story late at night, when you are supposed to be sleeping. On many mornings you wake up with a pen stuck to your back, and crinkled papers to your side, the aftermath of falling asleep while you were still working.

"Who Me?" humorously conveys the lived experience of Johnny, a boy who is about to transition to the fifth grade/middle school. Johnny has a couple of handfuls of great friends. Yet, he also often feels different than, and distant from, most of his schoolmates. He doesn't feel like people at school understand him, and he often feels uncomfortable when around them. One day Johnny decides he is tired of listening to and worrying about others, so he puts several cotton balls into each of his ears. The ways in which this tactic helps Johnny to block out others helps give him relief and lessens his rumination. Although others might detect what he is doing and find this coping mechanism to be odd, maybe even teasing him more for such an unusual thing to do, Johnny figures he will at least be able to finally be happy, unchained and free from the distraction of others.

You never share "Who Me?" with anyone. Yet, you're proud of the story you've created. Writing this first autoethnography has helped you feel a bit better about your life.

Methodological Dilemma

I am sitting at my office desk writing emails to students whose stories I would love to include in the book. One student, Renee, and I have already exchanged several emails. Because her story focuses on the death of a family member, she has expressed concerns. In her last email she let me know she has decided to not participate. I write her this response:

> Dear Renee,
> Thank you for letting me know. I will miss not being able to include your story. As I mentioned to you at the end of the semester and in our recent emails, the account of your cousin's suicide that resulted from his being bullied is powerful, not to mention heart breaking. I cannot imagine what this loss must feel like for you. You have my sincere admiration for your being able to muster the strength necessary to write the story for class. It is a testament to his life. Your being comfortable is my first and foremost concern, so I respect your decision not to participate. If you should happen to change your mind, and I hope you might, do not hesitate to write or call me. I would be honored to include your story in my research.
> Warmly,
> Keith

I never again hear from Renee, but her story continues to trouble me. What I write to her in the above email is sincere. No story or book is worth risking harm to a participant. Still, in my note to her I omitted important details about the deeper ways her story, and my being unable to include it, makes me think and feel. So, I decide to write her a more detailed email:

Dear Renee,

I cannot stop thinking about you and your story. I stay up late at night thinking about what happened to your cousin. Now when I see bullying stories on the news or the Internet, I think of his suicide. I must admit: your story has consumed me and I do not truly understand how to make sense of what I am feeling.

Once I graded your story, I just knew I had to have it as part of my study. Frankly it excites me. I feel as though a book with bullying stories must have at least one suicide story, if it is to be a "good" book, right? At the same time, I want a suicide story in my book so that readers can understand how deep the despair from bullying can be. I need your story, and sometimes it feels as though I need it badly ... too badly.

I also feel this way about other students' stories. There's this one student who ... I'm sure you remember his story from class ... wrote about the boys who horribly bullied him in high school for being gay and "out." Over the course of a semester at school these boys repeatedly called him "ugly duckling" and "fish face." They even would tell him he has "a mouth that is perfectly made for sucking dick." The horrors he must have felt when hearing these words, and experiencing this violence! He has never responded to my invitation for the study, and no matter how hard I try I cannot stop thinking of him. I object to what the boys called him and feel sad about the despair their words instigated for him. But I also want that story. I don't have any other story like it, and the graphic language, as horrible as it is, is ... perfect.

Renee, at times I feel obsessed with these stories. They have an allure that makes them difficult to resist. I feel close to them and am struggling to let them go. I am disappointed by not being able to have some of them. In fact, not being able to include them makes me want them even more. I crave these stories.

Maybe I have already gone too far in what I have shared with you, but there is more to say. Craving disturbing stories like these, and in these particular ways, also feels, to me, to be dirty, embarrassing, and shameful. What type of person becomes so obsessed with and excited by pain and suffering? Who gets so disappointed when learning "good stories" are not available? What does it mean to want to "use" people's stories? What gives me the right?

I should end this note here. Concerned by how I might look, I have drafted and redrafted this email many times. I feel like I am pushing you, and that is

the last thing I want to do. I hope you understand. And if by some chance you should change your mind, I am still open to including your story.
Unsettled,
Keith

I never send this email to Renee.

Note

1   My use of second person in this story is inspired by Pelias (2000).

3

PURE EVIL ENTERTAINMENT

JESSI

Reared as an only child, Jessi found it essential to regularly communicate with her friends during and after school. As she writes in her story: "They were the closest things to siblings. At home I didn't have anyone my age going through the same things as I." Jessi and her friends were close and always in contact. Being connected meant having support, and knowing that as long as she and her friends were in touch, she would be okay. One of her closest friends was Maria, whom she met a year before her story takes place. Jessi describes Maria as athletic (a softball player), attractive to most boys (long, blonde hair and the ideal mix of "girlyness" and "tomboy"), and always with a boyfriend. Jessi admired Maria's ability to attract boys, even though they were never boys she would want to bring home to meet her parents. One of Maria's boyfriends was Mike, described by Jessi as part skater boy and part rebel, who had trouble staying out of trouble but who had a good heart. Maria and Mike broke up after several months of "high school love," but they remained friends, and he continued to be in the circle of friends.

Soon after the break-up Mike began seeing Amber, a tall, dark, aspiring model who had great cheekbones and the curvy body to make her appear twenty years old, instead of fifteen. In Jessi's eyes, Amber was an attractive young girl with an unattractive personality: "Every word that came from her mouth left you with a bad taste, and she had a general disdain for everyone and everything except herself." Amber was the type of high school person who looked annoyed when interacting with others, the sort of girl who left those with whom she had been interacting feeling intimidated by her.

The circle of friends was complex and complicated and grew worse when Jessi started to take an interest in Mike while he was still dating Amber. Jessi struggles to remember why she might have been interested in Mike. Granted, she thought he was cute. However, she was an excellent student who kept out of trouble, and he was the rebel. Still, she pursued him, much to the chagrin of Amber. Seeing Jessi talk with Mike made Amber jealous, which began to stoke the fires of anger that would soon disrupt the world of Jessi and her friends.

An additional and central character to this problematic circle was "Instant Messenger" (IM), the online technology that allows people to chat in real time. IM fueled Jessi's need for connection and the technology was a firmly embedded practice in her daily ritual: come home from class, get changed out of her school clothes and into something much more comfortable, go to the kitchen and make herself a snack, and then retire into her computer room until dinner. She would spend hours chatting with friends, and re-designing her "About" section, the portion of IM that describes a given user: "IM was an obsession that I believe most kids my age went through. I would talk to my best friends, and I would talk to other friends I didn't know so well at school, but somehow had received their screen names." She was hooked, and connected, as were her girlfriends.

One day after logging into IM she noticed a message sent from her friend Maria:

Maria: I NEED TO TALK TO YOU ABOUT AMBER!!!
Jessi: Now what?
Maria: She IM-ed me today and was talking shit about you again…
Jessi: What did she say?
Maria: She said you're a bitch, and that she doesn't know what he sees in you anyways.
Jessi: Seriously?
Jessi: And what did you say? What's Amber's screen name?
(Maria disappeared from IM.)

Jessi was mad. She could feel the anger and pressure building up inside of her with each breath. *Nobody* talks about Jessi to her friends. Who did Amber think she was? She knew she had to confront her, so she got Amber's screen name from another friend and messaged her.

Jessi: Hey this is Jessi … Maria told me you called me a bitch?
Amber: Yeah … I did … and you are one.
Jessi: You're kidding, right? I'm nice to everyone, and all you do is sit in class and complain about everyone around you. You're always miserable.
Amber: Maybe. But you're not even that pretty, I told Maria that I didn't know what Mike saw in you and it's true. He likes me better, plus I have a better body than you.

The last line of Amber's message affected Jessi in ways to which she was not accustomed. She writes in her story:

Until that moment, I never gave much thought into what I looked like. I looked like your average 15 year old: I'm 5'3", weigh 115 pounds, and have Hollister and American Eagle shirts hanging in my closet. My morning "get-ready routine" consisted of brushing my hair and applying some silver eye shadow, which all of my friends also wore with me. I never considered having a "body image." Now when I looked into the mirror, I saw that Amber was right.

Amber's message struck a chord in Jessi, activating powerful insecurities in Jessi concerning her appearance, feelings that would stay with her throughout high school, and linger even today as an adult. Was she ugly? Did she have a terrible body? Jessi now felt as if she was in a competition over bodies, and she was the weaker opponent. As she writes, "My body was nothing compared to hers. I couldn't compete!"

Later that night Jessi went over to Mike's house. Sitting together on his bed, in tears she told him what Amber had said to her. Mike tried to comfort Jessi, holding her in his arms and assuring her: "You know what she said about me liking her more isn't true, right? I told her yesterday that I didn't want anything to do with her." She remembers shaking her head "no," but still did not understand why Maria would tell her these things. Amber's words—just a few basic words—had hurt her. Although Mike was helping, Jessi also could not understand why Maria was speaking with Amber in the first place:

She told me she didn't even like Amber. So why would Amber tell her what she thought about me, and why would Maria listen? I knew something was up, but I couldn't figure it out. Maybe I didn't want to know.

At lunch the next day, Jessi relayed to Maria what had occurred during the conversations with Amber and Mike. "Amber's a crazy bitch," she fumed. "Mike doesn't even like her. He told me that he told her the other night that he didn't want anything to do with her anymore, and that he liked me … not her." Maria replied, "Yeah, she was talking so much crap about you last night! She doesn't even know you!" Nothing more was said.

At home later that day Jessi grabbed her snack and hurried to the computer. There she signed into IM and waited for Amber to come online. She sat in silence, debating whether or not she would confront her. She went back and forth, staring at the screen, occasionally practicing what she was going to say with other friends who also were online. Soon she saw Amber's name pop up on her list of IM friends, paused, and thought: What did she want Amber to hear? Was confronting her worth it? What good would it do? Jessi then saw Amber sign online, clicked on her screen name, and quickly began typing a message, trying to beat her to the punch. Yet she had moved too slowly. Suddenly a message from Amber appeared on Jessi's screen:

AMBER: So I'm a crazy bitch now?

JESSI: You weren't already aware of that?

AMBER: I know you went to go see Mike last night, and I know what he told you. He's lying to you...

JESSI: So now you're a stalker too?

AMBER: Um, no. Maria told me.

Suddenly it made sense: Amber had confirmed Jessi's suspicion of foul play. After all, how else would Amber know the details of these conversations? She knew it was Maria who was manipulating both Amber and Jessi: "When I was talking to Maria she hated Amber, and I'm sure when Maria was talking to Amber, she probably hated me, too!" Maria had betrayed her, which left Jessi devastated, and confused:

> Hysterical I called up my two best friends at the time, who were also friends with Maria, and told them about the situation. Like me, they were inexperienced in this type of situation. Until this point I never had a friend betray me, and especially someone I needed. She was my sister—I trusted her! Also, I had never been in a fight with another girl over a boy. I felt isolated and had nobody to talk to who could understand what I was going though. I couldn't tell my parents ... they just wouldn't get it.

She would have to sit with the problem; unresolved and angry, she felt more hurt than ever.

Jessi went to school the next day still feeling hurt by Maria's betrayal, and trying to put the pieces of the puzzle together: "Maybe they were in it together the entire time?" Walking into class she spotted Amber and Maria sitting side by side, looking chummy. She tried to play it cool and simply walk past them to her usual seat, but did not have much success: "I could feel their eyes glaring at me. I could hear the faint sounds of whispers, which I only assume involved me as the topic. Miserable, I sat down and waited for the day to be over." Yet fifteen minutes into class, someone from the other side of the room passed Jessi a note, which was folded into a little square. "To: Jessi," was written on the front, with handwriting that Jessi quickly identified as Maria's. After opening it, she realized the note was a conversation between Maria and Amber, including a range of harsh comments about Jessi. "She looks ugly!" "She talks and walks weird!" "Her hair is too messy!" "She tries way too hard!" "Boys will *never* like her!" Looking back, Jessi wishes she would have chosen a better response, one that would have made a bigger impact, like throwing the note in the garbage. Maybe that would have shown them how she was stronger than their hate, and how petty they were being. Maybe that would have been the "cooler" thing to do. Instead, she slipped the note into her bag and waited for the day to finish. Hands trembling on her desk, she tried to ignore them. She just wanted the situation to go away.

Once at home Jessi ran into her computer room, shut the door, and began to prepare herself for another fight:

> Once again I waited for Amber to log on, like she always did. This time I was ready for her. I was going to end this, and I was going to win. I was a force that could not be stopped, with my fingers typing words I barely understood, just to impress and upset her. By the time she logged on, I had pre-typed what I needed to say to her. The message was foul and something I'm ashamed of ever doing. My words were as hateful as the note that was passed to me earlier that afternoon. I called her every name I could imagine, and might have slipped in a few suggestions for her to end her miserable life, because nobody liked her. Of course, I sent a similar message to Maria.

The three girls feverishly messaged back and forth, and held no punches: "We called each other every name that fifteen-year-old freshmen could think of, and used every insult we could, no matter how terrible." It was electronic violence that occurred not only that night but the entire month:

> Every night after school, we logged into IM and went back and forth about how awful the other person was. I'm not sure how any of us came up with new material over such a long period of time, but we did. Over time it really wasn't even about Mike liking me more, Amber being a bitch, or Maria betraying me. Now we were fighting for pure evil entertainment. I was living for the battle. The bullying had sparked a fire inside of me that I couldn't extinguish. I wanted to have the last word. I needed to "one-up" them.

Each night Jessi would sit at her computer and await their responses. The other girls must have kept similar postures. What and how they fought varied: "Sometimes I would initiate the bullying, and at other times I would be the recipient. Either way, it didn't matter at this point." Their words hurt Jessi and she knew her words hurt them. Yet she felt justified because she needed to defend herself: "I wasn't going to go down without a fight! And if I did go down, so would these girls. I had a point to prove and so did they. None of us backed down."

Eventually Jessi's parents stepped in and worked to end their endless volleys of bullying, and she is now mindful of the need for their intervention:

> It would be safe to say that our fight probably would have continued for a long time if my parents hadn't gotten involved. They noticed how obsessed I was with my computer, and how depressed I was when I came home from school. They probably asked me over one hundred times what was wrong, but I couldn't, and wouldn't, tell them. This was my life, and they wouldn't understand. Finally, my mom caught a glimpse of what the three of us were saying to each other on IM, and banned me from the computer.

She was appalled at the foul language we were using and the ways we were treating each other.

Jessi vividly details the conversation she had with her mother:

> Mom took me outside to our patio. Suddenly she took a long skinny cigarette out of a pink carton, brought it to her lips, lit it, and then, as if she was doing it for effect, took a long inhale in and then slowly, ever so dramatically, exhaled the smoke from her lungs. We sat in silence for a moment, while I held back tears. I knew I was caught and that she was disappointed. Finally my mom spoke: "This needs to end, and this needs to end now. I'm not okay with what is going on with you and your friends, and I will be talking to Maria's mom. From now on, you can only use the computer when I'm home, and only for homework." Being a teenage brat, her comments did not resonate with me. I begged and pleaded that she not call Maria's mom. I told her it would ruin my life if she got any more involved, and she would embarrass me even more. She agreed to leave it alone.

While Jessi had lost the computer privileges that had become such a reliable and necessary part of her after-school life, she was spared from humiliation.

Jessi ends her story by reflecting on the power in cyberbullying to readily attack and injure another person's life:

> It was just so easy to say horrible words online without consequences. None of us ever had the guts to say anything to each other in person. We threatened each other physically online, but none of us said those same words to each other at school. Online you forget there is a person on the other side. You don't see their emotions, or their physical reactions. It's easy to forget your humanity, and to decipher right from wrong, especially when you are young and still learning, especially when you aren't face to face to see the impact of your choices.

In addition, through writing her story, Jessi now understands bullying, and herself, differently:

> If you were to have asked me back in high school if I considered myself a bully, or if I ever have been bullied, I would have vehemently responded "no" to both questions. Maybe at the time I didn't really know what a bully was, and maybe I didn't want to admit that I could be a bully. I imagined a bully to be a lonely jerk who gave "wedgies" to shy wimpy kids, and stole their lunch money. I wasn't either of those in high school so clearly I couldn't be a bully, or the victim. I now believe a bully is someone who deliberately inflicts pain on someone (whether it be physical or

mental) for any number of reasons—entertainment, reassurance, etc. With Maria and Amber, I recognize I was a bully, and a victim of bullying. I wrote mean and hateful messages to amuse myself, as well as to protect my pride. Most importantly, I didn't care if they hurt the receivers of those messages. I bet Amber and Maria didn't care either.

For Jessi, the moral of her story is to "think before you act," and to "be aware of the possible effects of your words." She realizes that the ways in which we choose to communicate with others have consequences. At the time she could not see it; she was too immersed in the back and forth attacks to recognize it.

Today Jessi remembers her communicating on both sides of bullying as lived experience that negatively shifted how she was able to live her young life: "I remember feeling depressed, and unable to express myself. I didn't know whom I could trust to tell about the bullying. In fact, I could trust no one other than myself, and so I felt very isolated." She is thankful her parents stepped in when they did, and that her mother was so firm: "If she hadn't, I'm not really sure how the situation would have ended."

ANALYZING JESSI'S STORY

"Now we were fighting for pure evil entertainment … The bullying had sparked a fire inside of me that I couldn't extinguish." Jessi's story shows some of the powerful ways cyberbullying can enable youth to lose control, and how even "good girls" like her can lose sight of others' humanity.

"Good Girl" Seeks Connection

Jessi's story reveals the importance of relationships in informing bullying and identity. By avowing the "only child" identity, Jessi shows a desire for a positive relationship to fill this absence, or the disconnection. Maria served as a chosen sibling, a friend on which she relied. This aspect of their relationship becomes especially relevant when reflecting on the hurt Jessi felt after being bullied and betrayed by her two friends, especially Maria. There is a way in which the hurt and confusion from being bullied takes on more significance because of the role Maria played in her life—the sister-like connection with Maria (pre-bullying) serves to magnify the pain she endured. The attacks are bad enough; yet, from Maria, her dear friend, they hurt even more. She would expect it from someone like Amber, but not Maria. She was "family." Further, that these attacks came from Maria influenced how much Jessi believed them. If her trusted friend was saying these things, perhaps the accusations of the attacks were accurate and perhaps she deserved them. Bullying hurts enough. Yet, when it comes from family, as Iman conveyed in greater depth in her story, it can be quite difficult to bear.

Jessi's identity as "good girl" and "anti-rebel" shapes her experiences with bullying. This pre-bullying identity is relevant in at least two ways. On one level, until she began to retaliate in response to being bullied, Amber and Maria attacked without provocation. Perhaps Jessi's interest in Mike angered or hurt Amber, motivating her to retaliate against Jessi. Even more intriguing, though, is the possibility that Jessi's "goodness" made her vulnerable to bullying in the first place. In this sense, staying out of trouble, being "clean," rendered her in the eyes of her bully as someone who would not be able to defend herself. Thus, Jessi's innocence might have suggested to Amber and Maria that she was weak, making her an easy target. She was damned for being good.

On another level, Jessi's identity change to a "bad" girl reveals how quickly a bullied victim can transform into a bully within cyberbullying. That transformation occurred impulsively and without reservation. She was attacked, and to defend herself and her pride she retaliated in ways that matched, if not surpassed, the intensity of violence coming from the other two (e.g., encouraging the two to commit suicide). Shaken, hurt, and continuing to be a victim of bullying, she became a cyberbully immersed in an "obsession" of attacks. It is debatable whether or not her "good girl" identity went away as she began to bully. However, her performance and identity certainly became layered, muddled, and in question. I am confident Maria and Amber no longer saw her as squeaky clean, if they ever did.[1]

"Unlikeable" Body

Jessi's account underscores the relevance of physical appearance to bullying, primarily in regards to issues of physical attractiveness. These bullies focused on the quality or nature of their victim's bodies, honing in on features that they feel are abject and, thus, subject to harmful treatment. As with the other stories included in the book, Jessi's lived experience with being bullyied shows how words hurt others (Kowalski, 2011; Vangelisti, 1994), and how the performance of verbal aggression entails communicative violence that cuts at the self-concept of the people against whom it is used (Infante, Riddle, Horvath, & Tumlin, 1992; Infante & Wigley, 1986). Often words are not "simply words," but ways of intruding upon others' well-being and greatly affecting their lives.

Jessi's story emphasizes the links between hurtful and aggressive words and bullied bodies. Take, for instance, the harsh things Amber said to Jessi during their initial IM chat—for example, that Jessi was "not really that pretty" and "I have a better body than you." Add to these, the cruel words Amber, and later Amber and Maria, said to Jessi, who repeatedly heard that she was "ugly" and "messy," "talks and walks weird," "tries way too hard," and perhaps most importantly, is someone whom "boys will never like." These instances use teasing and ridicule to mark and accentuate what is deemed to be a stigmatized, that is, a disfavored, unpopular or unacceptable body. In turn, their attacks were specific, personal, and invasive. Jessi's story does not suggest any sign of pause or equivocation in bullies' messages.

The harm created through their teasing and ridicule is revealed through Jessi's story in at least three ways. At a basic level, Amber and Maria's comments hurt Jessi's feelings. They were mean-spirited and demonstrated no positive valence in meaning. The hurt likely was greater to Jessi because she was caught off guard and vulnerable, given that she did not expect to be bullied by one of her closest friends. In addition, the teasing and ridicule served to activate Jessi's focus on and concern about the body. By repeatedly hearing them, she came to internalize and believe what they said, learning that she had a stigmatized body that affected, and was going to continue affecting, her relational being. Consequently, bullying changed Jessi from generally being a confident and assured young girl to someone who lived with self-doubt and looming personal questions that made her feel uneasy. Finally, their hurtful words isolated Jessi. Similar to Iman's experiences, she did not feel comfortable speaking with anyone about the bullying, including her parents. This desire for having the bullying remain private is further complicated when we consider Jessi's role in bullying Amber and Maria. Had she opened up to parents or others, she would be "outing" herself as a cyberbully, which would be counterintuitive to continuing the "good girl" identity. Like Iman, Jessi's choice to seclude herself left her feeling alone and depressed.

Jessi's turn to performing as bully showed her resourcefully relying on words to hurt her victims, a layer of this discussion that works in at least two ways. First, *in spite of* the hurt she experienced by the bullying, she was able to punish them in return. That is, no matter how far they had knocked her down, she mustered the strength and communicated in ways that shamed their bodies and pursued self-harm. Perhaps she even did so because she was exhausted and confused, not really remembering that she was someone who tried to stay out of trouble and not hurt others. Second, *because of* the hurt she experienced from their bullying, she injured them in return. This second wording is related but different. It suggests motivation and a deliberate plan of hurting the two girls through the words she chose. Regardless of who she had been in the past, they hurt her, and she retaliated. She was no one's helpless victim. Their words had hurt her so much that she was now furious, and was going to respond in kind. The story suggests to me that this second strand is more of what Jessi wanted to convey by her story.

Youth in Combat

Jessi's portrayal treats bullying as a battle. The girls fought on multiple and interrelated fronts, bullying at school and cyberbullying. Attacks against Jessi within the classroom, for instance, served as exegeses that energized and motivated her to be ready to sign on to IM at home. Also, the violence was prolonged and significant. Over the thirty days of war, the girls communicated intense back-and-forth attacks, particularly online, wherein messages were meant both to hurt and, seemingly, to "hurt better" than the previous attack. In addition, each combatant had an axe to grind, and an identity to bolster. As she writes, "I wasn't going to go down without a fight! And if I did go down, so would these girls. I had a point to prove and so did they. None of us backed down." Statements like this in the story show a battle with high-stakes roles, combatants who spared no horrendous condemnation. Virtual death to other was their shared goal; yet, each person was out for the win.

This war significantly changed the identities of its combatants in several ways. The cyberbullying allowed the girls to increase their ridiculing of each other, including the number of insults they could exchange in regards to their bodies, and who they were as people. It provided a forum for the ongoing ascription of identities (Goffman, 1963), consecutively, message after message, making the other person more fully into the "other," the stigmatized being who was disfavored and unlikeable. The cyber-nature of this bullying intensified the impact of the violence. Unlike bullying using the spoken word, cyberbullying entailed typed messages that appear on a screen. Unless deleted, these hurtful messages would remain on the given device's screen, and, thus, could be relived by victims and bullies. In this way, cyberbullying helps to create a lasting memory of the attack, and perhaps a site to which to return to feel more prideful (for bullies) or shameful and alone (for victims).

At the same time, Jessi's story shows how bullying rendered these young women as aggressors. They bullied each other without reservation, and in ways that draw each person's identity into consideration. For instance, Amber performed as aggressor because she was known as being prone to trouble making. Her performance was a continuation of who she was prior to the bullying. That Maria became an aggressor is significant, again, because she was not the friend that Jessi believed her to be, and the performance required Jessi to reconcile significant dissonance concerning their relationship given the duplicitous and manipulative ways Maria decided to communicate. Jessi performed as aggressor as a result of being bullied by Amber and Maria, and due to Maria's deceit and betrayal. Her actions were understandable, yet, relationally unhelpful.

The story further speaks to ways cyberbullying can escalate to levels of conflict at which the point of the battle is to battle. At a certain point it is no longer about settling the specific reason or motivation that made the attacks "necessary" in the first place. As Jessi describes, her battle with Amber and Maria eventually became more about the pleasure of the continued attack, the "pure evil entertainment," rather than, say, "Mike liking me more, Amber being a bitch, or Maria betraying me." In this sense, cyberbullying had rendered them aggressors who were aroused and consumed by the conflict, and fixated on the bullying *process*. Regardless of why they began to bully each other, the bullying continued, and the ability to hurt the other, and hopefully in ways that were better than the other's hurt, "evil" as it was, became amusing and far too easy.

Jessi uses her story to lament how far the battle of words got out of hand within their cyberbullying. She writes in ways that ask readers to take seriously how the three teenagers became obsessed with hurting each other. Further, she invites careful consideration about how the mediated conditions of cyberbullying make for a unique, and distressing, mode of hurting (Kowalski, 2011; Vangelisti, 1994). As she writes:

> It was just so easy to say horrible words online without consequences ... Online you forget there is a person on the other side. You don't see their emotions, or their physical reactions. It's easy to forget your humanity, and to decipher right from wrong, especially when you are young and still learning, and especially when you aren't face to face to see the impact of your choices.

Here Jessi offers profound insight about bullying. Cyberbullying is consequential. Her insight vividly speaks to the ways in which the conditions for relating, and for being accountable to one another, are unique to the mediated context. Even more, the mediated context allows participants to (re)shape their bullying and, thus, to (re)imagine who they and others are, and for that matter, what the stakes of bullying are, or are not (Ong, 1982). In this way, one more readily loses sight of the other, and the importance of relating with her/him without harm, or for that matter, trying to relate with care as much as possible. Cyberbullies are less likely to be required to face the same pressures that are made possible by the immediacy of relating in person; they can perform more directly, brashly, and violently. Indeed, they are freer to relinquish responsibility to care for the other, to treat her/him like a unique and valuable being, or a "Thou" (Buber, 1970). Instead, the other becomes an "It," an object who solely exists in these embattled moments (and weeks) of cyberbullying for the "I's" pleasure.

Mom for the Save

The turning point in Jessi's lived experience with bullying appears when her mother intervened. It was good that she took action, because the consequences were significant and escalating. This is shown by Jessi's mentioning of how bullying led her to become depressed and unable to open up to her parents. She also infers that it was likely that a more tragic ending would have occurred, had her mother not stopped the bullying. Perhaps one of the teens would have pushed harder for the other to commit suicide. Thus, the intervention served as a way to snap them out of their consumed state, and to cease their ferocious battle. Interestingly, given the intensity of the bullying, and the young women's vigilance and obsession with hurting one another, the story leaves me wondering about any residual bullying that may have followed the end of the battle. Did Jessi sneak back online, perhaps just once, to send one final message? Did Amber and

Maria still send Jessi hurtful messages? Although the cyberbullying ended, did bullying still take place at school? Did they remain friends?

While the ending scene of the story is brief, it provokes a number of reflections in regards to identity negotiation in the context of intervening in cyberbullying. Specifically of interest is the mother's statement: "This needs to end, and this needs to end now. I'm not okay with what is going on with you and your friends, and I will be talking to Maria's mom." Here the mother is aptly performing as an assertive parent, and Jessi is the child whose harmful and inappropriate behavior is discovered and needs to stop. However, what is interesting are the possible ways the intervention works to negotiate Jessi's identity. For instance, Jessi pushes back on her mother's initial conditions because she is fearful of being humiliated if her mother made good on her threat to contact Maria's mother. As the story shows, her mother agrees not to contact her. It is in the acquiescing that Jessi's identity matters, particularly in terms of issues of face (Goffman, 1959). By agreeing not to call the mother, Jessi is spared the embarrassment of being the "one kid" whose mother called, the kid who is in trouble. By sparing her from the call and embarrassment, her mother ostensibly saves her face, perhaps in an effort to spare Jessi from becoming any more vulnerable in a situation that is already out of control, and with Jessi already being weakened. In this same scenario, Maria's face is also saved.

How does Jessi's mother's response make sense? Perhaps the mother viewed this, albeit terrible, incident within the larger context of Jessi's prior ability to stay out of trouble. She probably felt the punishment was enough. Still, there is also the possibility that the mother did not go far enough. For instance, if she would have contacted Maria's mother, or for that matter, Amber's mother as well, although Jessi (and the other teens) might have lost face as a result, there would be more transparency regarding their cyberbullying—what had occurred, the harms that occurred, the ongoing risks, etc. Similarly, by choosing to not take news of the cyberbullying outside of Jessi's immediate family, presuming her mother told her father, also helps Jessi to pass. That is, unless the other parents know of the cyberbullying, Jessi's name, face, and reputation, particularly as someone who was caught and is "in trouble," are spared. As a result the "good girl" identity has a greater chance to survive, rather than her becoming known as someone who actively and obsessively bullies others. Of course, unless she ends up talking about it with the other moms, or anyone else, Jessi's mother's face is also positively preserved as well. In this sense, she, too, gets to pass, but as a mother who doesn't have a child engaged in vicious cyberbullying battles.

How Jessi's Story Could Have Ended

Jessi's story speaks to the ways in which cyberbullying shapes words and people in especially dynamic and destructive ways. It invites entry into a relational world that is often kept off the radar of adults. Yet it is no less violent. That said, Jessi's story does end rather well, or at least better than it might have ended. Not all stories of cyberbullying end well, and many of these battles do not involve bullying that is reciprocated. Rather many cases typically involve a bully, or bullies, attacking an innocent victim. I end this chapter by briefly describing one such case, the so-called "MySpace Suicide Hoax" (see Collins, 2008). It shines a light on the dangerous and life-ending extent to which cyberbullying can escalate, if proper intervention does not occur.

In October 2006, Megan Meir, a thirteen-year-old girl living in O'Fallon, Missouri, met Josh Evans, a boy around her age, on "MySpace," the social networking site. Meeting Josh was just what Megan needed. She had recently transferred to a new school after painstakingly trying to fit in at her old school. There she has been teased about her weight, lived with mild depression and, at times, lived with suicidal impulses. Even with the impulses, she never attempted suicide, and was being treated by a psychotherapist. Although the two never met in person, she felt Josh was attractive. Megan was thriving in her new school, and meeting Josh helped her to feel better. Then one day everything changed, when Josh said in a MySpace message to Megan, "I don't know if I want to be friends with you anymore because I've heard that you are not very nice to your friends." This was one of several such statements, which were also shared online with others. The last message sent by Josh, this time through America Online Instant Messenger, stated, "Everybody in O'Fallon knows who you are. You are a bad person and everybody hates you. Have a shitty rest of your life. The world would be a better place without you." Megan replied, "You're the kind of boy a girl would kill herself over." Twenty minutes later Megan's dead body was found hanging by a belt in her closet.

There is more to this senseless loss. A few weeks after the suicide, Megan's parents learned that "Josh Evans" was not actually a boy. The name and the MySpace account had been created by Lori Drew, mother of one of Megan's former "friends" at her previous school. Drew and her daughter created the account to see how Megan felt about the daughter, and to "mess with her." When the "MySpace Hoax" hit cable news, not until a year after Megan's death, Drew's name was largely kept out of the news. Drew claims not to have known about the terrible messages sent to Megan; they were sent by Drew's temporary employee, eighteen-year-old Ashley Grills. There were no criminal charges filed at the local level. Drew was later convicted federally for having violated the Computer Fraud and Abuse Act; however, the conviction was deemed wrongful, and later reversed. Although free from legal punishment, she and her family have been punished socially. Internet bloggers posted their personal information online, including photographs, telephone numbers, email information, and home address. Also, they were shunned by their neighbors.

The MySpace Hoax story is important because it stresses and underscores how bullying can lead to reprehensible and grave outcomes of harm. By conveying her narrative, Jessi understands in hindsight how lucky she, Maria, and Amber are that Jessi's mother intervened, and that the bullying stopped. She realizes the consequences of cyberbullying are real and material, showing a mindfulness that is present now, but was absent within the battle. The Hoax story is also instructive because it shows how cyberbullying can escalate with tragic results.

Note

1   When Jessi reviewed this chapter with me (see Appendix), she told me she doesn't see the "good girl" aspect of her bullying story as being all that significant. I've decided to leave that theme in the analysis, with her okay, believing some readers will identify with how youth who ordinarily do not participate in relational aggression can suddenly find themselves immersed in such bullying.

ROPE BURN

Reflexive Interlude 2

"What's fifth grade gonna be like?" I ask my mother.

"You'll love it," she replies, as she adds a couple of packs of number two pencils and a big eraser to our shopping cart. It is the end of August and a new school year starts next week. Since fifth grade in my school district means being in middle school, and going to a different school, I don't know what to expect.

"Will I have my own locker?" I ask.

"No, that starts in sixth grade, when you also will start changing classrooms for different classes. In fifth grade you'll still just have one homeroom and one main teacher."

"I'll be in … 5-C with Ms. Cheek"

"Yes, and she is a fantastic teacher—patient and kind, and she loves sweet little boys."

"I am sweet?! Awww, shucks." I press my finger to my cheek, trying to be cute. Mom smiles at me and gently rubs the back of my head, as she puts packages of doubled-spaced loose-leaf paper in our cart.

"I cannot *wait* to have a locker. I'll have a secret combination and will organize and decorate the locker exactly how I want it. I also cannot wait to roam the halls, to be free and on my own between classes. Anyway, I already feel like I'm in sixth grade, maybe even seventh. What do you think?"

"I think you're a wonderful fifth grade boy and you shouldn't grow up too soon."

"But what if I wanna be older?" I say, lifting my chin up in the air. "Well, I *feel* older."

"I know. You're very, *very* mature, honey." Even sarcasm sounds sweet coming from Mom. "But you'll have plenty of time to do all that soon enough. Enjoy fifth grade … be happy with where you're at."

"Okay, I will try. But do I have to be in gym class?" The cart stops and Mom looks at me. I already know her answer.

"Yes, you'll have to take gym each year until you graduate from middle school, and probably in high school, too." She returns to pushing our cart down the aisle.

"*Please* isn't there something else I can do instead of gym? I'll help teachers, or help in the office, or go to the library, or even do extra homework. I'll do anything but gym." This isn't the first time she and I have talked about gym. She knows I am serious, but that there is nothing she can do to fix the situation.

"Tell me again what it is about gym you don't like?"

"When I think of gym I feel a big pit in my stomach and my chest tightens to the point where I feel like I might not be able to breathe. You know I don't like the athletic activities they make boys do."

"I didn't like gym when I was you're age …"

"Yeah, but you're a girl! I mean, you were a girl. It is different for boys. People think boys are supposed to like gym … that we're supposed to be good at it, and if we're not, then there's something wrong with us. I suck at gym. I hate it."

"Language …" Mom looks around to see if anyone heard me.

"Sorry."

"Is this about what happened to you last year with the rope climbing?"

One day during gym in fourth grade, all boys were required to climb a long and thick rope that hung from the ceiling. Our gym teacher marked a point on the rope at least half way up, to signify the height to which boys are expected to climb. When it was my turn, the whole class watched me struggle to climb, and the teacher kept yelling "Come on, come on, get up there!" I only made it up a few feet and my hands and arms burned. Exhausted, I fell from the rope to the thick orange safety mat positioned underneath the rope on the ground. Looking over to the teacher for encouragement and support, all I saw was him shake his head in disgust. As I ran to my seat on the gym floor, I overheard a boy say to his friend, "He must not be a real boy … how pathetic." I sat down, buried my face in my hands, looking toward the ground. I was ashamed. I should have been able to climb higher. I wanted to be able to climb higher. I couldn't.

"That must have been so hard, honey."

"Well, it definitely wasn't fun. Everyone was looking at me!"

"Here's another good thing to look forward to in middle school: you will have a different teacher, named Mr. Sylvester. He is gentle, encouraging, and knows what it takes to teach boys in helpful ways."

I don't say anything and simply listen, as I look at all of the supplies on the store shelves.

"You'll be okay," she says, trying to get me to worry less. "You know that, right?" Her voice is not as certain as she has been in the past. I know that Mom knows she cannot fix this one for me. All boys (and girls) who are physically and mentally able must take gym.

I take a moment before responding: "I do, Mom. By the way, I need markers. Can I have the scented ones?" I change the subject but truth is I don't know if I will be okay. In fact, I am pretty sure I will *not* be okay, and I will hate everything about gym, except for being able to talk with my friends.

"Go ahead and grab a box, and grab one for your sister, too. Let's finish our list and go have some lunch."

"Lunch out at a restaurant … weeeeee!"

I don't suspect many kids make the transition between elementary school and middle school without feeling at least a little nervous. After all, the familiar comfort zones— favorite teachers, classrooms, and playground equipment—are suddenly replaced with new people to meet and spaces to learn. I feel excited and nervous about my transition. I am becoming a "middle schooler" and revel in the esteem I associate with this new identity, the new possibilities that dwell ahead as the little professor gets a little bigger and starts a new chapter.

I lose the ability to go see Mom during school days when I am not feeling well. I also am leaving behind Ms. Linderman and other teachers who have helped me prosper and stay well (enough) in elementary school. To be sure, new challenges for how I perform are fast approaching, and the ways in which middle school will affect how I feel, and who I understand myself to be, remain unknown.

SMA!

I am seated at my desk at the beginning of another school day in fifth grade. Many kids are still arriving to homeroom. Like most days, I arrived a bit early and have already begun to get ready for the day. I initiate my mental checklist: *My coat is hung up on the coatrack. Lunch—bologna with cheese and mayonnaise sandwich, bag of chips, and an apple—is in my backpack, which is hanging by my coat. Books are neatly organized in the shelf underneath the top of my desk. Two freshly sharpened pencils are on top of my desk, in the groove on the top of the desk, alongside a worn eraser and a few erasable pens. Where is my multi-colored click pen? Oh, it's at home, so no one in my class tries to steal it. Homework that is due today is complete.* I am organized and ready to begin another school day.

Enter Ms. Cheek, my homeroom teacher. Ms. Cheek cares about her students and has a dynamic presence in the classroom. As she walks through the room her long, straight, and flowing black hair bounces from one side of her head to the other. She looks like the actress Lynda Carter, who stars as Wonder Woman on television, a show I have loved for the past couple of years and have watched daily during the summer. She is smart, upbeat, and funny. Yet, she is also the type of teacher whom good students love and bad students fear, because she doesn't tolerate games. Personally, I fell for Ms. Cheek on the first day of school, and I would like to think she feels close to me as well. Maybe we're close because she knows I work hard as a student. She grades most of my work with a 4/4 score. She also knows I easily get nervous at school and often feel like I don't fit in with others. Regardless, when she speaks with me, her voice is calm and nurturing. She is quick to praise my work, too: "You're doing so well, Keith." "What a creative young man you are, Keith." I am at peace when I am around her and beam whenever she calls on me to answer a question in class.

As I sit at my school desk on this fall day, I am working to complete an in-class writing activity. I am fully engrossed in the experience and have assumed my usual posture: body leaning into the desk and hovering over the desktop; gut pressing up against the desk; one hand holding up my head with that hand's fingers grabbing onto my bangs; and my small brown glasses are barely catching onto my nose as I look down at my paper. Also, the tight grip I maintain on my pencil is so intense that by the time I finish middle school, it will have created a 1"x1" bump of skin directly below the nail on the left side of my index finger. The bump, which teachers tell me is a "writer's bump," will never go away. My mouth hangs open and my tongue is hanging partially out of my mouth, something I do often, but without realizing it. Every once and while I drool a little bit, which alerts me that my mouth is open, and I need to close it. Drool is, of course, one of the more gentle reminders I receive.

"Look at him ... he looks like a dumb ass!" Zach and Tom, two boys sitting directly to my right say repeatedly, as they point and laugh at me: "You are such a dumb ass." Their teasing feels like a spotlight is shining on me for the rest of the class to see, and their voices exude judgment. Put simply, the two scare me and always have. Zach and Tom are each other's best friends. They are rougher and more athletic boys and look like they could easily win a fight. They are the sort of boys whose chests stick out, or maybe they purposefully stick them out, so others will be impressed by their toughness. I am not friends with them, and they have barely said a word to me since the school year began. Nevertheless, today is their day to come at me.

Zach continues, "Look at Berry's mouth—it is wide open and his tongue is hanging out."

"My name is Keith, thanks very much," I say without looking at them. My hands are trembling, not only because of their meanness, but because I actually talked back to them. I usually don't talk back. It is too risky.

"Berry ... fairy, ya we get it," Tom adds. I say nothing and continue to look away.

Perhaps not getting the rise out of me he desires, Zach decides to escalate their attack, and says, "Fairy Berry, you're such a *SMA!*"[1]

Until now I have only heard people use SMA against other students. Yet, now Zach and Tom are naming *me* SMA. Still seated and looking down, I begin to panic and try to quickly figure out how I might respond. *How do I escape? Do I ignore them, like Mom and Dad tell me I should do with mean kids? I haven't witnessed ignoring stop bullying against other students. Do I say more to them? If so, what would I even say? I'm too nervous to even think of a smart sentence. Also, my first response did me no good. What if they want to fight at recess? I don't want to fight. Even if I wanted to fight, I wouldn't even know how to punch someone. Maybe I can kick them. Then again, if I did that they might say I was acting like a girl. Where's Ms. Cheek?* Ms. Cheek is helping students across the room, so she cannot see us. Scared I might choose the wrong response, and with both boys showing no signs of retreat, I freeze. I want to tell them off, but say nothing. I want to flee, but go nowhere.

Their taunts continue, as if to egg me on and make me fight back: "SMA has nothing to say. I guess he's speechless. Maybe he doesn't know words. Maybe that tongue of his is so fat it's clogged his mouth. That's why his mouth is always open. Wait, maybe he is not even a 'he' at all. That's it—Berry's a *she.*"

I focus on my writing, hoping they will leave me alone. Thinking it will help, I slowly shift my body to the left, so they will only see and be talking to my back. Still, they continue to ridicule me in chant form: "SMA SMA SMA SMA." My face and neck are beet red, and my hands are now shaking as I continue trying to write, pressing the pencil even harder against my index finger and onto the page. With my back to them, I am unable to see what they are doing. I fear at any second they will charge and punch me in the back. Still, I cannot look at them.

"Gentleman ... Zachary and Thomas," Ms. Cheek yells. "How is your writing coming?" She says nothing about what they were doing to me, but her confrontation stops them in their tracks. They return to doing their writing, and leave me alone. Hands still trembling and face still flushed, I exhale as I turn my body back to its usual direction, facing the front.

Still trembling a few minutes later I walk over to Ms. Cheek and ask, "May I go to the bathroom?"

"Of course, sweetie, just make sure you take the pass and come right back to the room. No wandering around like you did last time," she says with a smile. It took longer than normal to return from the bathroom the other day. I had an upset stomach, so it took me a while to finish in the bathroom. I also toured the hallways for a while, prolonging the trip and my time away.

"Okay, I'll come right back." I grab the wooden pass that dangles from a hook on the side of her desk and exit the classroom. I don't need to use the bathroom. I just need to get out of the classroom. I wasn't able to concentrate. Even more, I figure the longer I am away from class, the more likely my bullies will move on to other victims.

I arrive to the bathroom and am relieved to see I am alone. I make my way into the stall and close the door behind me, making sure it is firmly locked. I take down my pants and sit on the toilet, just in case I unexpectedly need to go. There in the stall, away from the fray of tougher bodies, hurtful words, and my own inability to stand up for myself, I sit content. Amid the particles of feces left in the bowl from the last user, and traces of urine that have built up on the seat over time, I feel safe. Yet, this safety is not enough, as I begin to ruminate, trying to figure out what had happened, and to calm myself. *Why me? I am one of the good students and did nothing to them. They must be troubled and come from bad families. Maybe they're jealous because I am close to Ms. Cheek and they are not. I wish I could change seats. Then again, changing seats will probably draw attention to me and make them bully me even more. Will they be waiting for me when I return to class? I wish I could go home.*

After a few minutes pass, I pull up and re-button my jeans. I flush the toilet, wash my hands, and return to the classroom. Ms. Cheek notices me return the pass and says, "Thank you, Mr. Berry. Well done." I see Zach and Tom are by themselves, on the other side of the classroom, goofing off. I return to my desk and quickly get back to my writing.

A few minutes later, as I get back to work, I notice my mouth is wide open and my tongue is hanging out. *SMA! SMA! SMA! BERRY'S A SHE! BERRY'S A SHE!* Fearing a reprisal of the bullying, I quickly pull my tongue back into my mouth, close it, and look around to see if anyone noticed. *Why do I do this with my mouth and tongue? Maybe Zach and Tom are right, maybe I am a "retard."* Thankfully no one saw me this time. I am safe, for now.

Zach and Tom will continue to bully me over the next couple of weeks. Their attacks usually hone in on the way in which I sit or walk, often with my mouth wide open and tongue hanging out. I become their personal SMA and favorite bullying target. Their weapons, though, are not limited to words. Sometimes when they walk past me, for instance, when students are lining up in the lunchroom for hot lunch, or to get jackets to go outside for recess, they feign like they are going to punch or choke me. Sometimes, when teachers aren't looking, they actually punch me in the bicep or stomach, often hitting hard enough to knock the wind out of me and draw tears to my eyes. Even though I am in pain, I fight hard to keep my tears hidden. If they see me cry, they will know how defenseless I am, how defenseless I feel, and will attack me more. They know how to get to me, and they're good at it.

As a result of their bullying, I begin to secretly train myself to never have my mouth open and tongue hanging out when I am at school. I tell no one of this training, because I don't want to risk anyone else making fun of me. For weeks I walk around with my lips pursed, to assure me my mouth is closed. From time to time, when I notice my mouth is open and tongue is hanging out, I instantly say out loud, "Stop it!" I never had noticed or seemed to care about this habit of mine until I was bullied for it.

Silent Treatment

I am at home sitting at the dinner table with my family later on that day. My family eats dinner together on nearly every weeknight and often on the weekends. It is Friday night and, therefore, it's pizza night. We're eating "garbage" pizza (loaded with all kinds of vegetables), mostaccioli, meatballs, garlic bread, and tossed salad. A few minutes into our meal, Mom interrupts our conversation and says, "Okay, let's go around the table and share the most memorable thing that happened today." We perform this ritual almost every night at dinner. I can tell Mom and Dad love it, based on how they beam at each other and us kids when we say something funny or special.

When it is my turn to share, I put down the slice of pizza I'm eating and say, "I don't have anything to share. There was nothing memorable today."

"Nothing?" my Dad probes.

I thought quickly to myself for a second about how I would respond. "Oh, Ms. Cheek told me 'well done' after I went to the bathroom!" My brother and sister both laugh. I can see my parents holding back laughter.

"Good job on doing well with the bathroom," Dad responds.

"Thanks, Dad." We smile at each other. My father is a man of few words, but his smiles show so much love and pride.

"You're welcome."

Turning to my brother and sister, I say, "Did you two go to the bathroom well today?" They both laugh again, and my brother hurls a piece of crust at me.

I am hoping my humor will take the attention off of me and keep me from needing to share anything serious. I say very little for the rest of dinner, as I have a lot on my mind. I am still thinking about the highly memorable experience of being bullied. I can hear Zach and Tom's chanting *SMA! SMA! SMA!* in my head, and when I think about what happened for too long, I start to feel anxious and quickly become overheated. I don't want to talk about what happened today. I just want it to go away. Still, I cannot stop thinking about their actions.

After dinner it is my turn to help Mom load the dishwasher. She and I are standing at the sink, scraping the remaining food off of the plates, rinsing them off, and then loading them into the dishwasher. "You were quiet at dinner tonight," Mom says to me. "Actually, you were also quiet when you got home from school earlier. Everything go okay at school today?"

"Ya, everything was fine," I quickly reply.

"You sure? You know you can tell me if there is something bothering you."

"I'm sure, I'm sure ... and yes, I know I can tell you anything." As we talk I am looking at the dishes and not Mom. If I look her in the eyes, I won't be able to continue fibbing. My secret will be blown, and I know she'll push me even more to talk about what is troubling me.

"Good," she responds in a tone of voice suggesting she is not convinced by my response. After a minute or two of silence, she adds, "You're a *special* boy, you know that, right?

"Yessssssss..." I say, embarrassed by the attention.

"Well you are ... a very special boy. We never have to worry about Keith." She closes up the dishwasher, rings the water out of the dish rage, and tosses it back into the sink.

I am still too shaken to let others know Zach and Tom bullied me today. They hurt me and made me scared to see or be around them at school. I am no match for them physically and don't want to fight in the first place. Also, if I wanted to talk back to them, I fear any words I use will sound like gibberish. My friends tell me the best way to stop being bullied is to respond with meanness. However, I don't like being mean and am no good at it. Yet, maybe I am also not ready to speak about being bullied because discussing what happened will be too shameful. Also, perhaps it was just a fluke occurrence, a one-time thing in my new school. Why talk about something that isn't an ongoing thing? If I don't speak to the bullying, maybe I can convince myself it never happened in the first place. While Mom wants me to talk, to help me feel better, opening up to her may make me feel worse.

Mom regularly tells me I am a "special boy." As I get older she will often tell me I am a "special young man." She leaves notes on my dresser, and signs greeting cards from her and my father with this message. Knowing of my proclivity to worry, she uses this message to affirm and love me. Perhaps she also says this for her own benefit, as a mantra that helps her worry less.

The Ruminator

"Just think of nothing, Keith. Before you know it, you'll be asleep," Mom says, several weeks later, after the boys have stopped bullying me. I am standing in our family room at home, where my parents are watching television and reading the *Chicago Sun-Times* newspaper.

I respond, "Can I just stay up a little bit longer and watch TV with you guys? Just a little bit longer?"

"Fifteen minutes, and then you're hitting the sack."

"Yes!" I say, as I grab my mother's *People* magazine from the table and hop onto the couch. I am stalling.

Fifteen minutes speed by and I hear my father say, "Okay, Keith. It's time." My mother stares at me, confirming my father's decision.

I say looking at my mother, "I won't be able to sleep. I just know it."

Mom replies, "You'll be okay, now go. It is time."

Realizing they're serious, I begin to walk out of the room.

"Remember, just think about nothing," she adds. This technique is one of her most prized suggestions on nights when I am unable to fall asleep, which is frequently. Her advice is counterproductive, however, because now I have to think about thinking about nothing.

Once in bed, I lay on my back, pull the sheets and comforter up to my chest, and begin to stare at the ceiling. I try to think of nothing by picturing a black screen in my mind. I see the blackness, but soon after I start to see bright rainbow colors. As these images amplify, random other thoughts creep into my consciousness: running across the lawn with our dog Candy; sounds of my dad opening another beer upstairs; back to trying to see nothing; then back to Zach and Thomas; then to tomorrow's piano lessons; then to wondering if other kids have these sleeping troubles.

Sometimes the thinking of nothing technique works, and I am able to fall asleep. When it doesn't work, I usually turn on the light and read a book. Soon after I begin I often find myself becoming sleepy. To seize the moment, I quickly turn off the lights, close my eyes, and fade into sleep. Sometimes this technique fails; and I fall back into the cycle of rumination.

In fifth grade I begin to ruminate, especially when I am in bed or at school. I think about situations through which I have recently lived, primarily experiences that are troubling me, or simply things I am trying to understand. I ruminate about upcoming and anticipated interactional situations. This thinking often exhausts me. I get lost in incessant thinking, feeling tightness in my chest and a pit in my stomach. Sometimes my ruminating persists to the point where I shake my head quickly from side to side, as if to snap myself out of thinking and back into the present moment. While my imagination and ability to visualize has often served me well, my practices of ruminating remind me that sometimes my ability to think through stuff can be incapacitating. Sometimes I wish I could simply turn off my thinking.

Methodological Dilemma

"Write your stories in ways that paint a vivid picture of your lived experience with bullying—the bullying practices through which you lived and their consequences. Make it creative, personal, and impactful."

As I lead students through a mid-semester, in-class writing activity, I am emphasizing writing with "thick description" (Geertz, 1973), and vulnerable and evocative storytelling (Bochner & Ellis, 2016; Ellis, 2004). Most students appear, to me, to be excited and ready to practice autoethnography. Yet, the more I invite them to write openly, the more I see many of their eyes widen, suggesting they are beginning to figure out that this genre requires hard work and personal risks. Moreover, writing in these ways on the topic of bullying compels them to candidly speak to their relationship to violence and the vulnerabilities of talking about being harmed or harming others. As a result, it will implicate them in ways that may not feel good.

A student asks, "Just how open do these pictures need to be? I mean, how deep do we have to go?" In some form or another, many students will ask me this same question during the semester in class, through email, and during office hours.

"Thanks for the helpful question. Can you tell me more about your concern?"

"Sure. You've told us we get to choose what we disclose in writing our stories. We shouldn't convey thoughts and feelings that we don't feel safe in disclosing. However, to write good stories we need to openly convey difficult experiences that involve tough emotions."

"Correct. I hope that you're already asking yourselves some of these tough questions, and reflecting on the limits you may want to put in place for yourselves."

Another student jumps in to say, "I want to write a good story, but writing in this way is definitely new to me. I am not sure how I feel about telling people how I felt, and how I feel about how I felt."

"Cleverly stated," I respond, smiling. "To be sure, the questions we're asking ourselves in this process will likely resist easy answers. I bet you'll experience a lot of uncertainty and encounter competing or contradicting questions and answers.

"Like wanting to be open, but not knowing if we can do it, or how open we want to be. Or excited to write in these ways, but scared about what it will be like to go back to times in our life that were so terrible."

"Yes, I understand."

"While at this point we may not know how the process of writing your personal story will end, I do believe that it will be a powerful experience in which you come to understand your lived experience with clearer detail. Also, don't be surprised if you begin to think more clearly and feel more confident about those experiences, and about yourself, through the process."

I see a few students smiling and nodding their head, telling me they are thinking through or connecting with the ideas. Many begin to pack up their belongings as we've reached the end of the class meeting.

"Remember: I'll be with you, helping you along the way. You'll help each other, too. Okay, that's enough for now. Have a great rest of the day!"

As the students get up to leave the room, many are wide eyed and have blank expressions on their faces. Their looks lead me to feel as though I have walked them up to the end of a pier and assigned them to jump into unknown water. I will be with them in class throughout the semester to answer questions and give direction and encouragement, but ultimately they will be managing their own reflection and writing process.

This methodological dilemma is rooted in the unique teaching and research experience of immersing undergraduate students in autoethnographic inquiry, which asks them to revisit painful lived experience and to possibly experience new pain as a result. How do I maintain "control" of the classroom within this context? Is control even desirable? My students trust me to be a compassionate and protective teacher, yet adding researcher to this identity creates additional issues to be reconciled. What becomes of *my* identity through this relational process?

Note

1   "SMA" is a professional acronym I first heard in elementary school that stands for "socially maladjusted." It is a category of students who live with special needs, or people who need extra attention and accommodation from teachers and staff. As if this meaning isn't harsh enough, when students in my grade say SMA, they mean to call someone "smelly mentally affected." The term is a widely used epithet that, in essence, is used to mean "retard." Bullies use it to target and ridicule others liberally, seemingly without at all caring about its harmful consequences.

4

FLYING TOMATOES

Cruella's Clash with the Dalmatians

JEZEBEL

Lunch for Jezebel meant feeling nervous, which she routinely felt from the moment she entered the lunch line.

> I never quite understood the anxiety that comes from hearing the ring of the lunch bell. Upon each ring, I think, "Great, it's that time again to scramble and find the nearest friend to stand in the lunch line with so I don't look like a weird loner." Unfortunately today, I couldn't find a single friend, so I ended up standing in the lunch line alone for what seemed like hours. Getting a chicken patty like you do every day shouldn't be this arduous and grueling, right?

The mundane practice of taking a turn and receiving food, for her, is a tenuous ritual requiring careful attention and movement. She already feels like she stood out, and this makes her uncomfortable. Trying to be inconspicuous, Jezebel inches her way forward in line and then to a table, making sure to look only at her cell phone, not make eye contact with others. She knew what to do: look busy and distracted, and then others won't notice how lost you are, and how lonely you feel. Stay on guard. Don't let them see you, as she writes, "a lonely little middle school kid sitting at a table, slowly gulping food and death-staring at the clock, wishing you had the ability to speed up time." Stay on guard and lunch shall pass, she hoped.

Pressing questions pervade Jezebel's lunchroom existence. If I have no one with me in line, with whom will I sit during lunch? How will other kids treat me … if they even talk with me at all? Will I eat in peace? Will they include me? Will they leave me alone? She continues the forced look of distraction, working to hide or lessen how nervous she feels:

> I feel like a puppy at an aquarium. I knew very well that the other kids thought I was a complete "weirdo," someone who doesn't fit their archetype of "preppy," "popular," "Aeropostale brand clothes-wearing" socialites. I knew it from the judgmental glares, the random IMs I would receive on AOL: "You're fucking weird, nobody likes you." I knew how they felt about me from the muffled giggling in the hallway that would scratch away at my ear.

Others have hurt her in the past, and she figures they will do so again in the future. Sensitive and uneasy, she must be ready.

Jezebel regularly wore a "Naruto" headband around her neck. Naruto is anime, a "manga" (comic) series created in Japan that centers on the ninja monk character Naruto Uzamaki. Wearing the headband helped her to reconcile the ways she has ruminated about feeling alone. She writes with pride about the headband and what it represented: "It takes a lot of guts to parade around like an open book, trying to be unashamed of the things I like. The headband is a metal plate, with a leaf insignia encrusted into it. It acts as a sort of armor." At the same time, wearing it entailed risk. "Ironically, this armor only seems to attract more attackers," she writes. "I know that because I don't always have a buddy around, I am an open target." Indeed, the armor that was meant to bring her greater protection often made for greater problems. Still, she cherished that headband and would always wear it.

Jezebel's lived experience with bullying took the form of a viscerally and emotionally charged series of attacks that spanned three days. The bullying came in blasts that increased her insecurities. It also made her question a relationship of hers that she treasured.

Day One

Standing alone in line Jezebel was relieved to spot her closest friend, Rose, walking into the lunchroom. She beamed while calling out to her:

> "Rose!" There Rose was, stumbling around like a lost puppy, someone I identified with. I instinctively waved her over in a reeling sort of motion with my hands; I needed her help. I could feel the dark fog, the grimacing stares around me clear away as I realized I was not alone. With a bright smile that almost creased all the way to her eyebrows, her shoes turned into pogo sticks as she gleefully bounced over to me and joined me in the line. Safe, I was finally safe. I could breathe a sigh of relief as the loneliness and worry evaporated away from me.

Jezebel felt she and Rose were kindred spirits, connected by the comfort each friend gave to the other. With Rose, she was less lonely, and could relax. Rose was her sunshine. She knew Rose felt similarly about her.

Such comfort would be short lived on this day, however, as Jezebel remembers a shift in the climate; storm clouds moved in and covered up the warm sunshine:

> I was in the middle of taking this invigorating breath, until a nasty, snarky voice screeched and interrupted, "UM … NO." I had made a grave mistake. Daringly turning around to match this ear-splitting, malicious voice to the face of its owner, I craned my head up to see the scrunched up, distressed visage of my unwanted new enemy.

The enemy, to whom she refers in her story as "Cruella," is a much older student. Cruella regularly gets into fights at school, and, as Jezebel describes, is "your stereotypical popular, rebellious and self-absorbed diva of the school." Accompanied by the backup of an equally intimidating friend, Cruella shouted at Jezebel and Rose, "You did NOT just cut in front of us!" The two slowly turned around, as if they had not heard a thing: "We held still and strong, much like how a tree trunk doesn't budge even when a 5-ton car crashes against it." However, their response did not satisfy Cruella, who, to grab the attention of adults nearby, began to yell, "They … CUT! CUTTERS HERE! CUTTERS!" One of the adults walked over and escorted Rose to the back of the line. Jezebel was alone again, feeling unsafe without her lost puppy, and trying to understand what had occurred: "I kept pondering why it was such a huge deal that one person joined the line, when multiple people get served at the same time. It would have made no difference in their lives if she was there accompanying me."

Now several years later Jezebel feels confident that moment was not about food service, or whether or not she would get her food any sooner. She writes, "This was the day Cruella's desire for power over the younger and weaker grew." It was the day when she grabbed for power and authority by unsettling Jezebel and Rose, who already felt shaky about their social status.

Day Two

Jezebel, again, was standing alone in the lunch line. However, she was glad to see Rose, who had arrived earlier, and was saving her a spot at one of the tables. Soon after getting into line, Jezebel heard the voice of Cruella booming from somewhere behind her. Quickly her mood turned from happy to anxious. Once again she began working to manage her situation:

> I act as if I don't notice her, trying my hardest to gain the superpower of speeding up time. She notices I'm ignoring her, which is why she wanted to make her presence impossible to disregard. In the most abhorrent fashion

possible, she leers over me until I can feel her hot, predatory breath frizz the hair on the top of my head. Impulsively I start to comb away at my hair due to the unsettling irritation she has caused throughout my scalp, when my fingers brushed up against something other than my hair. It was knobby and had a rough and round surface. I knew something was wrong. It was Cruella's nose!

Cruella shouted, "Oh HELL NO you did NOT just touch my face with your greasy little hands!" Jezebel quickly turned around and mumbled, "I didn't touch your….!" Cruella stopped her before she could finish and yelled, "You JUST touched my face while you were messing with your ratty ass hair!" Jezebel just stood there, dumbfounded and silent.

Cruella seized the moment and continued her attack. "Now turn around," she demanded. Jezebel complied and turned around. Cruella responded, "That's a *good* girl." Jezebel was sunken and, again, felt small:

> It was just like how you'd speak to a dog; in this case, a Dalmatian. After I had turned around I heard her sidekick let out a snarling laugh. I felt defeated, as if there was nothing I could do or say to regain my self-esteem. I felt helpless. At that moment my silence was the loudest scream of frustration I could have ever made. My shoulders hung low, my chest caved in, and my head dangled downward until I finally reached the register to punch in my student ID numbers and receive my mediocre school lunch.

It had only been one day since Cruella's first attack, and she already had gained power over Jezebel. No armor would help. Cruella seized control with a few quick but sharp blows. She had won.

Day Three

On this day Jezebel was enjoying a rare lunchtime treat—Cruella wasn't anywhere in sight! As usual Jezebel was eating, talking, and laughing with Rose, whom she felt was not only a friend but also her safe haven: "My oasis was at the lunch table with Rose. There, I never had to deal with snarky, nasty mannered girls who pinched and scraped away at my self-confidence." There with Rose she felt more at ease and secure. They felt that way together, and because of each other. A few minutes later, Cruella and her friends sauntered toward where the two were sitting. Jezebel panicked, thinking to herself, "Please don't come over here. This isn't where you sit. At least, I hope this isn't where you sit. Oh my God—what if this is where she sits?!" Soon her fears became realized.

"UM … NO." Cruella yelled, just like the first time. "You are NOT sitting here, this is where WE sit."

Jezebel responded with silence.

"MOVE. Get OUT of the seat."

Jezebel shrugged.

Cruella's voice became louder: "You're seriously not sitting here, you aren't welcome here. EVER."

Jezebel looked to Rose. More silence. Nobody who was eating and talking at the nearby tables had any clue this was going on.

"Are you deaf? Can't you hear? MOVE!" Cruella's face reddened and scrunched up as she grew more furious. This time Jezebel took the heat and just sat there, refusing to give up her seat. Cruella relinquished by sitting down directly across from her. Cruella's friend sat right in front of Rose, and their guy friend sat down to the right of Jezebel. Jezebel was trapped.

Cruella and her friends turned up the heat of their attacks: "We hate you." "Your hair is ugly." "You're clothes are dumb."

Hearing these terrible words, Rose whispered in Jezebel's ear, "Ignore them; pay them no mind." Yet, Cruella had no plan to stop. Instead she barked at Jezebel, "Why are you even here? It's obvious no one wants you here. Why don't you just leave?" Jezebel sat there and didn't show them her face. She was no longer hungry. She looked to Rose for support, who had nothing to say, and chose to do nothing. Jezebel didn't budge. Instead she waited for this storm to pass. She was silent, but had much on her mind:

> I wanted to say so many things. SHUT UP! Get a life, get away from me, and if you don't want me sitting here too bad, why don't YOU leave? I was here first, you don't own this table, and you have no right to tell me where to sit. Why are you so obsessed with what I do and where I choose to sit? Why is it such a big deal? You're freaking out over nothing, I never did anything to you, just leave me alone. LEAVE ME ALONE!

There were many things she wanted to say to her. Instead, Jezebel muttered, "No one cares." Her words drew no response from Cruella, or her friends. Silence filled the air for the next minute or so, prompting Jezebel to feel like she had, yet again, made a grave mistake. "Um, I CARE!" blurted Cruella. The awkwardness of the situation grew, as did Jezebel's regret. More silence:

> I desperately tried to think of a topic to talk with Rose about, but no words would come out of my mouth. Cruella and her friends must have concluded their tactic of talking luridly about their revulsion for my existence wasn't working, because I wasn't budging. Soon they switched their method to a "silent" psychological assault, by scrutinizing me with scowling glares that attempted to pierce my resolve. Their approach crippled me with inner conflict and uncertainty: what are they thinking? What are they going to do? What are they looking at?

She chose to do what she had felt most comfortable doing in the past—disengage Cruella:

> My eyes wandered in every direction that didn't connect with their line of sight. Every item that was above their heads, or on either side of them, became infinitely more interesting to me. I never knew I could have such appreciation for a poster, a flyer, or someone else eating across the table. The object I looked at the most was the clock. Yet, as if the clock wanted to spite me, it turned its hands only leisurely, and so excruciatingly slow. It's as if Cruella had the superpower to slow time, so she could bask in her forty minute lunch period of power.

As lunch drew to a close, the glares stopped. Yet, the puppies knew this was not a time to feel relief. Certainly there was more to come.

Noticing that lunch was almost over Cruella started making jokes, particularly ones about Jezebel looking like garbage. Jezebel's ability to appear unphased continued, which meant Cruella needed to resort to advanced bullying tactics: physical attacks. Suddenly Jezebel saw her look down at the salad she was eating for lunch, pick out a baby tomato, and throw it across the table at her, landing on her lap—as if Jezebel were her garbage can. "Take that," Cruella sneered, "you piece of TRASH." That was enough for Jezebel. Looking down at the tomato, she knew she had only a second to a respond:

> I took the tomato out of my lap and rapidly set it in front of my tray. They took it and threw it back at me. I placed it to the right of me. They took it and threw it back at me. I placed it to the left of me. They took it and threw it back at me.
>
> What was I doing? Why didn't I just throw it on the floor? I was so rattled I couldn't make any logical movements at this point. Even Rose was looking at me with an expression that seemed to say, "What in the world are you doing?!" It was time to put this to an end. Without even looking I smashed the tomato down to the right of me, as far away as possible. Yet, I had made another grave mistake.

The gush of the tomato had landed in a pool of ketchup and French fries on the tray of one of Cruella's friends, prompting him to shriek, "GROSS!" The retaliation only further incited Cruella, who picked up the ketchup and tomato combination and threw it directly at Jezebel's white shirt. The shirt she was wearing, now soaked, was one she didn't usually wear. Instead of wearing her usual "Power Puff Girls" shirt, or one with Naruto on it, she had pleaded with her mother to get her a new wardrobe, something, as she writes, "a preppy, popular, Aeropostale-wearing socialite would wear." Seeing the gush on this new shirt, she questioned her desire to wear such clothing in the first place:

"What was I doing, why did I want to change, why did I think getting a new shirt would take the target off my back?" She knew something didn't feel right. This new armor wasn't working, she wasn't being herself.

Cruella's last volley of food drew an instantaneous reaction from the crowd, which horrified Jezebel:

> Laughter thundered throughout the lunch room. The tomato rolled off excruciatingly slow, like the clock's leisurely hands, leaving a bright red stain. I stared at the stain and everything it represented to me: shame, grief, and sorrow. At that moment, I wanted to be anyone but the person residing in my skin. These were all emotions I tried so hard to hide. Yet, here the feelings emerged in the form of an extremely noticeable and gaudy red blemish. Red like my face. Red like my bleeding heart. Red like my anger and frustration. Red like the traffic signal that shrieks "STOP. STOP. STOP. STOP."

Jezebel tried to remain calm, as Rose helped her to the gym locker room, so she could change into clean gym clothes. Once there and feeling safer, she was able to release. She sobbed and huffed, and tears flowed down her hot red face. Rose hugged her and said, "Don't mind simple-minded people." After that, she just let Jezebel begin to recover from the embarrassment.

Previously Jezebel had been able to avoid engaging Cruella. However, with the bullying, Jezebel's strength and resolve disappeared. She was humiliated and tired, and felt as though she had nowhere to turn:

> When I went home that afternoon, I collapsed to my knees. I clasped my hands together and prayed to God: "Dear Lord, I love you so much. Please, please I beg you to make her leave me alone. Please make her leave me alone, I don't know what I'll do if this continues. Please make her go away, or I swear I'll get violent. I don't want to be violent again; I don't ever want to be violent again, please."

Rising from her knees Jezebel began to reflect on this third day of bullying. She was thankful for not letting Cruella and her friends see her be so emotional: "I didn't allow her to realize the power she had over me, and the impact she had on my emotions. I feel like I won."

Jezebel also felt upset about Rose's involvement, or lack thereof, during these latest attacks. She wanted her friend to defend her. Instead Rose had been silent:

> She was a first-hand witness, and she made no effort to actively ease the situation. It was almost as if she was trying to embody a stranger, a bystander, someone who isn't expected to step in. Her own fear stifled her from being a hero to a close friend. In that moment she was a cold stranger to me.

Before Jezebel had relied on Rose, counting on her being there for her; after all, she was her oasis. Now Rose's absence made her feel alone and stranded, only intensifying the hurt she felt from being bullied. She writes, "This bothered me deeply. I was so frustrated that Rose had absolutely no desire to defend me. I felt betrayed for the longest time. I could see my safety net snap right before my eyes." Cruella's latest abuse humiliated Jezebel. Therefore, she didn't want to relive the moment, and so she never confronted Rose about not being there for her.

In writing her story, Jezebel is now able to understand the situation in more circumspect ways. She feels Rose was trying to focus on her own safety, and she couldn't simultaneously do that *and* defend Jezebel. She knew how hard it was to tolerate Cruella's attacks, how difficult it made lunch for people who already felt different than most people. They shared those feelings of difference together. She is now at peace with Rose's choice. The two remained good friends for four years after the bullying, until Rose's family moved across the state. They are still in contact.

Jezebel's circumspection is not the end of the story.

There was a fourth day conveyed in her bullying story. Although many of the same characters are involved, on this day action shifted:

> Cruella saw me that next day. I gulped. She looked past me. She continued to talk with her cronies like normal, not even paying any attention to me. She had no nasty comments, no malicious glares, not a single tomato to spare. From that day on, she never said a word to me again.

Cruella soon graduated from middle school and no longer continued to be a problem for Jezebel or Rose. However, years later, during high school, Jezebel saw Cruella coming toward her, which, for her, conjured up familiar feelings:

> I was paralyzed at the first moment I saw her. I was older and tougher now, but the blows she landed on me when I was most impressionable left long-term scars. Everything came rushing back to me, and all I could do was stare at her, wondering if she would even recognize me. She looked over at me, as did her crony. I braced myself for ominous glares, for terrible comments, and for the same roaring laughter I was so used to hearing from across the room. I prepared myself for the past to rear its ugly head at me, and to continue to haunt me as I go through what was supposed to be "the best years of my life."

While she was prepared for the worst, Jezebel was surprised by what she experienced.
Instead, they smiled at me.
They SMILED at me.
Both of them, they smiled and waved. They were genuine smiles.
She ends her story by stressing the significance of that moment: "Maybe that was their way of saying, 'We're sorry'—a slight moment of apology non-verbally.

Whatever it was, in that moment I forgave them. I forgave both of them instantly, and I have never felt so free since."

She also adds a little humor, writing, "They always *did* have ways of shocking me … and I do believe in miracles!"

ANALYZING JEZEBEL'S STORY

Cruella de Ville is a centerpiece of the classic story *The Hundred and One Dalmatians* and the character Jezebel invokes as the bully in her story. Cruella was an heiress who stole and skinned little Dalmatian puppies to sell their fur. The name "Cruella de Ville" plays off of the words "cruel" and "devil," which is a fitting appraisal of identity for a problematic character. Indeed, Jezebel's story offers a tale of two targeted "puppies" trying to save their skin.

Flaunting Spots

Being different mattered to Jezebel in ways that were at once similar to and distinct from Iman's negotiations of difference. As Littlejohn and Domenici (2007) write, "The meanings we construct in communication are rife with distinctions. We draw lines and make borders. We 'see' differences—between things, ideas, values, people, and groups" (p. 29). Difference can be an affirming and negative dimension to interaction and relationships, and is as much a social construction as it is a "real" and impactful dimension to lived experience that communicators negotiate (Allen, 2011).

Similar to Iman, Jezebel speaks to negative reactions from others concerning her being different, such as others treating her like a "loner" or "weirdo" and the glares she received from others while walking through the halls. The bullying and harsh treatment told her that being different, or at least the ways in which she was different, was not favorable within the more "popular" population of students at school. In these ways, they oriented to her difference by resisting and fighting it, as opposed to embracing it (and her). Consequently, like Iman, rather than feeling accepted and celebrated, others' judgment over time led her to feel like she did not belong and hurt her self-esteem. While we do not know directly from Cruella why she bullied her, the story shows that prior to the bullying Jezebel's identity felt marked as "other," thus, subjecting her to exclusion and attacks.

Jezebel's performance of being different was also distinct from Iman's, primarily in regards to how she managed the difference. Iman performed in more subdued and withdrawn ways while she was being bullied; that is, although she worked to be herself, she also did not blatantly accentuate the ways in which she felt, or others saw her as, different. In contrast, Jezebel's performance, especially in wearing the headband, accentuated her difference. She did not just feel different, and others didn't just lead her to feel that way. Rather, she performed in ways that openly and visibly put on display, or "flaunted" (Yoshino, 2007) her disfavored identity as "other." Yet, by stressing her difference in this way, she also made herself into a more clearly defined target for bullies. I am not suggesting she "asked for it" (the bullying); instead, by being more visible, others were able to seize upon the difference and her. Thus, by boldly flaunting her spotted identity, Jezebel performed as an especially vulnerable, even if prideful, little puppy. Indeed, she was tagged for skinning but determined not to let it happen.

In these ways, the pre-bullying identity of being "different," and someone who made difference more visible, works in ways that set a tone or a context for bullying. On one level, by introducing her difference, the story asks readers to understand how bullying did not come without warning. Jezebel had long been living with feelings of being judged and excluded. Cruella and others opted to take the violence to a higher level. In doing so, she calls attention to youth who self-identify in these ways, ascribing to them an "at-risk" status, if you will, for bullying. At the same time, the ways in which she introduces difference invites readers to live empathetically with her, considering what it must have felt like to survive and try to be well.

Performing Warrior

Jezebel's cherished "Naruto" headband provided her with a diverse number of ways in which to perform her herself. First, wearing her headband enabled Jezebel to openly symbolize her difference. She does not mention that anyone else wore one, or anything like it. I also suspect that the majority of her peers did not dress in ways that so readily and outwardly made them stand out to others. Yet, for her, it was meaningful insofar as it distinguished her from others, especially the "Aeropostale clothes-wearing" cool kids. Thus, by performing herself through the headband she avowed her identity as a different girl who was open to being unpopular.

Her performance says, "I am different than you, and I know it. I accept and am okay with this difference, as you should be able to clearly tell. I am this way whether or not you understand or accept it." This mode of performing identity is resonant with how many youth use their bodies to display their being different than the "norm"—for example, brightly colored pink or blue hair, piercings, "goth" make-up, quirky clothes. The shapes, modifications, and colors of bodies here serve as flaunted symbols of difference, drawing others into their worlds, compelling them to deal in some way with this difference. To be sure, it is brave and useful for youth to perform in ways that proudly flaunt their difference. As Jezebel writes, "It takes a lot of guts to parade around like an open book, trying to be unashamed of the things I like." Rather than attempting to hide, or to tone down, this difference, she strapped the headband around her neck, day after day, and roamed through the lunchroom and school energized.

Similarly, there is a way in which embodying the headband effectively "queers," or disrupts, normative positions on identity (Berry, 2014; Yep, Lovaas, & Elia, 2003). The queering is possible and necessary under conditions of communication wherein larger and more dominant ways of relating and understanding who relational partners are, or who they "should" be, prevail. Queering "gives voice" to ways of performing that were previously unavailable or silenced by normative convention and persons in power. In this way, wearing the headband is to say and ask, "There are many, equally viable ways of dressing, and of being a girl. Do you not see how you are trapped within a myopic way of orienting to the world? There is liberation, and freedom, to be found by breaking free from the pack." Troubling identity like this situates these performers at risk of harm. Yet, it also opens up the potential for a multiplicity of meaning in regards to living and relating to diverse bodies and beings.

Jezebel's self-identifying in these queer ways largely relates to how the headband symbolizes who she *currently* is, and in ways that are directed toward others as her audience. However, as is the case with examining all lived experience, this phenomenon is complex and subject to multiple interpretations. Thus, the headband meaningfully displays the young girl Jezebel *would like to be*, and in ways that direct the performance to herself as audience, or self-as-other. Her performances reminded her of her inherent beauty, a truth that her bully worked to dismantle. In addition, the headband was a reminder of the ideals of the Naruto warrior, with which she closely identified. Regularly wearing it prompted her to be a strong leader, even if the cruelty of others simultaneously made her feel sad and alone, and even when bullying led her to feel weak and confused. In these ways, wearing the headband meant performing as an *aspiring* warrior self, helping to point Jezebel in the direction she felt was right during times when bullying made her feel wrong. What might have been a silly headband to others, then, served as a way for her to maintain vision and try to be herself, even though it evoked bullying from those who resented or did not understand it.

No matter how brave Jezebel was, she was also a middle school student who was immersed in the process of feeling excluded and later on being bullied. She was a vulnerable warrior who needed protection. In the story, Jezebel speaks to this need when she references the headband as "armor," and suggests it helps her to ward off enemies.

Though she does not return to the headband after its initial mention, I cannot help but envision it as being critical to her survival. I visualize her standing at the bathroom mirror in the morning, checking the headband and further tightening it around her neck. With the headband fastened well, she felt safer and more secure; however, should it fall off around Cruella and others, she would be unarmed and at greater risk for and during attack. Also, I feel with her the added security that comes from having the backup of a symbol that is the source of one's great strength. I sense the physical contact of the metal encrusted insignia on her neck with her, as she's slowly turning around in the lunchroom line after another confrontation. I see Cruella noticing it for the first time and wonder if she ever honed in on it as an object to use in her bullying.

While Jezebel's performing the headband demonstrates creativity and resourcefulness, the headband had its limits. It could not prevent the warrior from being provoked into entering combat. In turn, while the story shows her enduring in resilient ways within conditions of psychic and physical stress, it also could not keep her from being bullied. In addition, as Jezebel writes, there was a counterproductive aspect to wearing it: "Ironically, this armor only seems to attract more attackers. I know that because I don't always have a buddy around, I am an open target." In this way, the headband donned to protect her also served to entice others and, at the very least, confirm their assumptions that she was "fucking weird." Indeed, performing the headband was met with contradictory outcomes. For when Jezebel was alone, or with Rose, the headband embodied everything they both loved and needed to enjoy in their young queer worlds. Yet, when she stepped fully into the formidable bullying space of the lunchroom, her headband was merely an abject object to bullies, as was Jezebel.

Appetite Lost

The three primary days Jezebel conveyed in her story comprise brief but powerful attacks that further speak to issues of identity within bullying, including the prominence of bodies, power, emotional toll, and the vital relationship of friendship in coping.

Bodies

There are two ways that Jezebel's account points to bodies being located at the center of attention in bullying. First, Cruella verbally attacked Jezebel's physical appearance, implicating her body as a site of critique. Similar to the stories of Iman, Jessi, Lauren, and Ena, here the bully honed in on the quality of her body, critiquing her "ratty ass hair" and "greasy little hands." In turn, the attacks escalated when Cruella referred to her as a "piece of TRASH" (to be followed later by her physically using Jezebel as a trash can). These were not "just words" that one peer said to another; rather, they were loaded words, uttered by a bully, and directed at a young girl who may have had the resolve of a warrior, but who was young, human, and vulnerable. Jezebel took the attacks seriously, and they made an impact, further demonstrating the power of words to hurt (Vangelisti, 1994). For instance, the attacks deemed Jezebel as someone whose body was dirty, gross, and undesirable. Also, Cruella only bullied Jezebel when they were surrounded by peers, which increased the chances others would hear what was being said, laugh, or perhaps join in on the taunts. In these ways, the presence of others compounded the embarrassment and humiliation that stemmed from the attacks. For me, the significance of the attacks is elevated when Cruella calls Jezebel "trash." Folk wisdom would suggest trash is not something most people typically like, cherish, and save; rather, it is something beneath us that should be eliminated. With Jezebel already feeling as if she did not belong, being ascribed this identity served to exclude her even more. Overall, Cruella's verbal attacks on the body disconfirmed Jezebel, leading her to feel even more devalued. Indeed, to Jezebel, the attacks effectively confirmed the meaningfulness of the glares and giggles from passersby in the hall: she was an outsider.

Second, Jezebel's story speaks to the visceral ways in which bodies exhibit force and exert influence within bullying. This pattern is visible in a diverse number of ways, including the roaring of Cruella's sinister voice that Jezebel felt within her own skin, Cruella situating herself, through her larger body, over and against Jezebel's smaller body in the lunch line, Jezebel's mistakenly touching Cruella's nose and, thus, instigating another attack, the physical trapping of Jezebel and Rose by Cruella and her cronies at the lunch table, and Cruella's hurling of the tomato from her salad at Jezebel, her trash can. Each of these instances is laden with ways of understanding bullying and embodiment. For instance, Cruella's trapping moment shows the bully using her body, and engaging the victim's body, to impose herself in the victim's space. The action prevented Jezebel from standing or sitting, or from peacefully interacting with a friend. In this way, her body was being used as a relational site of harassment, threat, and intimidation. Cruella's body was to be feared, and Jezebel's was to be treated as inferior, and subject to Cruella's domination at any pending moment.

Power

Intimidation and domination speak to issues of power (Wilmot & Hocker, 2011), which Jezebel stresses in her story after each round of eating lunch/being bullied. The account suggests bullies "win" power when they overtake "younger" and "weaker" victims and see their harmful impact on them. Victims win when they are not harmed by bullies and/or do not let them see such impact. We witness struggles for power occurring between Jezebel and Cruella and her cronies in a number of ways, such as when she refuses to leave her seat at the lunch table, and when she placed the food back on the table for Cruella and her friends to throw it back at her. Her defiance in these contexts symbolically shows the young warrior—even if fearfully—standing her ground and hoping for her win.

Jezebel's careful management of her responses to Cruella's bullying suggests an important need to cover vulnerability in bullying. As she suggests in regards to power, weakness, or letting Cruella know she had impacted her, is a stigmatizing behavior. It was important for Jezebel to tone down or make less obtrusive just how vulnerable she was, unless she wished to be further discredited, and possibly further bullied. Therefore, she performed in ways that tried to play it cool when feeling the heat of Cruella's actions. This attempt shows in various moments, including when she slowly turned around in the lunch line, didn't engage Cruella when trapped at the table, or decided to remain quiet rather than sharing with Cruella what she "really wanted to say."

However, maybe it was not very difficult for her. Whether Jezebel knew it or not, she was embodying the warrior: never making the first move, waiting for the opponent to commit and then move. Unfortunately, her inaction led to further torment because she also did not, or could not, use her voice to stop Cruella's behavior.

Emotions and Psychological Tolls

No matter how proud of being unique Jezebel was, or how open she was to display her difference, she paid a price for having been bullied. The story shows her suffering on emotional, psychological, and physical levels.

As is the case with all of the stories in this book, emotions significantly shaped Jezebel's experience of bullying. The attacks conjured up a broad spectrum of difficult feelings with which she needed to contend, including nervousness and anxiety over whether she will have to be around or make a "grave mistake" with Cruella; defeat over the ways in which she sees Cruella's actions as capturing power and gaining control over her; helplessness, fear, and fatigue when the bullying continues with no relief in sight; humiliation over the red stain on her shirt and how it might look to the others who surround her; embarrassment and regret because she bought the same shirt as a means of trying to fit in; and shame for violently retaliating with the tomato. Moreover, the emotional demands of being bullied understandably became more difficult as the bullying persisted. The persistence of Cruella's bullying weakened Jezebel over time, leading her to fall to her knees after the volleying on tomatoes. She was exhausted.

It is worth noting that Jezebel's experience of distressing emotions was complemented in the story by the presence of more affirming feelings. Of particular interest are the feelings Jezebel carried for Rose. As I explore more in greater detail below, she loved and trusted her, and these feelings helped to offset Jezebel's suffering. I mention them here to stress the multifaceted nature of emotions in bullying.

The toll of her problems was not limited to emotional issues. The story also speaks to Jezebel emerging from being bullied by performing as someone who is hyper-aware of others, of herself in relationship to others, and of her surroundings. Drawn into conflict situations rooted in intimidation and fear, and already feeling as if she lived on the margins, she was hyper-vigilant and her internal monologue served as an invaluable resource for survival. Where was Cruella? Rose? Why will the time not pass quickly? Why did I say that! Similar to Iman's worries in the locker room concerning Destroyer, Jezebel needed to be on guard and ready in case Cruella would approach and become aggressive with her. Staying prepared meant staying alert. Not staying alert meant the potential for error and a greater risk of facing more of Cruella's wrath.

Living within the bullying in these ways ultimately rendered Jezebel someone who experienced considerable self-doubt and self-critique, a noticeably different way of performing than the one she exhibited earlier in the story with her flaunting. The shift is visible in her conveying the "grave mistakes" she made with Cruella—for example, by touching Cruella's nose with her hand in the lunch line, and hoping she had not taken Cruella's seat at the lunch table. It also shows in Jezebel's feeling regret over convincing her mom to buy her "popular" clothes as a means of stopping the bullying. As she writes, "What was I doing, why did I want to change, why did I think getting a new shirt would take the target off my back?" Additionally, the transition into doubt and critique shows as she describes the ways she collapsed after throwing the tomato at Cruella. Being bullied left Jezebel treating herself in demanding and judgmental ways; she was unable to let herself off the hook for her actions, which were made under situations of major duress. Similarly, it also encouraged her to suggest that she held much of the responsibility for the interactions and their outcomes. If only she had not acted in a particular way, or if she were able to act in a different way, her situation would be better. In these ways the story speaks to how victims, who are already feeling dis-ease and worried about looming confrontations, sometimes (often?) are unable to see that bullying is a mode of relational communication. Therefore, interactions are shaped and meaning is created and used, by the choices of *both* conversation partners, and not just one individual. Further, the self-critique and over-attributing of responsibility fails to recognize the fact that it was Cruella who bullied Jezebel.

Similarly, Jezebel's experiences point to deeper ways that bullying conditions the lives of its victims. As is the case with the other stories in the book, this story shows her being consumed by Cruella and fraught with rumination. Although she had felt like an "other," and others had treated her as if she were for some time, bullying worsened the issue and further preoccupied her. Worried by how she erred in a past interaction, she ruminated on the past. Fearful of what might come next, she fixated on the future. Bullying prevented her from performing more fluidly and in the moment. She was imprisoned and longed for her freedom.

Rose to the Rescue

The beautiful ways Jezebel describes her relationship with Rose speak to the power of friendship in coping with the imprisonment of bullying. According to Rawlins (2009), "we feel comfortable in the presence of our close friends" (p. 1). Jezebel and Rose gave each other this freedom relationally, jointly performing as each other's "oasis" or "safety" in a lunchroom wherein their bullies did not have much care about their well-beings. If one puppy would be skinned, then both would be skinned, at least most of the time.

The spirit of mutuality that bonded the friends was so significant that it led Jezebel to feel deeply troubled when Rose did not step in to defend her. The absence of support, in essence, made Rose appear to be a neglectful friend, or the "stranger" or "bystander" who watched and did nothing. Yet, as time taught her, Rose was not leaving the friendship, nor did she love Jezebel any less; rather, she was taking care of herself within a complicated and dangerous situation, and she was free to do that. As Rawlins writes, "Friendship is founded upon connected, responsible, positive freedoms. It requires unforced yet mutually contingent choices to respond to each other as friends" (p. 9). While the fear and hurt of those moments might have led her to expect Rose to confront Cruella, the story shows a more mindful understanding of how this expectation, while understandable at the time, would be irresponsible of her as a true friend.

Who could say what made Cruella move on from bullying Jezebel, shooting her that forgiveness-inspiring smile. Maybe through her retaliation Jezebel effectively avowed an identity of no longer being "bully-able," so to speak. Perhaps time changed Cruella, or it's possible she moved onto her next Dalmatian. What's clearer, to me, is the meaningfulness, for Jezebel, of the smiles in that interaction—that it marked for her an apology and perhaps respect. That brief moment enabled her to let go, head band on, and fur (mostly) intact.

STRETCH

Reflexive Interlude 3

"The Stretch Armstrong doll? Wow, I got Stretch Armstrong—my favorite!!!"

After tearing my Christmas gift out of its package, I toss the wrapping paper to my side, plant a long kiss on the doll's lips, and then hold it close to my heart. Hearing my excitement, my mother and father look at me and smile. My brother and sister pause only for a second to see why I'm screaming, then go back to opening their gifts.

Stretch Armstrong is a popular doll for boys, which I've wanted from the minute I first saw him advertised on television. He is more than just a doll. He is a symbol of who boys aspire to be and a source of incredible curiosity for me. Stretch stands about eight inches tall. He looks like he's Caucasian, has wavy platinum blonde hair and a wide and bright smile. He is muscular and there is no excess fat on his body. Most importantly, as his name suggests, Stretch is strong. When I touch his abdomen a temporary imprint remains there for a few seconds. Even more, his arms stretch to great distances without being torn or snapped off. Once I stop stretching him, his arms slowly return to their normal position.

I quickly become attached to my new friend, Stretch. I connect with him in different ways than other boys relate to their dolls. The boys I'm friends with talk about how he is "so muscular" and "strong enough to beat up people" (their other dolls). In manly growling tones they add, "Stretch Armstrong is the ultimate man. He is muscular and plows through and conquers whatever stands in his way!" Some of my friends even grab their sisters' Barbie dolls, put them together in a kissing pose, and suggest the two are the "perfect couple" who are "destined to get married." I am attracted to Stretch's flexibility, particularly how he is able to be stretched to extremes that most human persons would not be able to withstand. He endures so much abuse, yet, once kids stop stretching him, he always returns to his original shape, to being himself. He's superhuman and no attacks faze him.

I also think Stretch is cute. His hair is wavy and perfectly styled and his smile is beautiful. However, I keep my attraction to him to myself, because I worry about what others will say if they hear me talk about Stretch in these ways. Boys aren't supposed to use the word "cute," and they certainly aren't supposed to think other boys or men are beautiful. At least this is what my father tells me, each time he hears me say the word "cute." Other boys and adult men in my life don't talk about cuteness, nor do I see males on television speak about same-sex attraction. They mainly talk about the toughness or strength of other males.

I realize that Stretch Armstrong is a doll, not a real person, but I am captivated by his resilience. I wonder how kids can constantly touch, poke, and prod him, sometimes brutally, without harming him. How can someone take so much abuse, but be so strong? Why can't I be him?

Rattled

Bam! Bam! [Banging noises]

I am standing at my locker, getting the books I'll need for my next two classes. It's early in the morning and only a few people mingle by the lockers. The lights above the lockers are still off, making the area awfully dark. I look around and see a fellow sixth grader slamming his metal locker door shut and his clenched fist hard against the door several times.

"Ha, that's right … what are *you* going to do about it?!" he says, staring into my eyes, puffing up his chest, and twice feigning like he is charging at me. His actions startle and shake me, so I say nothing in return and stare back into my open locker.

Mark is a well-known bully at school. He and I are not friends, nor are we in the same classes. Yet, he seems to know who I am.

"What are you gonna do, Berry?" he continues. Still shaken, I remain silent and stand still. I don't dare budge an inch.

"That's right, I didn't think so." Bam! Bam! [More banging.] Holding his schoolbooks to the right side of his hip, chest still tall and wide, he turns toward the hallway and struts away. He walks with confidence and a swagger that boys are supposed to have but I lack.

Even though Mark is gone, I am scared. I stay in the same position, still trembling and staring into the locker, struggling to figure out what just happened. *Maybe he was just trying to be cool or to joke around, but it doesn't feel that way. I've heard Mark looks for fights. Even worse, I heard he stuffed one of the band kids into a gym locker last week. The kid peed himself, but was too scared to report Mark, so he walked around for the rest of the school day with wet marks by his crotch. He was going to come at me just now. Maybe he was warning me, but about what? I've done nothing to him. What do I do next time? I know I'll do nothing and try to ignore him. That feels like the safest bet. Wait, doing nothing makes me look like a wimp. Boys are supposed to defend themselves.* After a few seconds pass, I gently shut my locker, trying to prevent my small mirror and cut-out smiley faces on the inside of the door from coming undone.

Holding my books at my chest, I hold my breath and begin to walk away from the lockers. Boys at school often tell me I "walk like a girl," because of the ways in which I hold my books (not at my sides like most boys), and how my hips swish as I walk. I walk this way because it feels comfortable to me. Continuing on my trek, I move toward the end of the locker aisle and carefully peak out into the hallway. I want to make sure Mark isn't still nearby, waiting to scare me, or worse yet, punch me. I see him all the way down the hall. The coast is clear. I exhale.

Mark is gone, but he stays with and "in" my body as though he never left. I still hear the ringing in my ears from his slamming and banging. I continue to feel his threatening eyes invade mine. He's accomplished his goal: he's gotten to me.

Acts of intimidation continue to happen to me several times each year until I graduate from middle school. Sometimes Mark is the bully, but not always. Bullying at my locker never leads to physical attacks, but scares me nonetheless. Administrators and teachers often stand by the lockers, suggesting they realize how trouble can occur in this space. But they cannot be there at all times, nor can they see everyone who moves throughout the maze-like rows of lockers. When I entered fifth grade, I was ecstatic at the thought of one day having my own locker. Now, the joy of feeling older and more mature is clouded over by the fear of being bullied. Being more independent is not all it is cracked up to be. As a result, I work hard at staying aware and on guard at my locker. If I see anyone suspicious, I finish getting my books and leave quickly.

Willing Target

I am the ideal target for bullying in middle school—physically, academically, and relationally. I am short and have a soft (non-muscular) body, and my head is big for my frame, tempting other boys to tease me. Even my brother and father often seem to enjoy calling me "head." The nickname makes me feel self-conscious. In addition, I have a soft spoken and gentle voice and love to stand with my hands on my hips, which marks me in the gaze of others as "feminine," or at the very least a boy who is not "masculine." But to me this embodiment feels natural and automatic. During these middle school years, my father and brother would often poke me in my stomach and beg me to giggle like the Pillsbury Doughboy, a popular character on television commercials with a soft middle section and angelic laugh. I acquiesce, giggling for them upon being poked. Though unaware at the time, I allow them to treat me as an object; I am an "other" whose body is commented on, assessed, and vulnerable to violations.

The ways in which I perform academically expand my profile as a target. I consistently do my schoolwork and stay out of trouble. I rarely receive bad grades, nor am I ever summonsed to detention. I don't create issues for teachers or staff, which leads some of my schoolmates to label me "teacher's pet." By no means am I perfect. I am awful at math and cannot stand science. Yet, I often think this aspect of my identity irks bullies. My enactment of "good boy" makes them look and feel lazy, shining a spotlight on their deficiencies.

I often interact and form friendships with the more "unpopular" boys and girls. These kids are dedicated students, the other "dorks" or "geeks" at the school's social margins. To my friends, I am "normal" and fun—I feel the same about them. When we are around each other, we are usually able to be ourselves and do not have to worry about being bullied. I like to be around and insulated by these friends with whom I feel protected and safe. But when they are not around, I usually keep to myself, ignoring others and doing my schoolwork. Venturing out and talking with students outside of my comfort zone happens as needed and briefly, such as when I need to ask someone what the homework assignment is for the next day, or to repeat for me what the teacher just announced to the class. But I do not try to make bullies my friends. I keep my distance.

In these physical, academic, and relational ways, who I am—and who I am not—puts me at greater risk for being bullied. It is not uncommon for boys to punch me hard in the arm or thigh, or kick me directly in the testicles. Some of the bullies threaten to choke me during class, say, if I don't give up my seat to them, or don't let them use the supplies I am using. Often these physical attacks or threats are complemented by violent language. They say: "Move out of that seat, you retard!" "Get out of my way, or I'll beat you!" Each point of contact with bullies and bullying draws me into interactions that are not good for me. I emerge from these encounters feeling weak and tired. They exacerbate my *fear* of being bullied. I see persons bullying friends of mine, persons who look and act like me, and wonder if I will soon be them. I am mentally immersed and consumed by memories of the times when I am bullied. I remember these attacks, sometimes viscerally, and fear the next one could happen at any minute and during any interaction. I live on guard.

The Burn

"Alright, gentlemen," yells Mr. Sylvester, our gym teacher, trying to talk loudly enough to compete with the echoes that bellow through the noisy gym. "As you know, it is Presidential Fitness Test week, and today is day two of the challenge."

"This is the worst day ever," I whisper in the ear of my friend, Will, who is sitting to my left on the school bleachers. Like the rest of the boys, we're dressed in our gym uniforms, which display our school name, Heritage Middle School, and school colors, red, white, and blue. Will is really smart at math and science and not afraid to flaunt who he is and what he knows. I admire his confidence. Unfortunately, he is also no stranger to being bullied. He looks like the classic nerd character in movies or on television programs—thick glasses, routinely flushed in the face, unusual walk, geeky laugh—and bullies capitalize on his demeanor. Although Will is more athletic than I, he also hates gym, which makes me like him even more.

"Let's just get it over with," Will responds. "You'll be fine."

"I hate these tests, especially climbing that rope!" I point to the long rope that hangs from the gym ceiling all the way down to a couple inches off the floor.

The fitness test is part of a national effort to improve physical fitness levels in youth. Yesterday during gym we did the long distance run outside. I lost all energy by the one-quarter mark and had to walk the rest of the way to the finish line. I felt humiliated seeing most of the class waiting for me and a few others at the finish. Gym class is a delight for the physically fit and kids who enjoy athletic activities. But "unfit" kids like me feel embarrassed and ashamed, not to mention bored.

Mr. Sylvester continues, "Today we'll be doing rope climbing. Boys usually love this one, so I know you'll have fun."

"Not this boy," I whisper. "I am a wimp."

Will responds, "No you're not, and don't talk about yourself in that way. You're awesome. Just do what you can. It's only a dumb test, and it doesn't even affect your grade."

Will is a good friend. I want to believe him, but I still feel like a loser for being so inadequate at gym and for being made to participate. I say nothing in response.

As I sit with Will, nervously awaiting my turn at the rope, my mind flashes back to several other uncomfortable moments from past gym classes. I return to my failures with rope climbing in the fourth grade, when I was shamed by my teacher and called "pathetic" by peers. Although two years have passed, I remember the embarrassment and humiliation from that day as if it were yesterday. I think about when we last played kickball in gym. During my turn at "bat," I went to kick the ball and completely missed. I kicked so hard that I fell on my butt in front of my classmates. I can still see the boys laughing and pointing their fingers at me today. I also remember a recent awkward experience in the locker room, the location at school I fear the most, because adults are rarely present, which encourages boys to more freely pick on other boys. I was at the urinal peeing when I saw four boys from the school basketball team showering about fifteen feet from me. They were fully undressed, soaped up, and laughing as they playfully slapped each other on the butt. They appeared to be comfortable being naked, fully exposing their bodies for others to see, and not afraid to show each other or anyone in the locker room their developing dicks and pubic hair. At the time I was just developing and was mortified at exposing myself. Pubic hair felt weird to me, even as it also made me happy, since it was a sign I was maturing. I couldn't take my eyes off of the boys' bodies. Although I was finished peeing, I stayed at the urinal, and pretended I was still going, so I could check out their bodies. I stared at their dicks, which were much bigger than mine, as they flung from side to side as the boys jumped around in the shower, and at their butts, which were far more muscular too. My gazing at them was about more than comparison. The more I looked, the more my own balls and dick tingled and my heart raced. I loved being there and looking at them, even though I was invisible to them. Fixated on their bodies, I stayed at the urinal, wanting the moment never to end. Suddenly, I heard a loud voice behind me yell, "Hey, don't take forever!" Startled and feeling as though I had been caught doing something wrong, I quickly put my dick back into my underwear, pulled up my shorts and left the locker room. I never mentioned the experience to anyone, but was sure that these boys saw me staring at them and would use it against me sometime soon. Thankfully they never did.

"Hey, are you listening to me?" Will asks, bringing me back to the present. "It's just a rope, you can do it."

"That is easy for you to say. Last year you went all the way up to the top and rang the bell, and people cheered for you!" He smiles, nods, and decides to drop the subject.

My anxiety continues to grow. I feel my stomach begin to rumble and my face and neck turn red. My body temperature grows warmer and sweat begins to drip profusely from my forehead. *If I am feeling this way now, I can only imagine how I will feel when I am at the rope, or after I fail to climb it. Why can't I be good at climbing this damn rope? Why can't I be a normal boy?* I consider trying to leave gym and think through the options. On the one hand, if I stay I will have to take the test. Although Mr. Sylvester believes we can all successfully climb, I know I will do poorly. Other boys will be watching me and I will, again, be embarrassed. On the other hand, I can tell Mr. Sylvester I don't feel well and ask to go to the school nurse. Getting out of here would be a relief. However, if others see me leave, I think they will know I didn't want to take the test, and that I was trying to get out of it. Even more, there's a good chance I will have to make up the test tomorrow. If that were the case, it would still be just me climbing and everyone else watching. I decide to stay and just do the test.

Will takes his turn first and makes it all the way to the top, without pausing even once.

"Mr. Berry, you're next," Mr. Sylvester says, asking me to come to the rope. Once I am by his side, he adds, "Good luck, son. You'll do well." He's so kind. Maybe he remembers how poorly I did during yesterday's run. I smile but say nothing to him.

I dip both hands into the large bowl of hand chalk that is positioned directly to the side of the rope. I apply lots of chalk to my hands, not because I believe it will help me climb much, but because I saw everyone else do so and think maybe it will help me feel more athletic. As I walk toward the rope, I see Will looking at me with a smile. Mark, the boy who has bullied me, is standing nearby and talking with Ricky and Paul, two boys in our grade who are his best friends. Noticing them looking at me, I quickly turn away and approach the rope. I place both of my hands firmly on the rope and tuck it between my legs, to steady myself.

"Climb whenever you are ready. The stopwatch begins when you start to climb."

Feeling a sudden burst of confidence, I hop up on the rope and begin to climb. I pull myself up some with my left hand, and then up a little bit more with my right hand. Yet after climbing only about two feet in total, I am stuck.

"I can't do it," I say, gasping as I speak and feeling as though I will lose my grip at any second and fall to the mat.

"Keep at it, Keith," Mr. Sylvester encourages.

"No, I can't."

"You can do it, I believe in you. Be tough."

I am able to climb one more foot before suddenly sliding down the rope to the mat on the ground. On my descent I feel a mixed sensation of rope burn and tingling in my testicles. "I'm sorry," I say to Mr. Sylvester, feeling as though I had disappointed him. "I am not tough."

"It is okay, you gave it a nice try. Take your seat." His encouragement falls on deaf ears. I have failed yet again.

On the walk back to my seat, I see Mark make a limp wristed gesture about me, to suggest I am a "fag." Ricky and Paul laugh and then, without missing a beat, feign limp wrists, and, looking directly at me say, "I'm Keith Fairy, and I'll be glad to hop on your big rope!" Other boys and girls around saw what they did and start to laugh at me. Looking down at the floor, I quickly walk back to my seat. Because Mr. Sylvester was packing up the mat from under the rope with a few students, he didn't see the boys teasing me.

"Don't give them a second of your time, Keither," Will says, having seen everything. "They're not worth it."

"I know. I just wish I would have said something good back to them. Something like: *Don't flatter yourself. I'm not coming near your rope!* Or *Big rope? Ha, it's more like a tiny thread.* But they caught me off guard and the words didn't come to me."

Over the next three weeks, Mark and his bully buddies will call me "Keith Fairy" and act like they're struggling to climb rope when they see me in hallways and lunchroom, or for that matter, anywhere teachers are not present. Each time they bully me I let them have their way. I don't ever say anything to them in return, nor do I tell my parents or teachers about the bullying. The boys know their teasing bothers me, and probably that I won't, and likely cannot, fight back. That's the point: they know I'm stuck.

Friendship of Identification and Shame

Derek is the type of boy whose ways of performing lead him to stand out to others at my middle school. He is 5'9" tall, thin, has long and flowing brown hair with golden blonde highlights, and silky smooth skin. He wears tight acid washed blue jeans that show off his hips and long legs and fashionable shirts. As Derek floats through classrooms and hallways, his hips shake from side to side. The words he uses are often dramatic and uttered with a beautiful and delicate lisp that often leads classmates to call him "girly." As a result, many classmates, boys and girls, bully him incessantly and label him "gay."

"Come on guys, leave me alone!" Derek begs, after boys knocked the books and Trapper Keeper notebook out of his hands in the hallways. They love to do this to him, perhaps because of the scene it creates. When they strike in just the right spot, papers from his notebook scatter all over the floor, making others stare and laugh at him, embarrassing Derek. Unfortunately, his pleas are usually met with more bullying. "Looks like our sweet ole' boy has dropped his books," boys say. "Derek, you really shouldn't be so clumsy—no one likes a klutz." Yet, boys are not the only students to bully him. As girls walk behind him in the hallway, I often hear them talk about him in mocking ways: "Which type of peroxide do you think Derek uses in his hair?" "Do you think his favorite color in dresses is pink?" "What do you think is his boyfriend's name?" They speak loudly enough that he hears what they are saying. The mocking works better in that way. Further, Derek is the prime candidate for bullying in the lunchroom. Boys cut in front of him in the lunch line, staring directly into his eyes, as if to simultaneously tempt him to react and warn him he shouldn't dare, ruin his lunch by dipping their dirty fingers into his food, and order him to "keep walking" when they see him approaching an empty seat at the table. Indeed, Derek is bullied more than anyone else I know in middle school. The bullying is so bad that I am amazed he still comes to school each day.

Derek becomes my friend when he and I are alone, say at recess or in class, or when I feel confident only he and I can hear each other talking. I relish our friendship. I get lost in the back-and-forth flow of our conversations and adore the clever jokes and stories we tell each other. I consider the voice that so many classmates ridicule just different and good. The grace with which he speaks, which others mistake as an invitation to bully him, disarms me.

When it is not only the two of us, however, or when he talks too loudly or dramatically, I feel considerably different. Then the ways in which he performs— the floating, highlights, lisp, and grace—unsettles and irritates me. I fear bullies will approach us and bully him, or bully both of us. Even more, Derek embarrasses me. I know how others feel about him—he's the school "fag" who deserves to be bullied and shamed for being so flamboyant. I fear bullies will see us together, getting along so well, and think I act like a girl, or worse yet, am a faggot, like Derek. In these times, I am ashamed to be friends with him, and often judge him in my head for the ways I am convinced others will judge me, for being so close to him. To help me cope with these difficult emotions, I often put more space in between us physically and relationally. For instance, I carefully monitor how closely I walk to him in the hallways, if I even walk with him at all. I won't sit as close to him in the lunchroom, if I decide to be around him there at all. I laugh less at his jokes, and sometimes I tell him his jokes aren't funny, and that he needs to "tone down" how he acts, even though on the inside I'm secretly laughing at his amazing humor and wishing I could be as brave as he is. I use fewer hand gestures that I believe others will read as effeminate and gay, play uninterested when he tells wild stories, and hope these choices will encourage him to talk less. In these ways I perform and feel quite different when Derek is around, and I expect he should do the same.

I was not aware in middle school that I was gay. However, I was taught to believe that being gay was wrong and sinful. Further, I knew that being perceived as gay put a boy at risk for being bullied and "othered." Therefore, I did everything I could to avoid having others categorize me in the same ways I saw them categorizing Derek. Others hurt him with their bullying, and I did not want them to do the same to me. I wasn't a loyal or "true" friend to Derek then, yet, like Rose felt when deciding whether or not to help Jezebel as she was being bullied, I felt in danger, ill-equipped to ward off attacks, and needed to protect myself.

The Devil's Other Face

"Keith and Mark, I'd like you to take this box of books down to the principal's office. Will you please run this errand for me?" asks Ms. H, our Language Arts teacher.

"Sure," I respond hesitantly. I haven't told any of my teachers how Mark and his friends bully me. Thus, she has no way of knowing she might be putting me in danger. Of all people with whom to pair me, she has to put me with him. Mark nods, but he looks irritated to have to go with me, or because he has to help a teacher.

"It's heavy," she adds, "so be careful."

Mark and I lift the box and head out the door. We say nothing on our way to the office and focus on not dropping it. I am a nervous wreck and do not make eye contact with him the entire way to the office. I also am barely able to hold onto the box and think I might drop it at any second. I hear Mark breathing, struggling to hold the box, too, which makes me feel better.

"Thank you, boys," Ms. Smith, the principal's assistant tells us, after we drop off the box in the office. "Now head right back to class." We both nod our heads.

"Did you see the big wart on her face?" Mark asks me, as we walk out of the office.

"Yeah, I saw it."

"Nasty, huh?"

"Ya, it was nasty, and so was her fat head." I feel bad to be saying these things about Ms. Smith—she has always been kind to me, and she is my mother's friend. Yet, Mark is talking to me in non-threatening ways, and that excites me.

"Definitely … fat and ugly." He and I begin to return to our classroom, as he continues to small talk with me. "So, you live on 190th St., right?"

"Yep…"

"You like it? I live near there. I love our block."

"Sure, I guess" I respond, surprised but happy he is not bullying me.

"Anyway, um…" he struggles, as if trying to remember my name.

"Keith … Keith *Berry*."

"Right, sorry. Anyway, I like your tennis shoes. That's a cool color."

"Thanks, I like yours, too." Mark is wearing worn out running shoes. Yet, I want him to continue being nice to me, so I compliment him in return.

We soon arrive back to the classroom. Once we walk through the door, Mark is silent and no longer acknowledges me. As he returns to his seat, he passes my friend Monica, and knocks the pencil out of her hand and tosses her papers to the floor.

I head back to my seat near Will, who saw Mark's antics. He says, "What a jerk, right?"

"Ya, totally," I respond. "But he was just nice to me when we took that box to the office—asking me questions and listening to my answers. He seemed … nice?"

"Come on, you're too gullible."

"Maybe he is ready for us to be friends. I like this Mark better. Maybe he's changing. Maybe he's actually a good guy."

"No way, he's a bully. He's shown you and many others who he is. He's a bad person. Don't let him fool you."

"I'm not being fooled."

"Be on guard."

I nod my head and we both get back to work.

Methodological Dilemma

"What do you think of my story?" Ena asks me after class. I recently finished reading the full rough draft of her bullying narrative. She adds, "Does it work?"

"You've done some beautiful work, Ena. It's a powerful account."

"Thanks you," she says as she looks down, as if she is embarrassed by my praising her. "But does my story work?"

"Yes, your story … works." I pause when answering her because her word choice intrigues me.

"Okay, I am glad." She exhales and appears relieved.

"Your story is compelling and important. It is difficult to read about the violence you were made to endure in being bullied, but your openness allows me to better understand the pain you experienced. Your story leads me to have an empathetic response, which is a sign of a helpful story."

She nods her head.

"But yes, they … work."

"Wait, you paused each time before you said my stories work. I feel like you're not telling me everything."

"Very perceptive—I paused because at times I have also worried about how open you all have been."

"But the instructions say clearly that we should only write stories about which we feel safe. These are *our* stories and our safety is priority. Right?"

"Correct, ultimately as storytellers you have control over what you write."

Ena just nods her head, taking it all in.

"Let me put it this way: the process of teaching and working with you on the stories this semester has presented me with some questions and issues I had not fully anticipated."

"Like?" she asks with a smile.

"Well, for starters, in most of the rough drafts I've reviewed, students have included candid detail on deeply personal issues concerning bullying. As I take in all of this brave and evocative writing, I also wonder if folks are being mindful about the risks that are inherent to this type of writing. While there can be great gains from the process, I also wonder about any losses that might occur. After all, you'll be sharing your drafts with your peer review partner, and I wouldn't be surprised if some of you will share your stories with others outside of class."

Ena says, "I for one thought carefully about every sentence I wrote."

"I feel confident most students have taken this process seriously. Still, what about the other risks that you might not have been able to identify? For example, do you care about how your story might make you look to others? Is being so open worth the risk, just to make the stories *work*?"

"It is worth the risk to me. I'm good by it." She pauses to think. "Also, you saw during our first class meeting how passionate students are about bullying and the need for us to do something about the problem."

"I understand and respect the dedication. Yet, I am also concerned about the unknown risks that may dwell outside your awareness, those that may not be important now, but might be significant later."

"There's more?" Ena asks with wide eyes.

"There is almost always more, if we are thinking carefully about complex issues."

She smiles and asks, "Should I be taking notes?"

"Ha, well, you can if you would like," I respond.

I cannot tell Ena all my concerns, because I could not disclose to her my plan to write this book (see Appendix). Even though all participants in my study will have a chance to revise their writing, and even though the book uses pseudonyms, I still am concerned about openness. For instance, if persons who are in the book choose to share their stories with others and let those persons know which story is theirs, how will their dedication to high levels of self-disclosure affect their identities and lives generally? How will the students and the persons whom they include in their stories come across to readers? How will they come to understand themselves, as a result of having been vulnerable? Yes, stories may "work" in many important regards, but at what costs? Also, in what ways will *my* Reflexive Interludes stories "work" for and against me?

"What I am trying to say is there is more to using autoethnographic writing than merely telling our stories. As we construct our stories we are also constituting identities on the page, ours and others'."

"Right, I remember," she says, showing me the spot in her notes from class about identity negotiation. She continues, "I feel like I am aware of the risks and am comfortable with what I have written."

"Terrific, I am proud of you for that."

"Thanks."

"Stories might *work* for the class … [much like they will *work* for the book] … but I am still concerned about the *work* that these stories might do on its storytellers!"

5

HIGHLIGHT GIRL

Finding Strength in Her Weak Soul

LAUREN

I begin Lauren's story with one of her diary entries, which shows a young girl who is fearfully anticipating graduation and the start of her next level of school, a transition that, as Iman's and my experiences also show, entails adapting to relational changes that shape bullying.

> August 12, 2004
> Dear Diary,
> Tomorrow is my first day of middle school, but I'm not looking forward to it at all. How could I be? All of my friends are going to Sunnybrook while I'll be going to school 45 minutes away. It's going to be so much harder than 5th grade ... I just know it. Mom keeps telling me that I'm "smarter than the average girl my age," and should be at a school that pushes me. Apparently, that's what Sunnybrook Middle School will do. She keeps calling it an "IB school," which she explains as being like my gifted classes last year. I guess those weren't so hard ... but what will I do without my best friends, the Johnson twins and Jenny? Sure, Nicole and Riley will be going to school with me, but I haven't really talked to them since the 3rd grade, when I transferred from Seacoast to Bakers. I'm sure they're really close friends now. I'll be left out ... I hate being left out.[1]

Lauren was worried, because she had been hurt in the past. Even though she had heard that moving to the fifth grade would be exciting, she was nervous about the peers with whom she would be relating.

★★★

At the heart of Lauren's story is her friendship with Nicole, whom she's known since kindergarten. The two lived near each other and were inseparable best friends. They did everything together, joined the same Girl Scout troop, enjoying play dates and sleepovers, and singing and playing dress up together. Lauren remembers this bond first being tested in the third grade, when she and Nicole were in the same class. She was ecstatic with the idea of being together with her closest friend. Yet, Riley, a girl who also was close friends with Nicole, but someone whom Lauren did not know, also was in the class. So, in third grade Lauren began to participate in a friendship triangle, a triangle of bullying, which would influence the relationship between Lauren and Nicole, and the ways Lauren felt about herself.

The bullying happened early on in their friendship. Lauren recalls Riley pulling her aside during recess one day, which she thought was a good sign they would become friends:

> I thought this talk would be of a positive nature; in the back of my mind, I figured Riley taking time to talk to me meant she wanted to be friends. Instead, she blatantly told me that she thought I was weird. She stated that she and Nicole wanted *nothing* to do with me, because I wore the school uniform instead of normal clothes, had a bob cut and glasses, and chose to run around the field on imaginary adventures by myself, instead of playing kickball during recess.

After dropping this bomb, Riley merely walked away, leaving Lauren alone, hurt, and in tears. After a few minutes she began to walk back inside from recess, and saw Nicole standing in close range. She writes, "I looked at her with tears in my eyes, and she refused to return my gaze." Lauren needed some sign of friendship from Nicole, something to help her understand Riley's hurtful words. But Nicole ignored her, and Lauren was devastated.

This dynamic occurred repeatedly over the next month: Riley would engage Lauren, say mean things to her, and then walk away, only to have Nicole watch the attack transpire, saying nothing in support of her friend. When Lauren tried to become friends with Riley, her attempts were met with the same result: Riley acted mean and Nicole remained silent.

One thing became clear very quickly: Lauren and Riley would not be friends. As a result, Lauren's relationship with Nicole became strained. If Riley was around, Nicole ignored her. "If I tried to talk in her presence," she writes, "Nicole would look right through me and turn away. However, if Riley wasn't there, everything was normal." The friendship triangle ended after third grade, when Lauren transferred to another school. That meant her time with Nicole would be spent devoid of a third party. Lauren was able to forgive the ways Nicole had been a bad friend to her. She soon felt like Nicole was her friend again.

★★★

Lauren couldn't shake the nervousness she felt about beginning middle school. She had become comfortable with her new friends, and loved being around Nicole again without Riley. However, knowing that Riley would be attending the same middle school made her worry, remembering how differently Nicole acted when she was involved. Since the two of them were now destined to be part of Lauren's life for the next three years, she hoped her best friend would not abandon her again. But…

★★★

February 22, 2005
Dear Diary,
I hate it here. I hate it here more than anything. I hate Nicole, and I hate Riley. Even though I've made new friends and try to stay away from them, they still manage to hurt me. They go out of their way to do it. It's like a game to them. They'll make fun of me as they walk by in the hallway and laugh about it. Of course they do it in a way that makes it seem coincidental that I'm standing there, just close enough for me to overhear them. Today they walked by and Riley said, "I can't believe her mom lets her leave the house like that … The worst part is she thinks she looks good." I know it seems silly to be upset … but I can't help it. The things they say make me question how I look, how I act, and, inevitably, who I am. Am I ugly and just not aware of it? Am I a loser and deserve the rude comments? These little things are definitely adding up.

The next two years of middle school were not easy for Lauren. Riley and Nicole continued to torment her, always following her in school. They still aimed their sly comments at her in the hallway, on a range of topics: "What is up with your hair?" "Your clothes are disgusting!" "You have NO friends!" "You're weird!" Also, any time she answered questions posed by her teachers in class, the two of them would laugh out loud. If she got an answer wrong, they laughed at her for being stupid. If she got it right, they laughed about how much of a nerd she was. There was no way for her to win, so she kept her head down, and tried to ignore them.

Lauren struggled to find a way to feel better. She remembered something her mother always told her for situations like these, to "kill others with kindness." If someone is hurting her, she should respond to them with a kind reaction, or by thinking positive and self-affirming thoughts, which would make it harder for them to continue to bother her. Loving and respecting her mother so much, Lauren tried to live in this way:

> When they would say passive aggressive things to me at lunch, or mumble something under their breath, I would smile and try to compliment myself in my head to counteract their words. If they said I was a "nerd" for getting something right, I would tell myself that being intelligent is something very

admirable. However, even though my mom's advice came from her heart, and she meant well, it didn't really play out in the ways she explained. They never let up; if anything, the duo increased their bullying to get the negative reaction from me, which they so badly desired. If I ignored their negative comments in class, they would be quiet for a second and then find something else about which to nag on me. They were relentless!

It became nearly impossible for Lauren to hide how hurt she felt by the ways Riley and Nicole bullied her. Also, the positivity fell short as a strategy, and actually further escalated their bullying. Lauren also grew tired of the response, as she writes, "There are only so many times that I could hear negativity and look for the positivity in it!"

★★★

Lauren's struggle with bullying hit her limits during her year in seventh grade, when the following poem about her became widely circulated at her school:

Highlight Girl
Oh highlight girl, you're so dumb
You look around and think you have pals
Oh highlight girl, no one likes you
Especially none of us gals
Your hair is stupid, just like you
We laugh behind your back
Oh highlight girl, highlight girl,
You really should wear a sack.

The poem first appeared in her school's "burn book." These books were made popular in the hit motion picture *Mean Girls*, a movie about vicious bullying, girls, and high school. Burn books are notebooks that students fill with demeaning gossip about other students. Handwritten and/or pasted images appear on its pages, and bullies design each page to humiliate a specific target of their bullying. Students secretly circulate the book around the school for students to review and for their amusement. Lauren was "featured" in the book at Sunnybrook that year, and the poem, written by Riley, comprised the section about her:

> It started as a shared joke between the members of the book, who began calling me "highlight girl" randomly throughout the second semester of the school year. I thought it was odd, but didn't really question it all that much. After all, I did have chunky blonde highlights in my hair, which were popular at that time. I stayed unaware of the burn book and poem until the end of the year.

Lauren first learned about the nickname online. At the time the social media website "MySpace" was popular. Many people's MySpace pages included a game, or a survey, that asked members to complete a fill-in-the-blank prompts based on their personal preferences. One of the questions was "You know you (blank) when (blank)," which someone at Lauren's school edited to read, "You know you're at Sunnybrook when (blank)." The new prompt encouraged Sunnybrook students to post things that were unique to the school, or stuff that only "insiders" would know. When she went on the website one day Lauren noticed a student's response to the prompt, which read, "You know you go to Sunnybrook when … *Oh Highlight Girl.*" Baffled, her mind went to all of the people at school who had recently started calling her by that name, and began to question the origin of the saying.

Lauren soon met with her dear friend, Glenn, to see what he knew about the name. He confirmed that she was the focus of the poem, and said he first saw it during a recent class period. Glenn saw Nicole circulating the burn book throughout the classroom, and grabbed it, to see what it was. He told Lauren that, instead of wanting the book back or feeling embarrassed, Nicole giggled as she flipped through the pages and showed him its cruel contents. With each giggle her pride for what she had done, and her lack of remorse, became more apparent. Lauren sat stunned. Reluctantly, Glenn then recited "Highlight Girl" to her, which hurt her immensely:

> With tears in my eyes, I thanked him for being such an honest and supportive friend, and then I called my mom to come pick me up from school early. I couldn't handle seeing anyone, especially now that I knew I was the topic of their jokes. I had no way of really knowing who saw the poem in the book, and I jumped to the conclusion that everyone knew about it … everyone but me! I was humiliated. I had to go home and stay hidden, and that's exactly what I did.

She didn't go to school for the rest of the week.

Lauren continued to be bullied throughout her eighth grade year. However, by this time she had learned to cope in better ways. Instrumental in the shift was her small group of friends, other students who were loyal to her, stayed by her side, and worked to keep up Lauren's morale. One of the most influential friends was Susanne, a new eighth grader to the school, who didn't have many friends. Lauren saw something special in her:

> Susanne had recently moved from South Africa and was living with her mom and her mom's new husband. Her family had a lot of issues, which mostly dealt with her biological father. Susanne never had a good relationship with him, because he abused her mother while she was growing up. Her dad also had a "bully" role in her life, just like Riley did in mine. When we were placed in the same homeroom, I reached out to befriend her.

There was something undeniably warm about Susanne. She was kind, and had lived through struggle, much like Lauren had. Naturally, she quickly became Lauren's best friend.

Lauren and Susanne had a trusting friendship in which they supported each other and were a positive influence on each other's life:

> We were there for each other throughout the day at school, and would talk on the phone all through the night. Whenever Nicole and Riley were getting to me, Susanne would get her older friends to drop her off at my house right away, along with buckets of ice cream. She would sit there holding my hand and remind me of my good characteristics. Sometimes, she would even write a list of good things about me for me to keep in my planner the next day.

Lauren had found in Susanne a new way to cope. She was able to ignore others' jabs more easily, which was like "mentally dodging them like knives." In addition, she made physical changes to assist her in dealing with others' negativity:

> To no longer be considered "highlight girl" I dyed my hair back to its natural color, getting rid of all highlights. I figured it would be smart to take away one of the main attributes they tormented me about, especially since it was such an easy fix. I told my mom I was tired of the highlights, so she gladly took me to the hair salon. I remember that day vividly. Sitting in the stylist's chair, I closed my eyes as she put the chemicals in my hair. My scalp burned, but I told myself the sting was nothing compared to the ways I would feel once my hurt was gone. Once she was done, the stylist let me look in the mirror, and the person I saw staring back at me was overwhelmingly soothing to me. I felt like a different person. The stylist had cut my hair differently, and now my simple brunette hair brushed stylishly against my shoulders. As I ran my hands through it, I got a little choked up. I assured my mom I was happy with how it turned out. Yet, I knew the true reason for my happiness: I was a new girl. I was untouchable.

The high Lauren felt from her transformation also sparked other changes in her experience of eighth grade:

> I switched to contacts and convinced my mom to go shopping with me for a new wardrobe. It amazed me what a couple of outward alterations could do to my ego and confidence. I began to be noticed by boys, got compliments from the teachers, and actually liked to look at my reflection as I walked out of the bathroom each day.

Riley and Nicole continued to bully Lauren; no changes in appearance would stop their attacks. Still, things were now different. With a new best friend and a different physical appearance, Lauren felt confident about herself. She was no longer faking her happiness just to pacify bullies.

★★★

July 27, 2007

Dear Diary,

High school is just around the corner now, and I couldn't be more excited. I know things are definitely going to be changing in my life. I can leave all of this behind and start over. Sure, Nicole is going to the same school ... but Riley won't be there. I feel like she was really the leader of the pack so, without her, Nicole's bullying will fade into the background. Here's hoping, at least.

★★★

High school was different for Lauren. She got the fresh start she needed to more fully move on from the bullying she had endured. At her new school she met an entirely new crowd of peers, who welcomed her for who she was. Not since elementary school had she felt like she was generally liked by her peers. Thankfully no one new stepped into the bully role Riley had vacated. Although Lauren wanted to keep Nicole out of her life, doing so would be difficult, because they went to the same small high school, were on the cheerleading team, and took some of the same classes together. Still, Lauren couldn't help but notice how different Nicole seemed:

> Without her leader, she seemed lost, searching for friends to fill the void. In between classes, she wandered through the halls by herself, seeming to mope. I could tell she felt alone; it was as if she felt abandoned by her prior companion. I'm sure, for her, it didn't help to see me now prospering, while she fell into the background of what used to be her kingdom, the school hierarchy. She got so desperate for attention and a way back in the social circle, that she reached out to me, of all people, to be her friend. She began to sit next to me in class, making little jokes to try to get a laugh out of me.

Lauren enjoyed this shift. She could now finish school happy, together with a loving best friend.

She ends her story by reflecting on these changes in the context of the relationship between her former bullies:

> Nicole was never the ringleader. She had no backbone and let Riley mold her into whomever she wanted Nicole to be. She was a weak soul. In some ways, Riley bullied Nicole as well—she took advantage of her identity by making her follow her lead, trying to force her to be another player in the bullying game she had created. Riley dominated their relationship, which made her the strongest social influence in Nicole's school life. This influence was much stronger than any influence I had on my long-lost friend, because I lacked Riley's hunger for power, and I didn't need to be

cruel to the weak in order to feel stronger. After all, that's what bullies crave most in relationships: power over the other.

Lauren now pities Nicole for bullying her. She writes, "I feel bad for the road she was pressured to travel down, and I forgive her. However, I also can never forget the things she did to me."

ANALYZING LAUREN'S STORY

What does it look like to attempt to reconcile significant relational transition within bullying? Lauren's story demonstrates the ends to which a young girl might go to cope and survive when the ways in which she's been taught to deal with conflict in the past do little, if anything, to thwart others' attacks in the present.

Changing Times, Changing Friends

Lauren speaks to the challenges inherent to being strong within bullying, a relational process that often is fueled by weakening others. There are two dimensions to her story—both rooted in matters of change and identity—that significantly shape the context for the bullying she experienced. First, there is the preoccupying transition she faces between elementary and middle schools. The diary entries stressing her worries about how alone she will feel at the new school show the complex identity negotiation in which she became immersed.

My own lived experience with this transition helps me to understand her anxiety. As I am writing this chapter, my eleven-year-old niece, Peyton, is beginning middle school. In the months leading up to the change, many of her family members, including me, spoke with Peyton in ways that tried to build her excitement. For instance, I'd tell her, "This is so big, Peytie! You're becoming a big girl!" Her lack of enthusiastic response led me to think that attempts to build excitement also apply pressure to an already pressure-filled change in her young life.

I stay with this sense of pressure when I explore Lauren's story, thinking about the heaviness of change for young people like her, and the need to reconcile uncertainty about what middle school will be like—what the transition means to her, who her friends will be, how others will look at her, and how she will view others. In these ways, change sets the conditions that make possible nervous or anxious selves who are, at once, excited about the transition and nervous about how they will feel and function. Similarly, the change can bring unstable footing; they find themselves searching for a more steady way of standing and moving through their new world, which can be further destabilized by being bullied.

A second transition conveyed by Lauren's story concerns the changes that occurred in her long-term friendship with Nicole. As neighborhood best friends, Lauren cared for Nicole, and counted on her as a positive person in her life. Yet,

Riley changed that friendship. The Nicole-around-Riley was a Nicole who contradicted the person she was when she and Lauren were alone together. The Nicole she knew and trusted was lost to Riley. Now Lauren had to deal with a duplicitous and bullying Nicole. The bullying from Riley and an altered Nicole turned Lauren into an anxious, sad, and hurt girl. Lost for Lauren was her level of assuredness, and the ability to be more carefree around others.

The changes in her friendship with Nicole compounded Lauren's transition into middle school. In turn, the newness interconnected with transitioning to middle school likely complicated Lauren's ability to reconcile the loss of Nicole. What is clear is how the experience of making sense of the changes created more uncertainty for Lauren in an already uncertain time.

Game On

Lauren's account emphasizes the "game"-like nature to how she was bullied. Prime targets in this most aggressive contest were her body and physical appearance, being a good student, and other objectionable characteristics that her bullies felt would prevent others from wanting to be her friend. Sneering looks and mean giggles from passersby in the hallway made the bullying feel worse, so much so that over time she began to question herself and wondered if their appraisals were true. Young, friendless, and vulnerable, the bullying weakened her resolve as a player in the game. Score was being taken and she was losing.

As part of this harmful game, bullies made demands on Lauren in regards to how she lived, a dimension to the story that suggests various possible identities being negotiated. At a more basic level, the bullies did not expect anything different from her. In this case, they simply used (what they felt was) her stigmatized identity on which to focus their bullying. In this case, Lauren existed for them merely as a target obliged to "take it." At the same time, the demands suggested she needed to change, or become someone other than who she was. This "someone" is a person whom the bullies deemed desirable and acceptable.

Who did they wish Lauren to become? On one level, the bullies were demanding that Lauren should act more like them. She should like the same things and activities that they liked, and look the way they looked. But on another level, their bullying may have been a demand that she cover her intelligence. This idea is more plausible when we consider that Riley and Nicole would bully her after she openly displayed or flaunted her smart self in class. In this way, the covering demand says to Lauren, "We know you're smart, but we think smart is not cool, so keep it out of our (less intelligent but cooler) faces. If you do not, you can expect similar bullying in the future." At the same time, the demand could also be that she pass or hide her intelligence. This alternative possibility in effect says, "Your unique identity contradicts what most girls perform; hide it and act "dumber." If you do not pass, you will pay."

But their taunts may have had little to do with Lauren being intelligent. They could have simply served as yet another opportunity to tease her. Regardless of the specific reason, their bullying harmed Lauren and led her to feel as if she was an objectionable "other," different in bad ways from the other students.

Limited Kindness

Lauren's "kill it with kindness" strategy reveals an additional layer to bullying and identity that concerns *responding* to bullying. Her response exhibits restraint in the face of bullying in an effort to downplay its impact. By complimenting the other or relying on internal monologues, victims refuse to retaliate, trying not to show bullies how much they hurt. In essence, "kill it with kindness" is a reframing strategy that allows the victim to understand and perform within a harsh situation by diffusing it, and trying to create more affirming and less hostile meaning for oneself and the other.

Consider some of the ways in which this strategy becomes a form of negotiating identity within bullying. On the one hand, restraining oneself effectively entails practicing performances of "being the better person." The victim works to be someone who does not "lose themselves," refusing to retaliate. Lauren's restraint also works in ways that help to manage the bullying. By not retaliating or showing them how they hurt her, Lauren tried to keep the conflict from escalating to more harmful levels. Thus, the strategy serves as a mode of attempted self-protection, which makes possible a caring for the self by a victim who first and foremost desires to be safe. As Lauren's account demonstrates, a positive response is not guaranteed to help. As she writes, "There's only so many times that I could hear negativity and look for the positivity in it!" Also, responding with kindness could also instigate further and harsher aggression from bullies. Nevertheless, "kill it with kindness" displays an effort to infuse more peace into the turbulent relating of bullying.

Lauren's "kindness" is an intriguing counter move in this "game." For instance, folk wisdom would suggest there is an efficacy to responding to bullying through retaliation. It suggests that victims need to perform in ways that show how they can defend themselves and are not weak. There may be value to this position. Responding with more assertiveness or aggression might have ended Lauren's bullying sooner, or at least allowed her to feel more comfortable as she endured the hardship. It might also have been really satisfying to tell the girls off, or punch one of them in the face. But an aggressive response risks escalating and perpetuating the "hurt" and violence, when de-escalation and healing is likely most needed and beneficial in the long term.

These reflections prompt me to consider other responses to bullying that similarly show contradictory ways of responding. I recall seeing a picture on Facebook that portrayed a young boy who was no more than ten or eleven years old. He was standing on the sidewalk at a busy intersection holding a sign that had "HONK AT ME: I AM A BULLY!" written on it in large red letters. The boy's face was flushed red and he was scowling. He looked angry. The woman standing to his right, whom I assumed to be his mother, stood stoically by her boy, arms folded and looking equally angry. It was clear, to me, that the boy was being punished for bullying. I suspect the logic informing this response was: the more cars that honked at the boy and the longer he stood out there for the world to see he was a bully, the better the punishment. He'd learn his lesson, case closed. The photograph, which was widely "liked" and "shared" on Facebook, shows another response to bullying akin to retaliation: fix them through tough love, and show them what it feels like to hurt.

This kind of response can be meaningful in at least two ways. On the one hand, the mother was trying to have her son take responsibility for having bullied someone, and more specifically, for communicating in ways that hurt someone else. As with Jessi's story, she was letting him know his behavior was wrong, that she would not tolerate bullying, and that he must stop it. In turn, she put his body on the line, requiring him to feel the heat of interactions, which, from the looks of him, certainly did not feel good. When I first saw the picture I felt happy the boy was being held accountable, like he was "getting a taste of his own medicine." I said to myself, "good parent!"

Yet, my glee was not without reservation. When reflecting more deeply on the photograph, I could no longer understand the situation without also believing the mother's specific choices implicated his well-being in risky ways. In addition to seeming uncomfortable and angry, the boy looked embarrassed and humiliated, like he had his pants pulled down in front of other kids, who responded by pointing their fingers at him and laughing. While the anti-bullying lesson spiriting the punishment is important, the specific ways in which the lesson was pursued also creates the conditions for the boy to feel tremendous shame for being "that guy," a bully so bad his mother dragged him out for everyone to gaze at, beep, and judge. The boy became a stigmatized "other" through an aggressive response to bullying.

Maybe it is okay to feel shame, or to shame others. Perhaps shame is something people earn and, thus, it is a justified strategy in some contexts. The issue is worthy of debate. However, to shame as a response to bullying is problematic and tantamount to a "bullying moment" in its own right. If our goal is to mindfully respond to bullying, fueling an aggressive problem with further aggression feels, to me, counterproductive and unkind.

On Public Display

Nicole, Riley, and others not only bullied Lauren, but also took the time to devise a nickname for her, which they used on multiple levels for their bullying. By calling her "highlight girl," these bullies honed in on an aspect of Lauren's appearance and made it into something to despise and ridicule. Her hairstyle went from something personal and lovely to something objectionable. In addition, by incorporating the name into the poem and posting it online, her bullies made the bullying public. They made Lauren and her abject hair a matter of public interest and spectacle. Indeed, everyone online had the potential to view the poem as much as they wanted, and to believe and spread to others the harsh things the poem said about Lauren. Yet, such aggression was not only cyberbullying. Everyone who saw or heard about the poem could also invoke it to bully Lauren face to face at school or elsewhere.

The "burn book" in which Lauren was included made the bullying she endured more intense. As with the poem, the book showed premeditation on the part of her bullies. It took time and energy to execute such an attack. Folks were committed to bullying her, and to letting Lauren know how they felt about her and further cluing her in to her status as "other." Including her in the burn book is to say, "Who you are matters so little to us that we are going to dedicate space in the book just for you, to stress to others that you are a horrible person." In these ways, the book socially located Lauren with a scarlet letter "L" (for "loser"), and put her further on display so others could gawk at what her bullies had documented as her most "disgusting" features.

Bullying Lauren in these invasive and highly visible ways deflated and weakened her. While the poem and book might not have been seen by everybody, and everybody who read them surely did not agree with them, to Lauren everyone saw the poem, and everyone believed the disparaging ways they portrayed her. Thus, these bullying tactics reminded her of their disapproval, and reminded the bullies and others of her disfavored identity. Perhaps her peers might dismiss their bullying as being "just" a name, poem, or book, or "just" part of the "game." Yet, their bullying tortured Lauren and embarrassed her to the point she was unable to show her face at school. She was in a bad place, and something had to give.

Get by with a Little Help from My Friend

Some of the most compelling moments in Lauren's story appear when she conveys the two turning points that helped her to relate to bullying differently and to negotiate a new identity. The first moment pertains to her developing a friendship with Susanne. Similar to Jezebel's close relationship with Rose, Lauren and Susanne were bonded by the power of shared experience, primarily because both knew first hand about how being bullied harmed their identities and lives. This was a different, and more supportive and stable, friendship for her. Through a friendship with Susanne, Lauren saw that she deserved to have a true friend (Rawlins, 2009) who would be there for her. Indeed, much like Jezebel, she found her "oasis." Even the tone of her writing about Susanne feels, to me, to be different and more positive. Her words feel lighter and more flowing, and she did too through her friendship with Susanne.

The second turning point relates to the changes Lauren made to her physical appearance in order to more easily handle others' bullying. These changes speak to issues of the body and performances of identity through the body within bullying. I see multiple and contradictory levels of meaning that inform her transformation.

Changing how she looked was the one thing Lauren felt she could do to alleviate her suffering. The need to feel better was significant, as indicated by her willingness to endure the pain caused by the burning of the chemicals on her sensitive scalp. As she writes, "[T]he sting was nothing compared to the ways I would feel once my hurt was gone." The need to endure pain in order to feel better is intriguing. Similar to Iman's cutting, the response feels paradoxical, yet also understandable. For Lauren, not removing the highlights, a primary source of her stigmatized identity, or not making the other changes to her physical appearance, would likely leave her open to more bullying. To change the bullying, she needed to change her body.

To feel better Lauren needed to conform to the same social criteria against which she was being judged and bullied. The story suggests that she enjoyed the highlights before the bullying; they helped her to feel good and like herself. Thus, getting rid of them at least in part involved working to get rid of an important aspect of her avowed identity, which she may or may not have done had she not been bullied. The return to brunette hair, and the new clothes and contact lenses allowed her to fit in, and to be more desirable. However, the changes were more on others' terms and, again, relied upon standards for which she was bullied. Thus, converting her identity in these ways, so as to alleviate the stigma and her suffering, involved acquiescing to standards that she did not initially set for herself.

At the same time, the transformation also speaks to issues of empowerment, even at Lauren's young age. The changes were something Lauren decided to do and represented a shift in performing herself. She set out to alter how others understood her, and how she understood herself. Granted, she could have tried to retaliate against the bullies; yet, doing so would have contradicted the caring and kind aspects of her identity that mattered so much to her. Moreover, it is possible she figured she would be less likely to change others, so making these personal changes allowed her to take ownership of her happiness. Unlike the failed attempt to feel better by changing her physical appearance demonstrated in Jezebel's story, Lauren's story indicates that she was, and still is, genuinely happy about how the changes helped her to change her life. As a result, she suggests a positive effect of being bullied.

Weakened Lauren found strength in ways that made sense to her. She lived through significant harm at an early age, and her difficulties were amplified by the changes present in her life at the time. With the added support of a new and true friend and her transformed look, she became a "new girl"; better yet, she felt "untouchable."

Note

1   Lauren organized her story in the spirit of a layered account, moving "in" and "out" of the diary entries comprising the story. I've used asterisks to distinguish between these different narrative moments.

OF FROGS AND FRIENDS

Reflexive Interlude 4

"How's school going, Keith?" Lynne asks me. We are sitting and talking as we sip Kool-Aid in her backyard by the pool.

It's fine," I respond flatly.

"Just fine?" she responds sounding surprised. "You're a great student and you love school. I bet it's more than fine, right? Students and teachers must *love* you." I start to blush and look down at the ground.

"Okay, it's … good. I like most of my teachers and am working hard."

Lynne lives next door with her husband, Mike, and their four boys. Our families are close, but Lynne and I are even closer. I love visiting with her and try to stop by several times each week, and more during summer vacation. She is a warm person and always seems to say things that make me feel loved and at ease. I maintain relationships like this with other parents on the block as well, especially with the mothers on our block, and particularly during middle school. The mothers consistently welcome me with open arms and I love that about them.

"Honey, why aren't you out playing with your friends?" she asks. "Don't you wanna play with the other boys?"

"Not really, I guess."

"Why not? Are they picking fights with you? Does your mom need to talk with their parents? Do you want me to talk with these boys?" I think she is trying to be funny, but I also know if I ever needed her in this way, she would defend me instantly—yet another reason why I love Lynne and feel like I'm one of her boys.

"No … nobody is trying to fight me," I say, chuckling, as I comically move my clenched fists in the air to emulate throwing punches. I respond with humor because I love to make Lynne laugh. I am not prepared to say that I fear some of the boys at school want to fight me. If I tell Lynne, or others, about these boys, they might make me report them. Maybe they'll want me to prepare myself to fight back, which I do not want to do. It feels safer to keep my fear bottled up.

"Good," she says, pausing and staring at me for a few seconds, as if to figure out if I'm being honest with her. "Cuz you're too wonderful of a boy to have people messing with you."

"So anyway... " I say, sipping from my drink dramatically and feigning spilling, again trying to make her laugh.

She smiles and says nothing, taking a sip of her drink.

"I do play with other boys, and with girls, too. We sometimes play baseball and softball in the field and go swimming at Lan Oak Pool. Sometimes we act like we're professional wrestlers in the WWF and wrestle each other in the field or front yards. I do a lot of 'boy stuff'."

"That sounds fun, and the wrestling sounds a little dangerous."

"Playing with the boys does get old. I have more fun just talking with you."

"Ya?" she says, as her smile widens.

"I hope that's okay?"

"Of course it is. I love your visits. There's nothing wrong with coming over, and don't you let *anyone* tell you otherwise. In fact, you should come over more often, if that's what you want to do." She gently rubs my hand while telling me this. Her touch instantly relaxes me.

"Just be you. Be who you are and do what you like."

"Be meeeeeeeeee!" I say in an exuberant, jesting voice.

"Goofy boy," she says, as she leans in to give me a hug. Her hugs are the best. She refuses to let go until we've had a long hug—at least five seconds, sometimes more—and her arms feel as warm as her heart must be.

Her encouragement makes me think about an idea I have been planning, leading me to jump out of my chair. "Okay, gotta go! Thanks for the drink. I'll visit again tomorrow." I begin to head down their driveway and to return home (eager to try out my idea).

"Good, I'll see ya soon. Hey if you see CJ anywhere, will you tell him I said to come home? He has homework to do." CJ is a sweet kid who is eight years younger than I. Like me, he's not at all a "boy's boy."

"Will do!"

"Thanks, honey, and please tell your mom 'hello' for me."

When I am with Lynne and other adults on our block, I am able to say things for which boys around my age would make fun of me. With them I can more often show them how I think and feel, and who I am, experimenting with my communication and ways of being without the fears of being ridiculed or stigmatized that I feel at school. I am able to be more of myself, uncovered.

I Can

"Hi," Mom says, as I walk through the front door. She's standing in the kitchen at the sink, getting dinner ready. "Where were you?"

"I was talking to Lynne," I tell her. "She says 'hi.'"

"Oh nice, did you have a nice visit? I should walk next door soon and catch up with her."

"Yep, it was fun. I love Lynne."

"How is she doing?"

"She's good."

"She's *well*, you mean."

"Ugggh, yes, she's *well*. Having a teacher for a mom is … *swell*."

Smiling and patting me on my back, she says, "Sweeters, you know that's one of my big pet peeves." Mom loves to correct me and my siblings when we say something grammatically incorrect. It's an obsession of hers.

"Right, you *is* a teacher, Mom," I say.

"Funny." She pauses. "But it's well, and not good."

I smile and give her a long hug. "Got it."

"You sure are upbeat. Are you having a good day?"

"I am."

"What did you and Lynne talk about?"

"Lots of things."

"Like?" she probes, trying to get me to share more and talk in actual sentences.

"She was asking me about school, the things I do for fun, and stuff like that."

"Nice."

"She said I should just be me. I should be who I am and do what I like, and that it is okay I don't always play with other boys or kids my age."

"She's right, you know," Mom says, stopping what she's doing to look at me directly in the eyes.

"I know."

"Make sure you remember what she said. It is important. Let's sit for a second," she says, putting down her spatula and oven mitt, directing me to sit at the kitchen table.

"Remember, 'I can't is the frog who drowned'." Mom is constantly telling this to her students, and to me and my siblings. Whenever she hears "I can't," she promptly responds, "I can't is the frog who drowned." The saying and cutout pictures of frogs appear throughout her classroom, on the walls and on her desk. It comes from one of her favorite children's parables. The story conveys a situation in which two frogs are trapped in a barrel of thick cream. The frogs are struggling to stay afloat long enough to climb out of the slippery barrel. One frog says to the other, "I can do it." The other says, "I can't do it." The one who believed he could was able to successfully climb out of the barrel and live. The one who believed he couldn't was not able to climb out and, consequently, drowned. Much like her mother did, Mom regularly teaches others about the power of positive thinking.[1]

"Of course I remember it, you say it enough!"

"I am being serious here. I say it so much because I believe what the saying means. I want you kids to believe it, too. You can do anything to which you set your mind. If you can imagine it, you can make it happen!"

"Anything?" I ask, smiling and leaning in close to her, resting my forehead on hers.

"Anything, baby doll," she responds, grabbing my hands, smiling, and kissing my cheek. "That goes for your school work, for the college you want to attend, and the type of job you want to have down the road. It applies to everything." I try to live in "I can" ways, but it doesn't always apply. After all, this frog cannot climb gym ropes.

"Okay, well, if you believe it, then I guess I believe it, too."

"Good, well I've got to get back to work making dinner. Dad will be home soon, and I still have a long list of things I need to do before we eat. I hear the boys playing across the street, if you're looking for something to do."

"Nah, I don't really feel like it."

"Honey, you should play with them more, they're your friends."

"Not right now. I wanna watch my shows." As Mom returns to completing the tasks on her list, I head into the living room. I've been wanting to try out an idea of mine for some time. My brother and sister are out playing with friends, and my father is still at work, so I will have total control of the television, and total privacy. The timing couldn't get better.

(Not so) Secret Princess

In the living room I see my duffle bag on the chair. I strategically left it there just before going into the kitchen. It is filled with supplies for a secret mission I have been planning for the past two weeks. Nobody knows about my secret, not even Mom or Lynne.

My mission is to spin like Wonder Woman, with music and wardrobe, during recess at school.[2] I treat this mission with adult-like seriousness, which means being smart about planning and acquiring the supplies I will need. Securing the music is easy, as I had just received a double-decker, double-cassette boom box last Christmas. When no one in my family is looking, I hold the stereo's tiny microphone to my family's 19" Zenith to record the opening theme music to *Wonder Woman*, a hit television show at the time. Acquiring the wardrobe is different, and, thus, requires more creativity. Wonder Woman typically wears star-spangled nylon shorts and a cape, a golden Lasso of Truth, bullet-proof bracelets, Golden Tiara, and bright knee-high red boots. I opt for a tight-fitting pair of shorts, a white clothes hanger rope lasso attached to my belt, gray duct tape bracelets, and a light blue nylon jacket as my cape. Imagination will fill in the rest of the details.

As her story goes, Wonder Woman is a "princess warrior" transplanted to Washington, DC, where she lives under the alias of Diana Prince and works for the government, tackling World War II evils. She possesses superhuman strength and stamina, as well as a handy invisible airplane that allows her to safely travel from place to place. Whenever she needs to transform into Wonder Woman, her secret identity, she simply extends her arms to her side and spins. Each spin, each transformation, is accompanied by music and colorful blasts of fire explosions as dynamic as the injustices she aims to topple.

I have loved Wonder Woman since the first time I saw her on television. Most of the boys I know talk about how pretty she is, and the ways her tight costume makes her boobs look big. While I couldn't care less about her boobs, I recognize how beautiful she is. However, I love her because she is strong and just. I also admire how Diana Prince, who is typically rather meek and deferential around others, much like I often am, is able when needed to transform into a superhero no one is able to stop. I also love the ways her bracelets allow her to repel the many bullets bad characters shoot at her. She makes defending oneself against violence seem so easy, which marvels me as a boy who often feels disempowered. I don't just love and admire Diane Prince/Wonder Woman, I often wish I could become her. I want to feel what that beauty, strength, and resilience feel like.

"Good night!" I say to my parents and brother and sister, as I get up off of the couch and start to leave the family room where we've been watching television. It is later that night and I am beyond excited for my spin, which I plan to perform tomorrow.

"Good … night?" my Dad responds, looking over at my mother in disbelief. They both know I often have trouble falling asleep. I have rarely ever gone to bed earlier, unless I was sick. Yet, I figure, the sooner I go to sleep, the sooner tomorrow, and my spin, will arrive.

"It's early, honey, is everything okay?" my mother asks.

"Everything is fine, Mom. I just wanna read and go to bed early. I'm tired."

"Okay, have a good sleep. See you in the morning."

"Good night."

After making my way to my bedroom, I hop into bed, shut my eyes, and begin to visualize my spin. *Where will I do it? Who will be around me? Do I ask for help from friends? This is going to be great!* I decide not to ask for help. This is my spin. Others can watch, but I don't want them to interfere and potentially ruin the mission. Given my excitement, I know I won't be able to easily fall asleep. So, I turn the light back on and begin to read my book. After reading only a few pages, I go to sleep.

At school the next day I can barely contain my excitement about the spin. I say nothing about this mission to my friends. Yet, I keep telling them, "I can't wait for recess today," and checking the clock on the wall in anticipation of our mid-morning recess. Finally, Ms. Cheek says, "Alright, folks, grab your coats and let's line up for recess." I leap out of my seat and grab my bag, which is filled with my wardrobe and boom box. I decide to position myself at the end of the line, to avoid detection by Ms. Cheek, who always leads the class outside from the front of the line. I figure if she sees me bring a duffle bag outside, she'll ask questions, and probably make me leave it inside, ruining my plans.

As the line begins to move, I am smiling from ear to ear with excitement. I have been waiting to do this for weeks. I want my friends and Ms. Cheek to see how much I love Wonder Woman. More importantly, I want them to know how brave I am, and how wonderful I am, or at least how wonderful I feel like I can be. Yet, I am also nervous. I hear my stomach grumbling and can feel sweat under my arm pits and in my groin area. This spin is important, and I don't want anything to go wrong. I know Ms. Cheek will protect me, if others start to bully me. Yet, I don't know how others will respond, and the suspense is driving me nuts.

Once outside I make sure to locate myself on the concrete area of the playground and close to Ms. Cheek and a handful of chatting, presumably safe(r), female classmates. I feel relieved most of the boys are playing a robust and distracting game of kickball away on the grass. Because they are not around, I will feel freer to really go for it as I spin. I am ready for my transformation, imagining how my typically hesitant and sensitive way of living will fall away as I spin. The conditions are right. My stage is set. It is time to spin.

I press play on the boom box and, as if in slow motion, feel the shifting of how those others around me appear. I close my eyes and began to spin, slowly at first, but then swiftly and more loosely. My face blushes and smile widens as the music plays and the wind kisses me. My cape falls to the ground from the force of my imaginary explosions. Although my eyes remain closed, I still can see others. I see them seeing me, and then me seeing them seeing me, spinning so gracefully and freely. I spin in that space of excitement and risk, compelled to continue, and carried by the winds, the energy cultivated from movement, and the chorus of the show's theme song accompanying me and making my heart burst with happiness.

Wonder Woman's story compelled me to perform in ways that unsettled my young cultural being. For in those moments of spinning I came to be a particular type of boy, a counter-normative boy within cultural spaces of conventionally lived sex, gender, and sexuality, just for starters. I spun unaware of my being attracted to the same sex, yet, again, aware I did not like girls in the same ways as other boys seemed to like them. Indeed, that spinning displayed my difference and aspects of difference previously unknown or kept invisible. Through spinning I called out to others, seeking recognition, change, comfort, and company.

That next day Ms. Cheek called my Mom to alert her to my schoolyard spin. Mom replies, "If it makes him happy, what does it hurt?" I wrote to Lynda Carter, who played Wonder Woman, telling her of the spin and my love for her. Her reply must have been lost in the mail.

It would be lovely to report that this performative event significantly changed things for me. That the conditions of the spinning and those fabulous rotations enabled me to feel stronger and less nervous and awkward than I usually felt. However, I have no memory of such change. I do not remember how my peers responded to me. I vaguely remember Ms. Cheek responding supportively to me as I put my materials back in my duffle bag. She did not reprimand me, nor did she try to make me feel as if I shouldn't have performed the spin. She certainly didn't tell me, "Girls, and not boys, spin like Wonder Woman," like I thought she might. Instead I believe she was surprised and also a little impressed at my spinning, the chutzpah it required. As I close my eyes in this moment of writing, I can still see her smiling at me, as she hustled all of the students back into school from recess.

I do not remember any of my schoolmates saying a word to me about the spinning, nor do I recall saying anything to them. Perhaps I didn't need to bring it up with them. After all, the beauty of the performance was that I wanted to do something I figured most people would think was different, if not odd. Regardless of how they might feel, I spun anyway. Maybe I was also scared to bring it up with others, fearing they might think I was dumb or weird, or worse yet, bully me for "acting like a girl."

I more clearly remember my own response to the spinning. I see myself trying to quickly put the materials back into my duffle bag and picking up the boom box and wedging it under my right armpit, so I could carry it inside. I am blushing, feeling warm and tingling from excitement. I also feel a strange combination of uncertainty and pride about what I had just accomplished. I usually perform as a reserved boy, especially when I am not around friends, and when it involves displaying for others the ways in which I felt different. Yet, spinning as Wonder Woman breaches this way of being, effectively putting my difference on display. At the same time, the pride I feel comes from doing something that is deeply meaningful to me. I spun just as I had wanted; it felt good; and others didn't keep me from doing it. As a result, in these moments I feel a bit looser and happier than I have in a long time. I think Lynda Carter would be proud.

★★★

"You did *what*?!!" Lynne asks me. It is the day after the spin, and she and I are talking while sitting at her kitchen table. While I wasn't comfortable discussing my spinning with people at school, I knew I could trust her.

I respond, "I spun like Wonder Woman. I love her."

"With a costume, and music … at recess … and others were there?"

"Yep," I say lifting my chest in the air. "It was fabulous!"

"Wow … good for you." She's excited, but her voice makes me think she has other things she wants to say.

"Thanks!"

"I told you the other day to 'just be you.' I guess you took me up on that advice, huh?"

"Are you mad?"

"Am I mad at you? Never! I'm just happy for you and wish I could have seen it." I comically feign wiping my head, as if I am wiping away sweat in relief.

"What did the other students say?"

"Nothing really. They just looked at me. Ms. Cheek smiled and looked impressed."

"Good, but did the boys give you any trouble?"

"They weren't really around, but no, they haven't given me any trouble about it … yet."

"Sweetie, that's good. Don't worry about the boys. I was just curious. I'm proud of what you did and am happy for you. Let's go outside. Grab your lemonade, some cookies, and let's go sit by the pool." I grab my lemonade and some cookies and hide several cookies in my pocket for later, following Lynne outside.

Lynne's encouragement makes me feel like I did the right thing in spinning. Yet, her questions also get me thinking more about the risks and the boys. *What if some of the boys saw me spinning? What would they think about me impersonating a woman, as a boy? What would the girls who were around me during the spin tell the boys or other girls at lunch or in class?* As much as the spin empowered me, it also exposed me and rendered me vulnerable to others at school, especially the boys. I am uncovered, which makes me feel at once alive and concerned.

Puffed Up

A few weeks later I am at recess when I spot my friend Noman across the parking lot. Noman is a petite Pakistani American boy who is in my class. He talks with a soft-spoken voice and his giggles are cartoonish, always cherubic and warm. I often see boys teasing him for "sounding like a girl" and not being at all muscular and tough. Noman and I spend lots of lunches together, engaging in the rituals of small talk or eating in quiet. I am comfortable around him, and I think he is at peace too.[3]

I see Noman standing against the brick wall leading to the school entrance. He is gently kicking rocks across the sidewalk and looks as if he is waiting for Ms. Cheek's cue for students to return inside. He has just spent recess staring at the ground as he walks around the parking lot. Though he tends to keep to himself, he is a good person and harms no one.

Noman smiles and nods "hello" as he sees me walking up to him. On this winter day, my eyes are fixed on his coat—a long, thick, and puffy winter coat—that is bigger than any I have ever seen. "Nice coat," I say sarcastically, as I poke at his chest, by his heart, feeling the sharpness of my fingers attempt to penetrate the puffiness. Nearly inaudible, he mumbles back, "[Something, I think, about] cold and [something about] snow." My pokes continue, and I yell, "I cannot hear you, No-man, talk louder!" He acquiesces to my aggression, his body goes limp, and he evades eye contact with me by staring at the ground. Still not satisfied, I grab Noman by his coat, my boy fingers barely able to cling onto his puffed up coating, and push him against the brick wall. "Owwww," he utters. His eyes are shut, seemingly to prepare for more roughness.

The pain displayed on Noman's face prompts me to quickly realize what I have done and leads me to stumble awkwardly through an apology: "Uh, oh, I'm sorry … my friend." He nods as I move away, the imprint of my assault slowing receding from the surface of his coat, replaced by puffiness. As tears begin to form in his eyes, he looks at me as if he is trying to figure out why I just attacked him. We walk inside, and never speak of the incident again.

This is my only memory of bullying a peer. Once was enough. I didn't just attack a "peer," I bullied a friend who was innocent, didn't provoke me, and only had my best interests in his mind. I do not remember what motivated my violence. However, I do remember how good it felt to bully him. I had a bigger body than he did, and I was a bit more athletic. I knew he was an easy target. I remember how easy it was in that moment to lose myself to the poking and prodding and verbal taunting of bullying. Bullying Noman helped me understand the adrenaline that comes from such violent acts. At the same time, I also remember how bad I felt afterward. By no means was I a perfect kid. Still, attacking him contradicted so much of the peacefulness I had performed in the past and much of the same ways I have performed ever since. I hated to see him tremble when I released him, even though I had taken such joy in the acts that had prompted the reactions only moments before.

I have no idea why I would attack Noman. Perhaps I felt as though spinning had opened me up to the point of my needing protection, feeling as if I could be bullied at any minute for going against what boys are "supposed" to do. Maybe my momentary exposure as a different kind of boy led me to feel in harm's way and, thus, in need of protection. For as much as my spinning uncovered me, perhaps it was by attacking Noman that I could return to being covered, or passing as a boy who didn't feel so different.

Methodological Dilemma

I am standing in the bathroom at home, looking at myself in the mirror. I have just gotten out of bed and am getting ready for another day of writing. My still-sleepy eyes focus on the lines between my eyebrows—the outward signs of work and stress that have been there for many years, and seem more prominent lately. I begin to think about the ways in which doing autoethnographic research on such a personal and impactful societal problem like bullying implicates me, and in so doing, complicates my ability to persevere and be well.

The choice to explore bullying through personal narratives has required me to engage with vivid details about situations of violent lived experience, others' and my own. I have encountered, and still continue to encounter on the page, bullies who take down their victims, seemingly without a care in the world for victims' welfare; in turn I see victims who desperately try to steady themselves in anticipation of the swift blows of their impending victimization, even though personal strength is the last thing they can envision being possible for themselves. This has meant confronting and staying with the emotional realities that bullying instigates, such as fear, helplessness, anger, apathy, desperation, and rage. Even though the stories also sometimes speak to positive emotions, such as pride, compassion, and hope, their emphasis on violence and painful emotions has at times made this research process quite difficult, even torturous. How much hardship can one autoethnographer endure?

It is common for autoethnographers to examine cultural life that involves pain and suffering (Ellis & Bochner, 2000; Ellis et al., 2011). For instance, my research and writing on the performance of aestheticized bodies among gay men, at the expense of those men who do not perform these bodies (Berry, 2007), and with being "out" in the university classroom, a space that is still conditioned by homophobia and heteronormativity (Berry, 2012), required me to directly engage and stay with unpleasant conditions. However, working with the stories on bullying in this book has presented me with a unique set of challenges. I have made it a point to become close with the students and their stories, so I can share and examine their accounts in as detailed and intimate ways as possible. Yet, the closer I have gotten to the stories, the more I have begun to internalize and feel the storytellers' pain. For instance, when I read and enter into Lauren's feeling of humiliation as a result of being cyberbullied, or the burning sensations she felt when her stylist applied hair dye to her scalp, I feel those experiences deeply. My chest tightens and my scalp burns.

Adding to these difficulties are the challenges I have faced in writing my own stories. Going back thirty-five years has involved going to the depths of my memory and at times struggling to remember how I lived with and through bullying—processes I have cared not to remember for some time. It has also meant re-living and feeling again the ways I suffered in my youth. Writing my stories has called me to be true to those experiences as I lived them, and that has meant needing to write with particularity and depth. I have chosen to return to these experiences through stories with mindfulness, which has called me to write with clarity, honesty, and feeling. I have needed to be open and ready to experience what came to me through my stories. Indeed, my students were not the only storytellers who performed vulnerably. Exposing my past experiences and selves has been as scary and sad as it has been exciting and important.

Further, because this research relates to writing a book, I have needed to stay with such pain and suffering for extended periods of time. As a result, the stories have at times fatigued me and have affected my body. Staring into the mirror this morning, I see the tiny scars I suspect might still be on Iman's body from her despairing acts of cutting and the feelings of inadequacy and humiliation from my experiences in gym. I feel it in the stress lines that have grown since I started the book. I also see in those lines how horrible it felt to be humiliated in gym class, to be taunted, rejected from being a legitimate boy because I was not able to complete normatively boy-like activities like rope climbing. These outcomes may point to the power related to using personal stories as qualitative inquiry. They also show how difficult such a research process can be, particularly in terms of researchers' attempts to manage how close we get, and how well we stay, as we immerse ourselves in the hardship that conditions cultural life.

How can autoethnographers stay mindful when working so intimately with complex stories of hardship? How do we negotiate a healthy distance from these alluring stories of violence, as we participate in an interpretive research process that importantly asks for us to reflexively and empathetically engage with stories and storytellers? Given the pain, how do we continue and stay well within the process?

Notes

1 Similar to Lauren's upbringing, my parents reared me by instilling the belief in the power of positive thinking. Thinking positively and performing positivity with others helped me cope and thrive in many ways during my youth, helping me to survive through hardship, such as being in the closet for so long. At the same time, as I became skilled at being positive, I was not simultaneously learning about and practicing how to engage and stay with negativity, in particular, and conflict, in general. When I was in my late twenties, I "met" the concept and practice of mindfulness. Practicing mindfulness has helped, and continues to help me to see the importance of working to reconcile the good with the bad, the positive with negative, and the joys with the pains. I tell some of this story in Berry (2013c). Though I do not extensively explore this issue within my bullying stories, I do still wonder how I might have responded to bullying, and how I might have lived through the struggles of being "different," had I learned these insights in my youth.
2 An earlier version of the Wonder Woman "spinning" story appears in Berry (2013b).
3 An earlier version of this story appears in Berry (2013a).

6

A NARRATIVE ON BULLYING AND RAPE

ENA

Ena's life began with violence, which was followed by years of feeling as if she were an outsider in her own family:

> Growing up I used to say I had no relationship with my family. I was one of seven children and was related, only by half, to one, my loving baby brother Liam. No one in the family ever spoke of my biological father, who had raped my mother when she was fourteen. Sometimes I wondered back then if my mother knew who he was. We got away from the abuse, ironically, to enter into a new family as the "other" with all kinds of mistreatment that came with this new situation. In this family I was undeniably different. My dark hair and eyes, large and genuine strait-toothed smile, and honey complexion contrasted with the golden blond and lively baby blue eyes of other family members. My desire to learn in creative ways confused a family of all math wizzes, and branded a target on my back, at which the entire family often aimed.

Ena struggled to be at peace as a child and adolescent. As she writes, "Now looking back, rather than saying I had no relationship with my family, I now believe that instead I was entangled in a damaging relationship with my family."[1]

★★★

Ena's experience of the dis-ease of feeling different was intensified by the relationship she had with her step-father. Their relationship was filled with sexual innuendo, which she recalls in vivid detail:

"Don't tease me like that" my step-father said to me as I sat on the couch eating a Popsicle. "Don't say that to her, she's only 9 years old!" my mom interrupted. As I finished eating my Popsicle, I began to figure out what he meant about "teasing" him. I left that interaction feeling faint and scared, because I honestly felt he might just be capable of atrocity like that. Also, my step-father often used the threat of sexual abuse against my mother, as a way of making her stay with him. "Maybe I need to be like your family and molest Ena, will that make you feel more comfortable?"

He said something horrible like this to antagonize his wife, knowing there were child rapists, or at least rape sympathizers, in her blood family. Ena's mother stopped communicating with that family when she met her step-dad. Thankfully he never made good on the taunt or threat against Ena.

The chance to help Ena with her homework provided her step-dad an additional opportunity to violate her:

Math was a challenging subject for me, but unfortunately mathematics was the only type of intelligence valued in my family, particularly by my step-father. Instead of simply helping, he criticized me the entire time. He would often use physical means of explaining or visualizing a math or science problem, such as putting a charged 9-volt battery on my tongue. He would tell me to close my eyes and imagine a large group of people standing on the middle of my palm. In seconds I screamed in pain as he pressed his thumb into my palm onto the metal coffee table with all his strength.

He also tried to overpower Ena when they played board games together:

We would sometimes play Risk, in which players fought against each other to conquer the world. Although he easily overcame me, I still felt a sense of importance when he would pay any sort of attention to me, even though he was fighting to conquer me. Who knows why I asked my step-dad for help, or agreed to play the game with him. Maybe it was because those were the only times when he would spend time with me.

In spite of the violence, playing Risk together is one of Ena's fondest memories. She loves remembering her step-dad dramatically performing all of the accents of the countries in the game, and Liam helping by rolling the dice for their step-dad.

★★★

Ena's life at school expanded upon the violent foundation her home life had established. She developed early, getting her first period at ten years old. This change made her a target for bullying:

I was 9 years old when boys began to snap the back of my bra. I can still hear the "clack" noise when I think about those boys. I would tell my teacher how uncomfortable it made me feel, how it startled me, and, even more, how much it physically hurt. My mom eventually came to the school to talk to the teacher, who told her I just needed to grow thicker skin. My mother's response: "Can I snap your bra then?" I still to this day remember that teacher, because her lack of properly handling such behavior allowed me to be sexually harassed at 9 years old.

Ena was bullied in unrelenting ways: she developed breasts at a young age, prompting students to often scream across the cafeteria at her, "Big Jugs!"; students regularly looked through her purse to check for pads; and when they found them, they displayed them to others, much to Ena's embarrassment and humiliation. She also recalls how the bullying turned even more aggressive:

> Once I was actually kicked in the vagina by a boy, leaving me on the ground crying. He kicked me as a test to see how different my parts were from other girls, as if it would hurt less or more; he and his friends said they were just curious. The teacher just told me to get up. I sucked in my tears, caught my breath, and got up.

Without the assistance from her teacher, the genitalia-focused bullying continued. She recalls one incident in particular, which involved five girls following her to the bathroom to look at her while she urinated. They wanted to further "inspect" Ena while she was on her period:

> I remember the scene clearly: the walls were black and speckled with silver bits that shined from the sun; the bathroom never, as long as I attended that school, had a light. I remember seeing their eyes widened to be able to see through the crack in the bathroom stall, staring at me as they expressed disgust, as if I was a dirty person for becoming a young woman. My heart pounded in an uneven rhythm out of pure fear of the consequences of their personal discovery—fear is the only emotion I remember feeling from within that stall. They seized upon the fear, making comments about my exposed body, about how I must never take a bath because of how "sickening" my vagina looked. I sat there mortified and catatonic, unable to move. I stayed in that stall for as long as I possibly could, because I knew what would happen when I went back into the classroom.

Ena's suspicion soon became a reality. Once she returned to class she realized the girls had told everyone about what they had seen, leading them to laugh at her: "They're laughter only made my humiliation worse. I felt like a tiny person as they laughed and pointed. I tried to sink down into my chair and disappear!"

The girls continued to make derogatory and offensive comments to her and others about Ena's development, particularly her vagina, for the rest of her fifth grade. As a result, she continued to suffer.

Once again Ena turned to her teacher for relief. This time she also sought help from the guidance counselor. Their collective response: Ena should reflect on *her* role in the issue, and consider what *she* did to prompt these girls to dislike her so much. They moved her desk to the opposite side of the room, where she sat alone for the remainder of the year. Their response made Ena's already substantial feelings of "difference" more intense. She writes, "I just wanted to be myself, hanging out with other kids, and not have to worry about being attacked." Their response didn't help, and it certainly didn't allow Ena to relax and be happy. The teachers had confined and excluded her, just as the other girls had done so many times before.

Ena also felt the school officials' response prompted her to react in hurtful ways to others:

> Soon after that issue was "resolved" I began calling other girls who approached my desk "bitches." I knew the consequence for using this language would be far more severe than the consequence anyone else received for their incessant sexually fueled bullying.

The condoning of the girls' bullying by school leaders told Ena that sexual violence is accepted and encouraged. Her resorting to harsh name-calling showed her the powerful ripple effect that sometimes results when people do not put a stop to violence.

★★★

Ena recalls in her story how much she liked to read horror novels in her youth: "They made me feel uncomfortable, but I couldn't stop reading them. I think there are certain parts of me that desired the feeling of fear, even to the point when I feel I started to attract it." She further writes:

> One day while the other kids at my day camp were playing kickball, I chose to sit alone in the dugout and read Stephen King's *The Shining*. Soon after I sat down, the camp's new counselor, a large man, wobbled over and sat next to me. He sat a little too close to a ten year old, and had a look in his eyes I will never forget. I grew rigid out of the fear I felt, feeling like I must have done something to attract this man without realizing it. He touched me a little and got very close; I instantly shook and felt flush in my face, knowing if someone didn't intervene he would certainly kiss me, and possibly more. He smelled like spit and body odor and had a look on his face that taught me for the rest of my life what sexual desire must look like. I responded to his actions in the shakiest of voices, asking him "What?" A female counselor

soon walked over and yelled something to the group. Hearing her voice the man jumped a mile in the air and landed on the other side of the bench.

Later that day Ena went to her mother to tell her what had happened. When approaching her she shook in fear of her mother getting mad at her, as if she had caused the man's advances. Her mother responded, "Ena, you are ten years old now, and you are old enough to tell the other camp counselors yourself. If you don't, he may end up doing worse to someone else." Ena never mentioned it to a counselor, or to anyone again.

Today she still wonders if her silence caused another girl the same problem.

Weeks later she noticed the wobbling counselor, or as she describes him, the "day camp pedophile," entering the same remote mobile unit on the camp in which Ena and friends were playing pool. She was shocked and frightened to see him:

> I had not seen him in such a long time, so I assumed maybe he had been caught touching others and fired. I had just begun to stop fearing him, and now this? I did everything I could to avoid him in that small room. At one point I saw him bend over to take his shot, only to expose the sight of white crusty material in his crack creeping up out of his basketball shorts. I remember feeling vomit come into my mouth. I was afraid and disgusted by this man. I was playing at the table next to theirs with a kind and fun Caribbean friend. Suddenly I heard the man scream. The inside of my arms shuddered and my hair stood on end, and I instinctively grabbed a purple billiard ball from the table and proceeded to ram it into the head of my friend. She shed blood and screamed for help, but I continued. I repeatedly hit her at least ten times, as if I was in a trance.

Ena attributes this violent attack against her friend to the man's earlier attack on Ena. As she writes, "Being reminded of the inappropriate moment I shared with that predator created a propensity for violence I did not yet know how to control."

Now almost fifteen years later, Ena says still thinks about the ways she attacked her friend at least once a week.

★★★

High school served as a place that expanded the ways in which others bullied Ena. She describes a series of these experiences:

> A senior in my class often went after other students, picking on superficial things like the clothes they were wearing, or their skin complexion. Behind me I would often hear this same senior guy pick on the freshmen. The other girls around him, as if on cue, would giggle at each of his attacks. The guy was clearly the leader of the group and no one challenged him or his behaviors, including me.

She was too new to the school, and too fearful to confront him. The teacher did not stop him either, which added to the confident swagger with which he moved through the class: "He had an air about him that told even the teacher, as well as the other students that he controlled the room and could act in any way he chose!" No one confronted the senior, and the bullying continued.

Ena's body continued to be at the center of her being bullied.

> My body was deemed as not being my own from a young age. Spankings, kicking the most private parts of my female body, and unsettling voyeurism of that body from peers of the same sex, supported that early belief. Entering into high school my freshmen year, not too long after I allowed a senior to fondle me during a lecture on contemporary architecture, all the while choking back what was left of my breakfast, and feeling like I was meant to be an object, I finally learned that bullying was far more than name calling on the playground; it was also violence. It entails verbal, sexual, and physical violence, and sometimes the target may be the most reserved parts of your body.

One day Ena noticed the senior bully wheeling his classroom chair over to her, moving with coolness as he wove in between the desks of other students, much to their glee. Soon after he arrived at her desk Ena felt his hands rubbing between her thighs. She went numb:

> I did not move, though I was screaming inside to do so. I never understood how fear could do that to bodies. I did not "fight," nor did I experience "flight." I just took it. The drafting teacher was a foot away, and the classroom was full as this senior molested me under the table. Although it may have only lasted for two minutes, it seemed to last an eternity, and two seconds was far too long. At the same time I felt guilt and confusion for the fact that I secreted and got wet. This was a sensation I had for the longest time associated with perversion, and something I believed I should have been able to control. Does that mean I wanted it?

Feeling invaded and stunned, Ena decided not to report him. Thus, he was never reprimanded by their teacher or another school official. He continued on with his bullying ways. A year later she saw him in the school courtyard. He grabbed her again, only this time he whispered in her ear, "Remember last year? You liked that, didn't you?"

She says she could still feel his hot breath as she wrote her story.

★★★

Ena currently lives with her mother while she completes her undergraduate degree and makes plans to attend graduate school. Her mother divorced the step-father several years ago, after he physically assaulted her (the mother). Ena and her mother have had a strained relationship for as long as she can remember. She says her mother is a decent person, and Ena is grateful for her support. She has also accepted that they will likely never have a "normal" relationship: "I have a hard time forgiving her for the things she did and allowed to happen. My mother is also sometimes very unpredictable and moody. I breathe a sigh of relief when I get home and she is not there." At the same time, her mother thinks Ena is "selfish and emotionless." To Ena, her mother struggles with their relationship for different reasons:

> Part of the strain between us is the way I came into the world. She was raped and here I am. I think I might resemble him in a lot of ways, because of how little I look or act like her side of the family.

Her mother has long since acted weirdly with Ena: "She acts kind of like I am adopted; I wonder if she prefers Liam, which I would understand."

During her senior year of high school, Ena became a member of the Sikh church. This positive turn brought peace and stability to her life. The teacher of her world religion course and his wife, both role models for her, encouraged her to join. Today she remains devoted to the religion, and feels that being a Sikh makes her life better: "I have a set of rules and a routine. The routine alone is very good for me, because I need things to be predictable and easily controlled." She feels nothing but unconditional love from her fellow Sikhs. Their love and acceptance makes her feel special.

★★★

Ena ends her story by reflecting on being assaulted and on assault in the context of cultural forces that promote violence:

> To think we do not live in a culture of violence, a culture of rape, and a culture of blaming the victim is to perpetuate something so problematic it causes young people to live through unacceptable harm.

She also shares an impassioned call for us to look at bullying and sexual assault differently:

> Sexual assault is often excluded in conversations about bullying, and that's a problem. I've brought it up to people, and almost every time they say I am being "dramatic," and that assault is on a completely different plane. But sexual assault *is* bullying because of the intense power it gives the bully, and the embarrassment it leads the victim to feel. Victims of sexual bullying, like me, feel guilt and shame. Our feelings are not present in "typical" bullying stories. It would help to expand our thinking on bullying!

Victims of this kind of bullying need to be understood and talked about with greater care as well:

> My story makes me feel the "fault" for this problem is bigger than any one of us. We all did this. Our culture says we need to "lighten up," "get over it," "grow thicker skin," and that "it gets better." Twitter and Facebook are overrun with the most heinous jokes about rape, or statements suggesting there's nothing wrong with bullying, or that bullying isn't an issue. Parts of our culture even suggest that victims "asked for it," or that we had as much of a role in the violence as perpetrators. Well, now I understand that as a young person I never allowed bullying and abuse, I just *endured* and *survived* it.

ANALYZING ENA'S STORY

The graphic details of Ena's story demand attention to a type of bullying that no one should be subjected to "endure" and "survive." She writes, "My body was deemed as not being my own from a young age." This statement speaks to her integration of bullying and sexual assault, and its meaningfulness concerning identity. What does it mean to negotiate a life of violence wherein bodies and identities are intricately intertwined, and sometimes painfully violated? Ena's story speaks to what it means to be an "other" whose identity is negotiated within the suffocating throws of violence, silence, disregard, and fear. She shows us what it is like to evolve from a bullying victim to anti-bullying advocate.

Unimaginable Beginnings

Solomon (2012) investigates stories of women who conceive a child during rape. He reports between twenty-five thousand and thirty-two thousand women become pregnant through rape every year in the United States, and at least eight thousand women keep their child. Solomon primarily focuses on the relational struggles inherent to mother/child relationships in these cases, and the ways in which rape brings stigma to both mother and child. That is, rape survivors and the children born within the violence in effect live with "spoiled," or discredited, identities (Goffman, 1963). The nature of their conception contradicts the "normal" and "natural" (non-rape) ways in which child conception and birth is "supposed" to occur. As a result, mother and child must negotiate added layers of struggle in their relationship. Solomon further writes, "A woman who keeps a child conceived in rape has a permanent tie to her rapist" (p. 506). She is prone to struggle with paradoxical feelings: the child is, at once, her offspring, an object of her love who she desires to protect, and a living and breathing reminder of her rape, someone who may conjure up disgusting memories and meanings. Thus, the historical violence that the mother endured can constrain feelings of closeness to her child.

Ena's story speaks to the painful aftermath of being "thrown" (Heidegger, 1996/1953) into life circumstances that require her to negotiate her identity as the stigmatized "other." On the one hand, the ways in which she lives are directly informed by how she "came into the world" (e.g., the added tensions and lack of closeness in their relationship, and Ena reminding her mother of her rapist). On the other hand, this stigma extends beyond the immediate mother/daughter connection. For instance, family members know of the rape, likely prompting added feelings of "otherness" for Ena, and others, to reconcile. Absent in the story are indications of warm and loving relationships in her youth.[2] Furthermore, Ena lives without a conventional (i.e., "natural" and "normal") birth story. Actually, she lives with the antithesis of such an account. This absence creates the conditions that make it necessary for her to be accountable for her "abnormal" identity. From birth Ena's "otherness" has informed much of her lived experience. She lives the consequences of a pre-birth violence that she never witnessed.

The stigma with which Ena lived extended well beyond how she came into the world. Her story reveals a diverse range of situations of being bullied during middle school and high school in which others rendered her "other." Other people's taunting and ridicule, just for starters, led her to feel as if she were on the outside of her new family, sexualized in the lunchroom and bathroom at school, and groped by the senior in class. Their "othering" had a toll on how she felt, and how she understood identity. Being Ena meant having her physical space and boundaries violated on a regular basis, adding to her feeling different, and dis-ease in general. Over time she came to feel that she existed solely to be messed with, dwelling frequently and precariously at the whims of others' invasive inspection (bathroom), amusement ("big jugs"), and invasion (senior stud). By claiming her body and being in these ways, bullies made an especially vulnerable girl unsettled and unsure, and feeling disregarded.

Ena's lived experience with the "otherness" that was created by her being bullied was also unmistakably conditioned the physical violence. This violence pervaded much of her youth in a number of ways including threats of sexual contact by a step-dad who liked to play rough, sexual, physical, and verbal abuse from peers at school, the camp counselor who fondled her, attraction to slashing violence in horror novels, which she suggests over time intrinsically fed her, and the primal bashing of her friend with the cue ball. Violence served as a pervasive pattern in Ena's youth. Absent in her story are examples of Ena feeling happy, relaxed, and free from the harsh imposition of others. Also missing are instances showing Ena being able to stand up for herself. Instead the story speaks to ongoing violence that became increasingly horrible over time. We see Ena living an identity saturated in violence and learning that violence was acceptable, and to be expected, especially for people who were "different."

The bullying that Ena experienced hurt her at the time her bullies violated her. Yet her story also speaks to the ways in which events can stay in and affect our memory, primarily how the sedimentation of past practices shapes how we negotiate life and identity in the present. She smells her senior bully when thinking of him and shakes as she relives the after-shock violence she perpetrated against her Caribbean friend. While the exigent circumstances of the bullying are "gone," the violence stays with her as does the "voice" of violence in her head.

Fallen on Deaf Ears

Ena's story reveals how inaction and silence toward bullies harm victims within bullying. Take, for instance, how Ena's teacher and guidance counselor told her to consider "her role" in the ways in which others bullied her, and why others might "dislike" her. Rather than supporting her, they responded with dismissing and evaluative comments that assigned blame to Ena. Moreover, they "cast" her as someone who is attacked because she is unlikeable, a response that hurts by devaluing a young and impressionable person. Or take, for instance, how her teacher moved Ena in class. I suspect the teacher's response aimed to disengage the bullied victims from bullies. However, neither the teacher nor Ena's mother were able to make Ena feel better. Rather, they excluded her, further isolating a girl who already felt as though she did not belong. Neither the parent nor the teacher took an opportunity to get school officials more deeply involved, and to establish and enforce a safer and more inclusive classroom climate. Instead they responded to the bullying like they were applying paper-thin bandages to seeping relational wounds. By attempting to cover the blood flow, they neglected the deeper injuries that necessitated more thoughtful, empathetic and caring responses.

The significance of this inaction and silence is more worrisome when we consider the mother's response after learning Ena had been sexually assaulted by the camp counselor. By telling Ena to report the attack to another counselor, she left an injured and unskilled ten-year-old child to secure her protection without a parent's or an adult's supervision. Granted, the mother might have felt great distress in that moment, by orienting to it as a painful reminder of her own rape. Living Ena's assault with her might have felt like she was re-living her own. I can only imagine how terribly difficult it must have been for Ena's mother. Nevertheless, she left her child to fend for herself, creating the conditions for scary experiences of vulnerability, risk, and dis-ease. Further, she responded manipulatively, inducing guilt by coaxing Ena into reporting the attack to prevent other girls from being attacked. Ena repeatedly had to reconcile contradictory messages. She was told to speak up, yet, every time she did so, she was responded to in unhelpful ways. Consequently, Ena continued to live and struggle within bullying and its aftermath.

These reactions to Ena being bullied perpetuated her stigmatized identity. This impact is particularly evident when Ena conveys how school leaders' responses (or lack thereof) served to "legitimize" and "encourage" sexual assault and bullying more generally. Indeed, their inaction was interpreted by Ena as a sign that sexual bullying was permissible. As she notes in the story, the very people who were supposed to protect her (parents, teachers, counselors) contributed to the continuation of the violence she was forced to endure.

Of course, the adults might have felt like they were doing the best job they could at the time. They also might have felt helpless in responding to such an awful problem. Nevertheless, the silence and inaction left Ena open to more threats and attacks. Instead of assuring her that she would be taken care of and safe, and making sure she knew the bullying she was enduring was wrong and unacceptable, they exacerbated Ena's trauma. Adults left her to question herself, and to feel the self-doubt, uncertainty, and shame that was traumatizing her. She felt anything but validated by their responses. Isolated, she became the "other."

Emerging Advocate

Ena's story demonstrates an evolution of identity that formed as a result of a disturbing history of relational violence. From the moment she was conceived, others ascribed to her the identity of an unwanted "other." From the time she was born she faced unrelenting stigma, requiring her to endure much hardship and uncertainty.

Becoming a Sikh represents a significant turning point in Ena's life. Her community members affirm her. She can be herself. Yet her ability to bring such a painful story to the page is an equally powerful identity-transforming moment, one I was not sure would happen. Shortly after our first class meeting, I met Ena at a local coffee shop to discuss her narrative. She conveyed her concerns about whether or not she could tell this story, or that she could make it through the process. Tears flowed in her eyes as she tried to tell me about some of the violence she had experienced. Given her concerns, I told Ena she could consider writing on a different topic. Yet, I could tell that accompanying her fear was a fierce determination to express the consequences of sexual bullying.

Ena is no longer a victim, but a wounded storyteller advocating greater awareness and responsibility concerning bullying. She is not just a statistic, but someone who highlights unimaginable violence and who makes the dark parts of bullying transparent.

Ena's body will never be someone else's again.

Note

1 Similar to Lauren's story, Ena crafted her account by using narrative layers or fragments. I've chosen to distinguish between her different story moments by using asterisks.

2 In the story Ena submitted for her class assignment, she interwove her account of being bullied with her brother Liam's story of bullying, which included sexual assault and homophobic bullying. That story conveys the loving bond she felt with Liam in their childhood and youth. I've omitted these parts of Ena's original story from this book, figuring it is Liam's story to convey and confirm, should he ever wish to do so. Like all names in the participants' stories, Liam is a pseudonym chosen by Ena.

BENNIES ON THE FLOOR

Reflexive Interlude 5

"BENNIES ON THE FLOOR!" "BENNIES ON THE FLOOR!" "BENNIES ON THE FLOOR!" [Chanting]

I am walking to my high school gym for a required, all-school assembly to kick off the new school year. The assembly is also my foray into what school life will be like for me as a new freshman. The high school I attend is a college-preparatory, Roman Catholic institution located thirty minutes from my family's home. Walking with me in a single file line are my fellow freshmen, or, to use the label given to use by sophomores, juniors, and seniors, "Bennies." Even though we are still a long ways down the hall from the gym, we can hear this chant—"Bennies on the Floor"—echoing repeatedly and loudly. My heart is racing and my mind is puzzled, as I have no idea what is in store for me. The blank stares on the faces of other freshmen tell me they are as unaware and unsettled as I am.

As we approach the gym doors, two teachers ask us to stop, saying, "Wait right here, please. We'll show you your seats in just a moment." Peeking into the gym, I can now tell that the chanting emanates from the bleachers, where the upper level students are sitting. I see them excitedly stomping their feet and clapping their hands in unison, each clap and stomp accenting each word of the chant. After just a few seconds in hold, all freshmen are directed to take their seat—on the floor. This is where we will sit for assemblies during freshmen year. Now that we have arrived, the chanting grows even louder and more enthusiastic.

"BENNIES ON THE FLOOR!" "BENNIES ON THE FLOOR!" "BENNIES ON THE FLOOR!" [Chanting]

Now seated on the floor, I feel as if I have entered into a strange new world. The space is lit by sterile, amber fluorescent lights, and feels old and dusty. Dressed in khaki pants, a button up dress shirt, and necktie, winter dress code for all boys,

I see waves of bodies—older and more established students who I suspect are far more comfortable than I and the other Bennies—filling every inch of the bleachers on both sides of the gym. All they are doing is chanting and stomping, to the point of my feeling overwhelmed and confused. *This is a mean way to greet the newest and most unskilled students in the school. I didn't want to attend this high school. Since most of my closest friends are attending the public high school less than a mile from my home, I had always assumed I would be there with them. Will it be like this for us the entire year? All four years? If so, I'm doomed.* The chanting is incessant, repeating over and over, seemingly becoming louder with each repetition. It envelopes me, drawing me further into a new academic space that makes me think about our freshmen identities. We are Bennies, the lowest beings on the school hierarchy. Indeed, we are smaller and weaker in status, so low that the only suitable seat for us is on the wooden floor on which players sweat during basketball games and bugs crawl at night.

"BENNIES ON THE FLOOR!" "BENNIES ON THE FLOOR!" "BENNIES ON THE FLOOR!" [Chanting]

The marching band, positioned on the gym's stage, begins to play the school's fight song. I am silent and look around to observe how other Bennies are reacting to the ways we have been received. Most are also silent, seemingly at a loss for words, and have blank stares and nervous grins on their faces. Some join in on the chanting, seeming not to care as much as I do, which adds to my confusion. *Why are they chanting? Do they like being mistreated? I will not chant. It's mean and not right.* I see nuns and lay teachers walking around the gym, monitoring student behavior. They are our leaders, the adults who are in charge of the school's moral code. Yet, they do nothing to stop the chanting. At least at some level they must agree with the hierarchy and don't mind the elders policing us. As a result, the chanting continues. Their inaction makes it feel as though the chanting, indeed, this hazing, is important and natural, not to mention something freshmen must tolerate.

"BENNIES ON THE FLOOR!" "BENNIES ON THE FLOOR!" "BENNIES ON THE FLOOR!" [Chanting]

As I wait for the assembly to start and the chanting to stop, I notice a small, shiny object fly passed my eyes, hitting the girl seated to my right on her forehead. It is a penny that came from the direction of the bleachers. Over the next few seconds, I see more pennies fly our way. I will later learn these offerings are "pennies for the Bennies," an added bonus to our "welcome" to the assembly, and the high school. As more pennies begin to bombard us, I cover my eyes with my hands and look down, trying to protect myself. At the same time I look through the cracks in between my fingers, trying to see what is going on. The barrage of relational currency only lasts for a few minutes, when a few nuns begin to circulate in front of both sides of bleachers, as if to identify who is chucking the pennies and tell them to stop. They do not catch any of the culprits, but the penny throwing stops. The chanting continues.

A few moments later, our school principal walks up to the microphone. Her presence prompts a slow end to the incessant chanting, only to be quickly replaced by thundering applause coming mostly from the bleachers. *Why are they clapping? Maybe they are showing excitement for the start of the assembly and another school year. However, people in the bleachers are laughing as they clap. It seems more like they are celebrating another round of bullying the Bennies.* The principal holds up both of her arms to silence the noise. She welcomes everyone to the first assembly of the year (more applause) and reports she is excited to welcome the freshman to the school community. She then leads everyone in a prayer: "In the name of the Father, Son, and Holy Spirit … Amen." No one utters a peep during her prayer, except to respond, "Amen."

The assembly lasts for one hour. It includes announcements about the latest school fundraiser and the first football game of the season. She also emphasizes the need for all students to work hard in their studies and to be a united school that works as a loving and holy community. *Loving and holy community? What about the chanting, and how "loving" was the hurling of pennies? Not one word about the welcoming the freshmen just received?* She ends the assembly with another prayer and wishes everyone in the school a great upcoming year.

I stand up with my fellow Bennies and quickly make my way to the exit feeling unsettled. Granted, the majority of the assembly was positive and upbeat. I even laughed a few times and had some fun. Still, I leave feeling demoralized. The last hour only strengthened my reservations about attending this school. I also feel confused, like the school's call for "oneness" is a lie, or at least something they don't take seriously. After all, how can the community be "one" when freshmen are treated in ways that cruelly split us off from the fuller student body? How do we comfortably find our way into the community when we are allowed to be ridiculed not for anything any one of us has done, but for simply being first-year students? I leave not feeling as though I am a welcomed part of the "one," but rather as someone who is an "other" dwelling on the margins of the school community. I and my fellow classmates perform at school at the expense of others' desires to ridicule, humiliate and shame us. In turn, such a stigmatized existence is allowed to occur. While some school officials may have tried to stop the penny throwing, none stopped the chanting. They will not try to do so at any other assemblies during my freshman year either. In these ways, the tradition is legitimized by the inaction of leaders. It is ingrained in the institutional fabric of the school, increasing the vulnerability I feel here.

I was already feeling anxious about attending this high school, but the assembly stressed and underscored my dis-ease. I was hopeful the transition to high school would eliminate the issues I faced in middle school. I hoped a change in location would allow me to feel more comfortable being the boy I was, or thought I was. However, that first assembly set a tone for what I felt was inevitable: a difficult high school experience. Moreover, it told me in no uncertain terms that my identity matters to my peers, and who I was, or wasn't, especially during the first year, will be publically scrutinized.

One might think the confusion and pain I felt during the chanting would prevent me from participating in the chanting the following year. This is not the case. Starting with the first assembly during my sophomore year, I chant at the Bennies. I do not throw pennies at the Bennies, but I chant enthusiastically and without reservation and continue to do so at each assembly until I graduate. I feel relieved and excited to be on the other end of the chanting. Now part of the more powerful masses of upper-level students, I yell and stomp and do not even think about how carrying on the ritual can negatively impact freshmen. The institution has worked its way into my nervous system.

It wasn't that I had forgotten how bad it felt to be victimized as a Benny. I merely liked how it felt to be the victimizer.

Knowing My Place

Starting on the first day of high school, students quickly form cliques that stay largely intact and influential until graduation. These social groups comprised a range of identity "types," including the pretty and popular students who look good and move through hallways with finesse, band members and thespians whose flairs for the musical and dramatic radiate from their bodies as they play the drums on their classroom desks, or orate a line from a play in hallways, "nerds" or "geeks," for whom books and learning are the center point of their friendships, and students who are present in class, but are more quiet and socially withdrawn outside of class. As the name aptly suggests, members of the cliques tend to keep to themselves; little mingling takes place across groups.

Athletes and cheerleaders comprise the upper echelon of the school's social hierarchy. This status is understood and seems to be adhered to by nearly everyone. Athletes seem untouchable. Their power is reinforced on game days, when they wear their uniforms to school and walk through the hallways with their chests puffed up and their entire bodies strutting to the movie soundtrack of *Rocky* playing in their heads. Further, the cheerleaders are pretty, fit, and spirited. Some of them may speak with non-athlete students. However, many still walk through the hallways as if they are floating on air, also untouchable. The athletes are tough and macho, and the cheerleaders are there to support them.

I primarily self-identify with the quiet and withdrawn students, and my friends are people I sit near during class. Our bonds involve brief conversations we have before, during, and just after class. I do not pursue deep relationships at school— my dislike for the school keeps me from wanting us to get closer. That being said, I develop relationships across social groups. For instance, my brother, Kevin, who is a senior at my school when I am a freshman, is a prominent member of the school's marching band. Like athletics, marching band is a tight-knit and esteemed clique, because members spend so much time together and the band is highly accomplished, having won national champion awards multiple years in a row. I benefit from the close relationships Kevin, nicknamed "Cecil," has with his bandmates. "Hey that's Cecil's brother!" his friends often say when they see me in the hallway walking by myself. I smile when they call my name, and nod my head to say "hi" in return. I feel a little better knowing my brother is at the school and that his friends often keep watch over me.

I am too young and naïve to realize the perceptions about the cliques at school relate to and reinforce stereotypical constructions of identity. The behaviors I have observed here are no less true, but they are also limiting. They tend to render us strangers to each other. As strangers we rarely have the opportunity to interact more deeply and perhaps even learn that we are more than the labels such cliques ascribe to people.

A Bitter Taste

"What is it, honey? What's bothering you so much? Is it school?" Mom has noticed me moping around the house, being more quiet than usual, and sits me down at the table to have one of her gentle-but-I-wanna-know-what's-going-on talks.

"Yes, it's school," I tell her. "I don't like it, and I don't think I am going to make it."

"What do you mean *make it*? I know you will make it and do well. You always do, when you set your mind to it."

"It's more than that, Mom. I am just not gonna be happy there."

"Why not, what is going on? How bad is it?"

"It's not bad, it's *awful*."

"Are you still thinking about the assembly? I wish there was something we can do about it. But remember, *sticks and stones may break my bones, but words will never hurt me*."

"No, as bad as that was, it's school in general. I want to be happy and to have fun. I am not happy when I am there, and that place is *definitely* not fun. Oh, and one of my teachers *prayed for me* in front of my entire class last week!"

"*Prayed for you*?!"

"Yes, it's the nun who chews on chalk while she is lecturing at the chalkboard."

"How can I forget her ... the chalk lady." Mom tries to infuse my anxiety with humor. It helps me a little bit, but I am feeling quite down.

"Well, I cannot forget her, so why should you!" I give her a little humor in return.

"So, tell me what happened."

"Sister was leading the prayer in front of the entire class, when she said *Almighty God, keep watch over our dear Keith Bear. Give him your guidance, and show him the way to better discipline. Help him to behave better in class, and to be a good child of God.*"

"That's very strange," Mom says after a long pause.

"You're telling me ... and she didn't even get my name right!"

"You *never* have had a problem with behavior, except for the flower incident."

My mother loves to tell the flower-picking story from my childhood. I love that she loves to tell it. I can tell she is about to re-tell it to me.

"I got a call one day from school," she says, with a wide smile on her face.

"Mrs. Berry?" the principal asks. "Yes, this is she." "I'm calling because right now I have your son in my office." "Oh my, which one?" "It is Keith."

"Keith!? That's impossible. He is not a troublemaker. Are you sure?"

"I'm sure, I'm sure. I caught him picking flowers on school property." "Oh, I'm so sorry, Mr. Kompier." (Insert dramatic pause.) "I just had surgery," she continues. "Keith was probably picking those flowers for me!" She loves the sentimental aspect of the story, and ends the story, like she normally does, with a beaming smile saying, "What kind of first grader does that!"

"I remember the story—it's a classic. The main character's a sweet kid!"

"A very sweet kid. So, I know the answer, but are you misbehaving in class?"

"No, nothing has changed."

"Of course not. Well, hang in there. I know you'll start to feel more comfortable very soon, honey. You'll start to make friends soon, too."

"I don't think so. I just don't see myself there and don't really want to make friends. Everyone I'm close friends with goes to TF-South." "South" is the high school near my house, where most kids graduating from my middle school, including my best friend, Robert, attends.

"I understand. Just remember it takes time for kids to adjust to new schools, and this school will help when you go to college. It's only the first semester. Will you give it some time?"

"Okay, I will," I respond quietly after a long pause.

"Good, okay I need to get some things done. Where's my list? And honey, why didn't you tell me about all this earlier?

"I don't know. I guess I didn't want to worry you."

"Nothing you share will worry me. Period."

"Okay. Thanks, Mom."

I get up from the table, walk out of the kitchen and through the living room, and head out the front door. I sit by myself on the front porch for the next hour, not thinking about anything in particular, just sitting there, staring off into the distance. I am checked out and in a fog.

I don't know what I wanted to happen from sharing my feelings with Mom. I didn't expect my parents to let me transfer schools. I don't think that is what I even wanted to happen. Maybe I wanted her to simply tell me that things were going to get better, that I was going to be okay.

Missing Story

In high school and its surround social environment, we learn who should love whom (read: man and woman) and what this love is and should really be about (read: procreation and the perpetuation of the Christian and Roman Catholic faith). My classmates and I repeatedly hear stories about how "happy" and "right" married men and woman are, and more importantly, how unmarried adults are unhappy and lost. In addition, we are repeatedly told about the wrongs of abortion and are required to watch a fear-mongering anti–abortion film. The film ends with a close up shot of an aborted fetus that sits on top of a clinic room tray, just having been extracted from a woman's body. Absent at my high school are different types of stories that offer a more inclusive understanding of diverse human beings.

The religious stories present and absent at my high school lead me to feel as if I don't have a story. Or at least I don't have a valuable story that is as beautiful, just, and normal as the normative story I am learning about and expected to follow. I am not aware of my being gay in high school. It is likely I am repressing many of the feelings and thoughts I have on the possibility of love, relationships, and happiness with the same sex. The religious teachings are mandating that I repress sexual thoughts, lest I wish to live in sin and go to hell. Nevertheless, in high school I am searching for a story that makes sense to me, and that doesn't make me feel as if I am an outsider. I am pursuing a happiness that I cannot name at this point in my life.

My Personal Oases

My days spent at school are not entirely bad. At least three areas of support allow me to stay happy enough and well enough.

First, I revel in the idea of speaking a second language and work hard to master Spanish. I take advanced placement classes and study my vocabulary and grammar on a nightly basis. In between classes I walk out of my way so I can see and say "hello" to Ms. Hinkey, my Spanish teacher for my sophomore, junior, and senior years, as she stands outside her door monitoring students in the hallway. I roll my "r"s with gusto and try to enunciate with precision as I speak Spanish in class, hoping she'll notice my efforts and be proud of me. When I am in other classes, bored or nervous, I often think of Spanish and Ms. Hinkey. Both bring me great happiness and help allay my worries. Ms. Hinkey and I have a teacher/student relationship, but we're also very close, which makes me feel like she and I are friends. She's like an academic mother.

Second, I eat lunch each day with a group of girls who are fellow members of the marching band with my brother. Knowing of my troubles adjusting, I figure he encouraged them to ask me to sit with them. As most students eat inside the cafeteria, the girls and I sit at one of the tables just outside the cafeteria by the vending machines. As we sit and eat, we small talk about school, other students, and life generally. There is softness, kindness, and warmth to these interactions. With them I experiment with how I interact and who I am. They laugh at my jokes and seem enthralled by my stories, and this makes me happy. Around the boys, I often try to speak with a deeper and more "masculine" voice, and I try to suppress my Pillsbury Dough Boy giggle. Around these girlfriends, I easily flaunt my giggle. I tell them about my love for Wonder Woman and my spinning performance at recess in fifth grade. They respond with acceptance and gush with praise: "You must really love her to do that!" "You are so brave!" "You are too cute!" In these ways, lunch with the girls serves as a safe haven for me, and I suspect it is for them, too. For one hour a day we are able to step outside of the hyper-masculine boy climate of the larger high school experience. Lunch means openness and peace.

While this support often helps to make school more enjoyable for me, there are still times when I feel especially nervous or sad, as though I need to get away from other people and classes. Therefore, a third source of support often helps. I ask to go to the school's infirmary. The infirmary at my high school is a secluded and dimly lit room located around the corner from the main administrative office. The space is filled with several smaller private rooms, and each has its own bed and a door that shuts. I have never seen a staff member here. When I arrive, I hop into one of the rooms, keep the lights off, and relax on the bed. I am never able to sleep, so I just hangout, away from the outside noise and pressures. Sometimes I visualize being home with my family, or spending time with friends. I think of Wonder Woman on a number of occasions on that bed, and remind myself of the importance of staying strong.

Rattled Dude

Bam! Bam! (Loud noises come from over my head at the locker.)

It is my sophomore year of high school, and I've learned a routine for moving through the halls in ways that help me feel comfortable. When I see people I know, I say "hello" to and usually walk down the hall with them. Otherwise, I mainly keep my head down and to myself.

Bam! Bam! (More loud noises sound a few seconds later, now from a few lockers down.)

I try to ignore these noises. I know what they are and who made them. Chuck, a junior, whom I just know by name, slammed his fists several times on the metal door above my locker, and then on the door a few lockers down, creating a loud, rattling noise. Chuck is not an athlete, but he's friends with many of them, and we share gym class together. He's a tall boy who has a chiseled chest and jawline. The chisel complements the acne that covers much of his cheeks. He tries to cover up his acne with cream, but his bumps and scars can't be fully hidden. For the past month and a half, once a week or so, he has banged on the lockers like this while passing by me in the hallway. I don't know Chuck, but he has certainly taken notice of me.

Once he slams on the second locker, and I look up, he sneers at me as he walks down the hall, usually saying something like, "Ya, that's right, Dude!" "Dude" is a word first made popular in the cult hit movie *Fast Times at Ridgemont High*, starring Sean Penn. Many boys have been using it ever since the movie became popular. The deeper and thicker their masculine voice can get in saying it, the better. This is how they remind each other they are guys and how good it feels to be guys. I hate the word and find it stupid. I don't say it.

"Don't pay him any attention," my friend Julie says at her locker, immediately to my left. "He's just trying to play with you. Don't fall into his trap again."

I shake my head in response: "I know. I just don't get it—why me? I've done nothing to him. I don't do anything to anyone."

"That's the point, dear. You stay out of trouble, do well in school, teachers like you, and you won't fight back."

"I wouldn't know how to fight back if I needed to. And if I did know how, I don't think I would fight. I guess I'm not *dude* enough."

We laugh as Julie closes her locker and heads off to the class.

I often see Chuck sitting nearby me at lunch in the cafeteria. He doesn't say a word to me. However, I'll sometimes catch him looking at me, waiting for me to notice him. If I look at him, he sneers back at me and snorts, as if he is a bull blowing smoke out of his snout. I take this to mean Chuck is warning me to never step out of line. He is watching me and will come after me if I do. One day I saw gobs of disgusting snot spray out of his nose when he snorted at me. He must have had a cold. Everyone around us noticed what happened. I loved it.

I never find out why he is watching me, nor do I learn exactly what the line is that I shouldn't cross. It doesn't matter, because his attempts to intimidate me work. I am afraid of him and, as a result, feel the need to regularly look over my shoulder during the school year to see if he's going to come up on me.

I let my parents know that I was being bullied by Chuck, but not until the end of the school year. I didn't tell them sooner because I thought they would contact the school about the bullying, and in so doing, create a bigger problem for me. I figured ignoring Chuck was the best policy, as it involved less risk. Because he continued to bully me, and since he and my brother knew each other casually, my Dad asked my brother to talk with him. I never directly discussed with my brother what happened during his confrontation. Yet, I suspect he told Chuck in no uncertain terms to stop bullying me. I also am fairly certain his words were accentuated with threats of physical violence, to help protect me.

Chuck never bullied me again. When he saw me in the hallways, he quickly looked away, as if he didn't see me. I was someone whom he could no longer bully; therefore, I didn't exist to him. I do not have any other memories of being bullied in high school. Yet, the remaining years at school were still informed by bullying. After all, I feared that Chuck, or guys like him, could bully me at any time. The fear was made stronger by the fact that, similar to my days in middle school, I was unconfident in my ability to fight back. Also, even though I knew that as a boy I was supposed to be able to be physical in these ways, and probably even like it, I had no interest in being aggressive. As a result of the continuing fear, I spend a lot of time scanning the environment as I move through hallways and the lunchroom and participate in gym. I routinely anticipate the possibility of aggression and conflict. I'm routinely on edge, far more than any teenager should be.

★★★

In the process of writing this book, my mother shared with me more details about the bullying-ending conversation between Kevin and Chuck. Apparently Kevin overheard Chuck make plans with his buddies to hang me by my belt inside my gym locker. If I wasn't wearing a belt on the day they planned to attack me, Chuck figured they could use my neck tie, and tie it around my wrists, or maybe my throat. "Nothing too serious," Chuck reportedly clarified to his friends. "We'll just cinch the tie enough to scare the shit out of him and make him piss himself." Luckily my brother intervened, and I never was required to face this extreme depth of bullying.

As my mother conveyed this story to me, so many years later, my hands trembled. In my lived present I was in no danger, yet I felt unsettled. I was safe within that storytelling, but memories of the bullying, and locker doors being slammed and banged on, came back to me instantly.

Methodological Dilemma

It is early morning in Tampa and the newly risen sun is shining brightly through my windows, invigorating my work. I am nearly finished with the book and am primarily focusing on the writing choices the storytellers use to resolve their accounts, that is, what their endings say about bullying and, even more, what they might prompt us to think about the challenging task of reconciling the hardship and suffering of bullying via personal storytelling.

For the last several weeks I have been unable to shake a nagging feeling I have had about their endings. Save for Ena's account, each of the stories ends with some sort of an affirming or positive resolution to the storytellers' account. These endings may not necessarily all be "happy," but they illustrate rather "neat" or "tidy" conclusions. That is, problems are more or less figured out, and storytellers convey their being able to emerge from horrors of being bullied and/or bullying others with a definitive answer, and they suggest they are satisfied. They've learned their lessons. A sense of closure is created. While the storytellers clearly show through their stories how bullying has had a major and long-lasting impact on their lives and their identities, and while not one of the accounts, to me, feels as though the writers were holding back to save face, absent in the stories are portrayals of themselves as emerging from the bullying confused, lost, or still searching for answers.

I am intrigued by what the students did *not* write as part of their endings. Are there messier and sadder dimensions to the resolution of their bullying experience that have been left out? If so, what is missing and why? Faced with the likelihood of multiple possible ways to end, why these resolutions and not others? What does it mean to want different endings?

7

OPENED

Bullying Communication and Identities, and the Power of Stories

"You folks are energized! It's wonderful to see you on our last day of class."

As I wait for students to quiet down so we can begin, I look around the room, much like I did on that hot and humid August day when we began the semester. However, now the smile on my face has grown wider. Many of the students seem different. The lack of familiarity present when we started the class has evolved into bonds that feel more intimate and interconnected; many students who were quiet and reserved in August have become more talkative and comfortable. The fearful looks displayed when I first introduced the bullying story assignment are now gone. Students now seem happy and prideful, and also tired.

"Where do I begin? It has been my pleasure to work with you this semester. The class has exceeded my expectations." My words bring smiles to many of their faces.

"Do we look like we've been tested?" asks the same student who, on the first day of class, humorously asked if there would be tests in the course. Several students chuckle, while many nod their heads, confirming they have, in fact, been tested.

"You've got the look of storytellers who just completed a personal journey back in time, re-living difficult experiences to better understand your story, yourselves, and bullying."

"Then we passed the test?" he says sarcastically.

"I don't know, I still have a few more papers to grade," I say with a humorous tone.

"Kidding aside, it has been exciting to be with you on this journey. In addition to working with you on your stories, I have also been working on my stories. As I suspected would be the case, going back thirty-five years to my youth has been challenging. Yet, coming to terms with my stories, an experience shaped by the ways you have come to understand and convey yours, has opened me in helpful ways. Writing helped me identify and come to terms in ways with the bullying I experienced and the personal struggles I faced as I worked to be happy in and out of school.[1] Exploring these memories at times made me sad. I, too, have been tested." Students' smiles get bigger.

"There is so much I want us to discuss. Since our time is limited, let's get to work."

In this concluding chapter, I convey narrative scenes that show significant aspects of the dialogue with which the students and I ended this class. I accompany these scenes with my reflections on bullying communication, bullying identities, and the power of stories for bullying research. I also share some of the most salient ways in which reflexivity and mindfulness helped me to respond to the "dilemmas" I faced in the research. I end the chapter and book by brainstorming with students about ways of continuing a response to bullying like the one we created together in this class.

Bullying Communication

"One of the most helpful aspects of your stories is the way they allow us to get closer to the inseparable relationship between communication and bullying.[2] From the violent acts of bullying, to the ways victims respond to bullies, to how friends, family members, teachers, and administrators try to intervene in bullying, and to how persons talk about bullying, such as through stories, bullying does not, and cannot, happen without communication and communicators. So, how do you now think about the role and power of communication in bullying?"

"Well, I keep thinking about the power of language," a student says from the back of the room. "On our first day of class, I remember someone taking exception to the adage, *Sticks and stones may break my bones, but words will never hurt me.* This class has me still thinking about that line. It makes sense on one level: others' words don't *have to* hurt you since the communication of bullying is relational, right?"

"Yes, keep going," I respond.

"But words are also crazy hurtful and are far more powerful than I think I realized. The scars from the words used against us can last a long time. Telling my story helped me to realize that changing bullying must include changing how we think about words. Words matter. Words harm in particular and powerful ways."[3] I see Lauren smiling and nodding her head in agreement, and remember she is the student from the first day of class who mentioned this adage.

"Well said," I respond.

This conversation makes me think about the ways in which stories in the book differently show the power of words in bullying. For instance, Iman's hearing that she "suffers from severe depression" and that she is "too white" worsened her already existing distress from feeling different in her family and at school.

The absence of supportive words from Rose while Cruella and her cronies bullied Jezebel led Jezebel to feel abandoned by her trusted "oasis," and at risk of more bullying. My mother's repeatedly calling me "special" over time allowed me to feel that while I was still trying to figure out what was wrong with me, and feeling bad, at least she saw me in such a loving way. Yet, it also might have kept her from digging into the deeper issues I was facing, and from needing to worry about me. Words are never empty "things"; rather, they are infused with meaning that defines, organizes, and evaluates situations, people, and stories (Wood, 2015).

Ena enters the dialogue and says, "I agree language is destructive in bullying…"

I interrupt, "It can also be significantly empowering in helping persons who are trying to cope, and to helping bullies understand the harms of bullying."

"That makes sense," she says. "But I hope we don't ignore the power of bodies in bullying." I hear Iman say, "Right?" and see her nod her head in agreement, as do many other students. Ena continues, "My story made me better understand the ways bodies are vulnerable in bullying, and the invasive ways boys *and* girls use bodies, their own and victims', as weapons. It sickens me. The power of bodies is maybe more forceful than with language."

"Remember, communicators experience and understand our worlds through bodies, ours and others.[4] Bodies most certainly aren't "absent" in bullying.[5] They are ecstatically present and serve as ways of knowing." To respect students' privacy, I don't disclose to the class what students have written about bullying and the specific issues they have faced.

"Your stories also illuminate the prominence of bodies in bullying," I continue. As I say this, I think to myself about how the color of Iman's skin, indeed, the largest organ on her impressionable body, served as a bullying target, while at the same time provided her with a way to cope through cutting. Ena's body was a constant target for her bullies, most prominently in the form of vicious sexual assault and the girls' peering through the cracks of the bathroom stalls, inspecting her body parts. The rotations embodied by my spinning as Wonder Woman provided me, if for only those few precious minutes, a liberating space in which to feel freer than I had in some time, and to know myself in different ways than I had been accustomed.

"So, what are some of the things we learn about relational communication from the stories?"

"Our conversation here reminds me of Carey's notion that communication constructs 'reality.'[6] Recall that his definition tells us that bullying interactions are not just a matter of 'transmitting' information between persons through communication; rather, persons use those interactions to symbolically create, and re-create over time, what bullying *means*. In this sense, words and embodiment of bullying are powerful because they affect what and how we understand about bullying or being bullied. In turn, how we understand things affects the good and bad ways persons feel about them. Thus, a communicative approach to studying bullying and identity requires us not only to carefully look at the words and embodiment of bullying, but what those symbolic messages *mean to the persons involved with, and affected by the bullying.*

"Also, remember communicators are diverse beings who bring different backgrounds to interaction … and communication is a joint accomplishment, meaning both conversation partners contribute to the process. Therefore, what a given moment or episode of bullying means to one person likely will be different than what it means to others.

"So … looking at bullying in terms of communication involves exploring how these worlds of meaning come together, and how people work to make sense of them."

Lauren asks, "Instead of telling victims or bullies—or anyone—*how to* understand bullying, it is helpful to listen and stay open to how bullying is *understandable to them.*"

"Yes, that makes the most sense to me as a relational communication teacher and researcher. Listen to persons' stories, which reveal how bullying makes sense to them. This doesn't mean their stories are the only sources of insight we need, nor does it mean they are infallible. It means stories provide the intimate and detailed vantage point we need for responding well to bullying.

"Does anyone have questions or comments?" No one speaks up.

"Okay, then, before moving on, I want to stress one additional idea. It is important to keep in mind one of the axioms of interpersonal communication that we discussed at the beginning of the semester: 'One cannot not communicate.'[7] This assumption tells us there is not a finite starting or stopping point for the making and using of meaning in relational communication. Conversation partners are often making meaning in ways that fall outside of one or both partners' awareness. As a result, people may be harming one another, even if such harm wasn't 'intentional' or 'deliberate,' as much of the bullying research often emphasizes. This axiom, along with the idea that relational communication is always already something conversation partners enact together, tell us the communication so essential to bullying is often far more involving, and uncertain, than we might originally realize."

Negotiating Bullied Identities

The stories in this book demonstrate the relationship between communication and bullying, and the creative making and remaking of identity. This process of identity negotiation is a tensional process informed by social constraints, including stigma. As youth co-create "realities" concerning the practices of bullying and what it means to live through them, they also explore ways of understanding themselves and others. In this section, I draw on the students' stories in this book to examine the *performance of selves* within bullying communication. These four performed selves—*invaded, juggling, persevering*, and *transformed*—speak to recurring ways in which victims perform or constitute themselves with others over time.

Bullying renders victims *invaded selves*. The "invasion" I have in mind speaks to the "encroachment" or "intrusion"[8] that personifies bullying, or the ways in which being bullied constrains and restricts the lives of victims. Indeed, bullying is "oppressive."[9] In this way, being bullied disrupts and diminishes victims' sense of autonomy; indeed, bullies connect themselves to victims in repeated and violent ways, diminishing their personal space and well-being. The aftershock of this invasion affects victims viscerally, in the given moment of bullying and they remember and relive the violence over time. In these ways, bullies forcefully insinuate themselves into victims' lives, compelling them to think and feel in particular ways, rendering them unsettled, in pain, and searching for comfort.

For Iman, being repeatedly and meanly told that she was "too white" encroached on her ability to perform herself as an African-American girl in the ways she desired. Ena's account demonstrates this performance in grave ways. Her bullies, often men, invaded her young body and being mentally and physically. Persons' lives are always in some way interdependent lives (Gergen, 2009; Schrag, 2003; Shotter, 1993). But these stories show how bullying intensifies such relationality in unwelcomed and violating ways.

Being bullied also requires victims to negotiate myriad social conditions while under duress, thus immersing them in the performance of *juggling selves*. Victims must handle a range of interactional activities or obstacles. They try to identify "right" ways of responding to bullies and the situation; to manage how they think and feel in that moment, if they can think or feel clearly at all; to identify who is around them physically who will notice or be able to help with the attacks, if they are even able to see past their bullies and concentrate on things other than their terror; and to consider issues of identity, such as who will emerge from bullying with the upper hand. They must also concern themselves with issues of identity. In these ways, the demand to juggle identities across contexts involves managing multiple, complex facets of identity in the face of violence, pain, and worry, and trying to remain hyper-vigilant to the emergent components of a bullying encounter. Moreover, the stakes are high in those moments: how one juggles often shapes future encounters with bullying, and how, or if, one will be subject to serious violence.

Jezebel's account shows a fitting example in which to situate the concept of juggling selves. Bullying required her to try to manage numerous factors, such as being a strong Naruto warrior in one moment, and a progressively weakened bully victim over time. She also needed to concern herself with the presence of Cruella, balancing the desire not to budge in her seat as she was being bullied with her desire to not be physically harmed. Jezebel also needed to figure out why Rose did not step in to defend her, and to identify a suitable way to respond as the bullying got worse (e.g., playing it cool or hurling the tomato). Ultimately, not even the powers of being a young and centered Naruto warrior could help Jezebel manage it all, leading her to fall to her knees in anguish.

Third, bullying also immerses victims in the performance of *persevering selves*. The repetitive nature to bullying, and the deliberate doing of harm, requires victims to find ways to carry on, and to stay well, or at least well enough to survive. They must do so, even though the constraints victims face while being bullied are often frenetic and, at times, feel insurmountable. This performance speaks to victims as resilient beings who did not give up, even though doing so might have been easier. Even when bullying takes victims to the lowest levels of their self-acceptance, and even if these individuals may not identify as such, they are tenacious beings.

All of the stories point to these women emerging from bullying as persevering beings. For instance, Iman spoke to how bullying led her to be suicidal. Yet, while her resorting to cutting was on one level counterproductive coping, it also helped to alleviate her pain without dying. Jessi persevered at the front lines of her cyberbullying, though much of her survival was conditioned negatively by her decision to be a bully-victim, to bully Amber and Maria in response being bullied.

Finally, bullying enables victims to perform *transformed selves*. Since identity is made and remade within communication over time, all communication is potentially transformative. However, the sense of "transformed" I use here speaks to significant changes in one's being as a result of bullying. These transformations can be positive. Victims may emerge as people who communicate using different styles of relating or word choices; orienting to and counting on relationships differently than in the past; and developing ways of coping they might not have considered prior to being bullied.[10] Whatever the change, for good and bad, bullying over time creates the conditions through which victims emerge performing themselves in novel ways.

The students' accounts show a diverse number of ways in which being bullied transformed them. Take, for instance, Jessi going from being a girl who largely stayed out of trouble, to someone who needed to defend herself against Amber and Maria, and then to a girl who bullied Amber and Maria in response to their bullying her. Or take the ways in which becoming friends with Renee allowed Lauren to emerge from bullying in helpful ways. Finally, it is by finding "self-love," a change accomplished most notably through relating with the open and affirming women at her all-black university that Iman is able to self-identify as a survivor, someone who no longer hates, but now loves herself.

There are additional performances shown in the students' stories worthy of considering. For instance, being bullied rendered these storytellers *isolated selves*, in that the aggression led them to be people who felt distant, and as a result, isolated from the people and activities that normally filled up their lives; *neglected selves*, insofar as the pain and suffering they endured, and the lack of faith they had in adults to properly end the bullying, often rendered them overlooked or ignored and thus harmed and in need of healing; and *self-doubting*, *self-hating*, and/or *self-shaming* selves, as not only did bullies turn on victims, but being bullied often led many girls to turn on themselves, calling into question and critiquing their actions and personhood.[11]

Where do we go with these insights? I am mindful of how victims' performances of selves within bullying are situated within a larger cultural emphasis in the United States that compels youth to "know themselves," and to have a positive understanding of "who they are." Indeed, self-understanding and understanding who others are are processes I too advocate through my teaching, research, and in everyday life. The stories in the book illustrate how bullying shapes this process in largely negative ways. Rather than coming to understand themselves as persons who deserve and experience acceptance, joy, and love, these victims self-identify in unsettled and disconfirmed ways as a result of bullying. These stigmatized beings face repeated and hurtful attacks, and also, understandably, feel bad about being victims. To be sure, there are likely many youth who are able to reconcile being bullied in less distressful ways. Also, time and distance has allowed the young women included in the book to understand themselves in more affirming ways, even though they still may feel frustration and/or anger about what happened to them. Nevertheless, their stories, and mine, show youth being made to feel miserable.[12]

I recently saw on Facebook a list of "4 Essential Elements of School Transformation": culture, climate, consistency, and community (The Bully Project, 2015). Naturally, I want to stress the essential nature of another "c"—communication—to these essentials. Laing (1967) writes:

> [W]hat we think is less than what we know; what we know is less than what we love; what we love is so much less than what there is. And to that precise extent we are so much less than what we are.
>
> (p. 30)

As human beings there is much that we don't realize about how we communicate, perform ourselves, and force others to have to perform themselves. Communication is the process of making known realities we might be overlooking or avoiding, and those that the limits of our thinking and feeling keep outside of our everyday awareness. I am not suggesting that communication is a panacea, or a "magic pill" that "fixes" bullying and the ways in which victims come to understand themselves. But it does provide a way to understand how bullying happens, and what happens to identities as a result of being bullied. The potential for communication to create positive change in how we relate to others and ourselves is one of the most significant reasons why I have studied communication for nearly two decades. Communication is the greatest resource I know for educating ourselves on how choices for interacting can and do impact others, and how we can come to relate with one another in times of duress and blatant violence. Indeed, drawing and keeping attention on communication and identity will not end bullying. However, it does create the conditions in which we can *more compassionately* understand the communicative practices and consequences of bullying, and seek to do something about them.

The Power of Bullying Stories

"Let's hear from folks who want to share something from your stories. I'd like as many people to volunteer as possible."

"I'll go," Lauren says.

"Go ahead."

"My story focuses on my being bullied by a (former) best friend and friend of hers. Their bullying focused on my appearance, especially the blonde hair I had at that age. They bullied me face-to-face and online, and it was terrible. Life improved when I met a new friend who helped me understand I was a confident and strong girl who doesn't have to let bullies bother me."

"You wrote a terrific story," I say. She smiles and whispers, "Thank you."

Jessi speaks next: "In my story I convey being bullied by a friend and her friend. They targeted my physical appearance, so strongly it led me to be self-conscious about my body for the first time in my life. After they bullied and cyberbullied me, I did the same thing to them. It's something I'm not proud of today. However, I now understand how it can happen."

"Bullying as a result of being bullied is not uncommon, Jess. Thanks for sharing."

"My story talks about bullying in the family and at school," Iman says. "I was bullied due to my race. I focus on how being different encouraged me to feel depressed, and how bullying didn't allow me to be myself. I learned a lot about myself from this process."

"Beautiful." As I wait for others to offer to go next, I notice how pleased these three look after participating. They have had a rewarding experience in writing their stories.

Students grow silent after Iman's contribution. After waiting for someone else to share, I decide to talk about some of the papers generally.

"The stories you've written explore so many important issues. Most focused on bullying that took place at school; however, several stories in the class conveyed bullying in other private and public places. As Iman's story shows, bullying takes place in families in real and impactful ways. Coming into contact with these different bullying stories allows us to expand our thinking regarding setting, and to remember that bullying takes places and changes lives and identities in a diverse range of contexts."[13]

As the students and I spend much of our remaining time discussing stories, the climate in the room is invigorating. Classmates are listening to each other's contributions, leaning in and offering affirming comments of support and identification: *Wow it must have been hard to write that scene. I don't know how you lived through bullying like that—what a strong person! What you had to endure reminds me in some ways of how I was bullied. It's good to know I'm not alone.* Rather than listening passively or defensively, they perform "compassionate critical listening" (McRae, 2015a; see also McRae, 2015b), embodying care and concern for others' lived experience. Missing from today's class is students playing on their cell phones, or watching the clock; present is more relational care that comes from shared time, energy, and investment on a mutual goal.

When it appears as though all students who wish to participate have had their chance, I move us on to the next topic.

"I'd like to say a few more things about the stories we've conveyed. These next ideas relate to the power of stories for studying bullying, specifically in terms of what gets made in terms of the stories themselves, and us as storytellers."

I read out loud a quotation from the course syllabus:

> [I]n our society, art has become something that is related only to objects and not to individuals or to life. That art is something which is specialized or done by experts who are artists. But couldn't everyone's life become a work of art? Why should the lamp or the house be an art object but not our life? From the idea that the self is not given to us, I think there is only one practical consequence: we have to create ourselves as a work of art.[14]

"This quotation from Michel Foucault is a continuation of our semester-long discussions about how people form and negotiate our identities within the lived experience of communication. But I love his emphasis on the ways this process renders people 'works of art'." Several students smile, raising their eyebrows.

"I love what/who you've created in this class. Through your stories you've taken risks and vulnerably opened and exposed yourselves for others, and in ways that might not have seemed possible or safe before." A few students fumble to grab their pens, so they can write down the quotation.

"Don't worry … it's on the syllabus," I say smiling.

"I included the quotation there, hoping it would encourage you with your stories. To think, how many of you felt nervous at the beginning of the semester. Many didn't know what your story was, how you would write it, and more importantly, if you could feel open to writing about the terrible bullying experiences through which you lived."

"Well, I was a mess at the beginning of the semester," a student shouts from the back of the room, "nervous as hell about what I had lived through and if I wanted to relive it."

"I understand and can relate."

"It's good to know I'm not the only one," he says smiling.

"Let me just say, the time and effort you folks have invested in this creating process, experimenting with creative and reflexive writing forms, is not lost on me. So many projects have resulted in stories that have left me … in awe. I want you to know the *risk* involved in telling your story is real, as you wrote about revealing and edgy issues. You boldly gave witness to the tenuous and harmful identity negotiation that pervades bullying. I'm thrilled to see the 'art' you've rendered, the art you've become by writing your stories."

"Clever tie-in," my "tested" student chimes at me.

"I thought you'd like that," I reply.[15]

"To continue, though, I want to mention something else: one of the powers of your stories shows in the attention you gave to writing with evocative detail and emotion. When I read your stories, I felt like I was with you in your experiences. As you wrote about all kinds of feelings, such as shame, humiliation, embarrassment, hope, and so forth, I felt many of them with you. Also, your emotional writing at times challenged me to reflect on and explore feelings that I didn't know I had, and maybe some that I didn't want to feel. In other words, your open hearts have opened mine."

As I write up this moment in the dialogue, I think about Iman, as she writes about tip-toeing through her house late at night, searching for the "right" blade for cutting herself. I cringe as her words allow me to visualize her cutting into the skin on her stomach. In addition, my face muscles tighten, like they do when I hear about unimaginable suffering, when I read about Lauren changing her appearance in response to being bullied. I, again, feel the burning of her scalp with her, even though I wasn't there in the salon, and have never felt the burn of hair dye. The students' attention to writing evocatively also takes me back to my youth when I would say certain words (e.g., "dude"), and avoid others (e.g., "cute"), or I would hold my chest up high, or avoid speaking in high pitched tones, all so that I might appear to others as "more masculine" and "not gay."

"Writing evocatively allowed me to return to the scenes of my bullying, to relive what I experienced, to remember what happened to me, and how I bullied other people," another student says, reading from jottings in her notebook.

"What was that like?" I say.

"It was fun … and helpful in some ways. It helped me to clarify experiences that had grown foggy in my memory."

"Writing in this way wasn't so fun for me," a student says.

"Why not?"

"I'm a pretty strong guy normally. But this type of writing made the memories of being bullying feel all too real. Writing brought back the pain for me, and, though you warned us, I wasn't really prepared to go to the places where I felt my pain was taking me."

"That's understandable. May I ask, what did you do when this happened?"

"I just stopped myself from going deeper. I figured that's as far as I could go."

"Sounds like a mindful response. I'm glad you stayed within your limits. Also, for what it's worth, you might also look at that 'point' as being something you want to keep exploring. Sometimes these moments have helpful insights to teach us."

"Maybe…"

"I want to say something different," another student says, saving her classmate from this moment. "I struggled with the number of things going on in my story, stuff that doesn't fit neatly together."

"You mean, the different types of experiences or meanings comprising bullying?" I ask.

"Yes."

I pause for a second, while looking for a related point in my notes.

"That's another aspect these stories capture well: the complex layers of experience that comprise bullying. In many accounts, we see personas that are public and private; aggression that is physical and relational; ways of coping that are positive and harmful; characters feeling okay in one moment and then terrorized in others; victims being violated by bullies and yet not staying away from them; and family, friends, and teachers and administrators who care for and assist victims at one minute and then turn their backs on them in another minute. Your stories put on display complex and contradictory factors of bullying."

"I'm okay with layers; it's the contradictions I don't like," the same student says.

"Contradictions represent tensions, and can make communicating with others challenging and uncertain. Yet, they are a regular part of relational communication, and several of the stories in the class show them to be a routine part of bullying.[16] This is a way autoethnography and personal narrative shine brightly, by allowing writers to show different, and often competing influences, and how communicators respond to these tensions. The bigger point is they show us that bullying is not a simplistic problem, but a complex one that requires a complex response. Good stories give us that complexity."

In this moment the students and I are coming to terms with the inherent "messiness" of bullying in terms of communication and identity: moving parts, flux of thoughts and emotions, vacillating influences, and changing people, at the very least. Bullying stories capture this messiness in vivid detail and allow readers to make sense of it. Yet, this process also requires readers to slow down and move through the stories moment by moment, layer by layer, considering what they mean, or could mean for youth's lives. In my lived experience, it is slowing down the decision to be mindful anti-bullying storytellers and advocates that is often difficult. As I suggested in Chapter 1, the emotional and unjust nature of bullying, and persons' desire to end the problem, often lead people to discuss bullying in abstract and generalizable ways, and to make claims about bullying that may not ring true as it is lived "on the ground." Indeed, we need more informed perspectives and strategies for intervening in bullying.[17] Stories create the conditions to slow us down and allow us to learn and respond well. They help us to experience and explore "with" storytellers bullying in the situated contexts of lived experience in which it occurs.

"Okay, before break, I have one more impression of your stories I'd like to share. Let me start with a favorite quotation of mine: 'Behind the story I tell is the one I don't. Behind the story you hear is the one I wish I could make you hear.'[18] I love this passage because I believe it beautifully expresses why it can be so difficult and risky to share stories. We may reveal some stories, while also keeping others hidden. Sometimes the pain and risk involved with storytelling makes it easier to keep them to ourselves. Also, we may muster up the courage to tell our stories, but that doesn't mean others will listen or like what we're telling. Yet, we need others to hear our stories; they can learn from them, and we can learn from their feedback. My point is that telling stories about bullying is complicated and rarely easy. Knowing of all these possibilities leads me to marvel at the stories you told." Many students beam with pride. They are also fidgety, and, I sense, ready for class to end.

"One *last* related point, I promise. Many stories of bullying remain untold. Maybe it's too hard for persons to think and feel through their memories of being bullied, or of bullying others. Or they may fear being seen in a negative light, revealing to others—or to themselves—how terribly they suffered as victims, or made people suffer as bullies. Or maybe some people don't think their stories will be taken seriously. Yet, you put in the effort, took the risks, and told your stories. For that, you have my admiration and respect.

"Let's break for ten minutes. When we return, we'll discuss where we go from here."[19, 20]

Dilemmas Revisited

I next return to the methodological dilemmas that ended each of my reflexive interludes, to describe how I dealt with each quandary in terms of reflexivity and mindfulness. While each response could fill an entire chapter, I describe them only briefly. I offer them in the spirit of a conversation with readers. I hope they provoke further discussion and debate regarding the challenges and opportunities of using of autoethnography in bullying research.

Reframing Obsession

Although I never sent the drafted email to Renee, the central issues of this first dilemma point to a significant struggle I encountered in working with students' stories. I've conducted the research informing the book in ways to closely identify with relational ethics (Ellis, 2007). Ensuring the welfare of the students who participated in my study, as well as those who opted not to participate, has always been my utmost concern. In turn, caring for the relationships I maintain with the students has been an essential factor in the study. In many ways, the students are research "friends" (Tillman-Healy, 2003), and their welfare is far more important than the book, or any research. As a result, the desires I experienced in wanting and needing Renee's story were new to me, and troubling. They contradicted how I normally engage with research participants, and who I understood myself to be as a researcher.

I addressed this dilemma by taking some time to reflect on how these struggles should not be surprising, given that I am using autoethnography, bullying is my topic, and I hope the book will contribute well to anti-bullying efforts. It shouldn't be surprising to have needs and wants that are deeply personal—autoethnography calls on researchers to vulnerably immerse ourselves in our examination of lived experience. In addition, "wanting" or "needing" stories feels appropriate, because including certain stories will likely speak to the bullying problem in ideal ways. This is all to say, I mindfully responded to the urges I felt by understanding my feelings more fully and gently. I worked to understand that my "obsession" to have Renee's story, or ones like hers, were indicative of my commitment and passion for studying bullying, and to being a thinking and feeling person who allows myself to feel and talk about difficult issues, and that may put me "on the spot" and open me to others' questions and negative critique.

I do not mean for this response to suggest my dealing with the dilemma was easy. The struggles were/are real, and my approach didn't necessarily "fix" the issue. My response helped me to feel more at peace and to resist judgment.

That said, today I sometimes still wish I "had" Renee's story.

Unsettling "Control"

In the conventional sense of the word, "control" in my classes and in research is not something I typically pursue. This does not mean I do not manage well on both fronts, nor should it suggest I do not hold significant power as a teacher and researcher (see Fassett & Warren, 2007). However, I do usually look at "control" as an illusionary pursuit in life. Trying to "be in control" can keep persons from staying open to the flux of lived experience that fills our lives, and the ways in which life comprises ongoing change, rendering these attempts futile. Still, how did I manage the tensions related to this dilemma?

Throughout the semester, I encouraged students to take risks, yet, only in ways about which they felt safe. We discussed how seeking to remain safe is ideal, since trying to remain comfortable sometimes (often?) prevents people from stretching our personal limits, testing comfort zones, learning from pain, and ultimately growing as persons. More generally, my encouragement took the form of nudging the students to go a little farther or deeper, or being more specific in key parts of their stories, keeping in mind that each nudge, each potential movement, farther and deeper into their pasts could mean the students might suffer from that work. Ultimately, I approached this aspect of the process by remembering that, indeed, I am their professor, and with this powerful identity I embody responsibility. Yet, I also practiced letting go, and tried to remind myself that my ability to "protect" students can only go so far. They are adults who will make and need to own their own choices and stories. I do not yet know how possible it is to let go, so I treated this practice as an ongoing work in progress.

You might wonder how I managed my identity as a researcher while teaching the class. My answer is carefully (see Appendix for a description of this issue).

Dilemma Re-worked

The concern about Ena's asking me whether or not her stories "worked" is rooted in the guiding principle of my book: communicators constitute identities within communication. Thus, as the students write (communicate), they are forming an understanding not only of the bullying actions that happened in the stories, but also of themselves as storytellers and persons generally. While the previous dilemma speaks more to students' reluctance to write deeply about their bullying experience, the current one relates to my concern that some students might expose themselves too much and get hurt in some way. While, again, I believe ultimately students are responsible for living by the choices they make, I also come to the classroom with more experience with autoethnography and personal narrative. I know more about the risks, and I take it as one of my primary roles to look out for them in these ways.

In some ways, "students are responsible adults" is too easy a way to respond to the dilemma. I am still concerned about the amount of disclosure in their stories. For instance, even though her story tells readers she is well today, I fear some readers will judge Iman because of the suicidal ideation and cutting she experienced. Also, I am concerned about the "work" stories might do to/on each of the storytellers down the road. Will they remain happy and proud of their stories? If they reveal their stories to others, will others replicate the kinds of behaviors that incited these feelings in the storyteller? Will the stories do any unforeseen "work" on the characters portrayed in the stories? Believing students are responsible adults doesn't preclude my need to remain infinitely concerned.

I encouraged students who I felt were going "too far" to let go of scenes of stories that I felt were too risky, or language that might cast them in potentially negative lights. I also continued to remind myself that the ownership of the stories is ultimately theirs, and that perhaps they are aware and strong enough to be able to defend their choices, and their stories, if need be.

I offered all research participants the opportunity to revise their stories, and all writings included in the study, before I began exploring them for this book. None sent any revisions.

Enduring the Promises of Hardship

How do we stay mindful when working so closely with pain and suffering? I must confess I am still trying to figure this out. Often I just continued to work, reminding myself that autoethnography at times will make distance and emotional stamina difficult. Stress and fatigue are associated with the work, especially projects that are sad and infuriating, like bullying, and with long-term projects, such as book writing. There were other ways I worked at responding to the issue.

Especially when working to convey and analyze the students' stories, and conveying my stories, I needed to remind myself from time to time that this research had me in the "throws of perpetual *doom and gloom*." This basic (and humorous) acknowledgment helped to keep me aware that there were reasons for my struggling. In addition, I also took frequent breaks. I also reminded myself that, although I was working on these painful stories in the "here and now," the violent events of the stories are a matter of the past. While the students may still struggle with their bullying experiences, and others are likely suffering today from similar problems, I am well and the students seem well. Indeed, I was in a relationship with this hardship and the amazing people who suffered. I reflected on the reality that in doing this research, I witnessed the pain and suffering of people about whom I care, including me. Thus, the sadness I felt was appropriate. Admittedly, the more I became immersed in working with/on these stories, the easier it became to lose sight of these perspectives. These "pull backs" helped considerably.

Why continue with this research, amid such struggles? Because the story is too important to let the pain and suffering that pervade bullying hamper my process. The stories are special and can help make lives better.

Conventional Happiness

I addressed the last dilemma, which focused on the issue of most students choosing "happy endings" for their stories, by keeping in mind that autoethnography usually is interested in, and relies on, "narrative truth" (Bochner, 2001). These truths are rooted in the ways that make sense to the storytellers who convey them. To question whether or not the students' story endings "truthfully" ended in the happy ways they conveyed is ultimately a less important question. I'm far more interested in the fact that most of the students ended in this way, and the point they wished to make by using such endings. After all, these are the endings they chose.

I have not followed up with any of the students to ask about their choices to end their stories as they did. Therefore, I can only speculate. There is a way in which these endings point to the cultural assumption that stories must have a definitive ending, meaning a "happy ending," or at least one that provides readers with a certain and acceptable sense of "closure." Their endings may also show efforts by the students to manage impressions (Goffman, 1959, 1963), particularly with me as the one who will evaluate and assign grades. In this way, these endings show bullying victims in largely positive lights, effectively saving face. This assumes that the socially desirable face to save is one that comes out of bullying with "lessons learned" and in stronger shape than they were within the throws of their bullying.

Looking Forward, with Stories

"Okay, the last issue I want to discuss with you about bullying, relational communication, and identity is…"

Jezebel dramatically says, "Say it is so … it's not over!"

"Endings can be tricky. This ending of our class is a conclusion of sorts, given that the class will soon be finished and we'll all move on in our different ways. Maybe (hopefully) I'll see some of you in other courses. Yet, I believe endings are also 'new beginnings'; they provide us with a chance to take what we've learned from each other, and the questions that remain, and try our best to put it all to good use."

"So, what's next?!" asks a student from the back of the room.

"How do we apply what we've learned and our stories?" He nods. "That's an important question. What are some ways we can continue to apply this work to our everyday lives? I'll start. One of the things I think we can do is talk about the stories with others. I've been talking to friends and colleagues about how well this class has gone, and how good your stories are."

"I've already shared my story with my parents," Iman says.

"Wonderful, what did they think?"

"They liked it and thought it felt true to them, even thought it was kinda difficult for them to read about me suffering. But they're proud of me and have already told family members about my story."

"I love that—a relational ripple effect possible through stories…"

I continue, "We can also re-write our stories, this time from the perspective of the bully/ies, or the parent, bystanders, or even the teacher or administrator." Students' faces cringe, probably from the idea of more work.

"While it might not sound desirable at this point to tell *another* story, doing so might expand what we understand about your bullying from a relational perspective.

"On a similar note, we can also advocate more autoethnographic stories be written, shared, and discussed about bullying as it is lived from additional standpoints, not just victims'." Students nod and smile, suggesting they like this idea more. "So, fill in the blank: I believe we need to hear more bullying stories written from…"

"bullies."

"a parent or parents."

"friends or family members of bullying victims who committed suicide."

"teachers."

"administrators."

"kids who *haven't* been bullied, to see how they escaped it all."

Responses fill the room.

"Wonderful, yes, more stories from these voices are needed and would be helpful. What we learn from them can open us to better understand and respond to their experiences with bullying, including how bullying has affected them."

Someone in the back says, "Good luck getting bullies, or former bullies, to write vulnerably and to fess up to their crimes!" Several students laugh and nod their heads.

"It might be difficult, but you never know. Let's not assume. After all, a lot of folks in our class wrote about bullying others, and they seemed to be okay with the vulnerability."

"Personally, I'd like to see groups of adults, like parents, teachers, and administrators for a workshop on bullying—one that introduces them to autoethnography and personal narrative as worthwhile paths for learning about and responding to bullying. I hear so many people criticize adults for what they are or aren't doing to intervene in bullying. I catch myself doing it sometimes too. But we need stories from them that allow us to step into their worlds and learn what dealing with bullying is like for them. Maybe even have a series of writing workshops where they write up their experiences. The politics related to the bureaucracy of teaching and schools might make this idea complicated, but it can happen and is definitely worth the try." I start to see a few blank stares on the students' faces. They seem ready to end the semester, and so am I, so I move us forward.[21]

"Okay, we have just a few minutes left, so who has some final thoughts or feelings you'd like to share? Something you've wanted to say but haven't yet had the chance?"

Lauren says, "I want this class to know that my story has helped me to gain the confidence I was missing in the past. I will be talking about my story in other classes. That feels a little weird to say, but I've embraced and feel close it, so I'm good with feeling that way."

"Great. With more time, I'd want to discuss why it feels weird." She nods and smiles. "Anyone else?"

Jezebel seizes the moment and says, "This conversation today is helping me realize that telling my story doesn't take power away from me, say, by making me vulnerable to those who may try to use the information against me. I'll admit I thought it might as I was writing the story. However, writing that story has actually put power back into my hands. I finally opened up about the bullying I endured. It's a victory that I went through something so … non-fabulous like bullying, but became a more FABULOUS person as a result!"

"That's beautiful. You all have been great. It doesn't always happen that professors miss their classes once the semester ends. But I'll definitely miss you folks.

"Maybe this is a perfect place to end. Thank you for being students whom I'll miss."

"Thank *you* for letting us write our stories," Jezebel says.

"You're very welcome. It's been my pleasure. 'Letting you', though? Thank you for *writing them*.

"Have a restful winter break. Thank you for a *fabulous*, story-filled semester that I don't believe I'll ever forget." Warm smiles abound.

"Let me end by saying this. As we start our new beginnings, please keep this in mind: I am certain more bullying stories are being lived as we speak. I cannot imagine the numbers of stories that have already been lived. With that bullying comes an awful lot of hurt. Yet, that hurt does not need to be felt in vain. We need to hear these stories, so we can get to know who the storytellers are, what they have lived or are still living, and to come to a deeper and more personal understanding of how bullying has shaped who they are. Let's keep telling our stories, and let the world learn about bullying in these ways."

Notes

1 For information on my lived experience after I graduated from high school, including stories of my "coming out" as gay, related and other experiences of identity negotiation

within relational communication, and my coming to see and use mindfulness as an invaluable framework and practice for everyday living, see Berry, 2006, 2007, 2012a, 2012b, 2013b, 2013c.

2 Pörhölä, Karhunen, and Rainivaara, 2006.

3 Additional research that focuses on the constitutive nature of language in bullying is needed. While the scars that often result from language in bullying can feel eternal for some victims, thinking about the issue in terms of meaning and the constitution of meaning within communication calls for consideration. Relational communication is a process that changes over time, and often from interaction to interaction. I assume the same about the language and meaning. In this sense, we are always immersed in a process of constituting new meaning for the words we invoke and use. As Stewart (1995) argues, meaning is constituted in moments of "articulate contact." Yet, conversation partners also draw on a surplus of historical meanings that is used and reused over time. Thus, words used in bullying, as weapons or in support, can mean similar things over time. This phenomenological understanding of the constitution of meaning reminds us that as we go about the important work of engaging with stories that convey the power of language, that language, like communication generally, is dynamic, complex, and subject to change. Relationally, that language is open to mean different things to different communicators.

4 Heidegger, 1996/1953.

5 Leder, 1990.

6 Carey, 1989.

7 Watzlawick et al., 1967.

8 *Oxford English Dictionary*, 2015.

9 Farrington, 1993.

10 Most of the students spoke candidly about there being positive aspects of being bullied, a layer of the bullying experience that merits more research.

11 Other relational partners (besides victims) likely also emerge from their involvement in bullying performing themselves in novel ways, becoming subjects different than who they were prior to bullying. The focus of this book leaves us without direct evidence of such identity negotiation. Still, how might bullies, for example, identify (or not) with the performances of selves I just explored? Do *they* feel like invaded youth? How do they embody tenacity? How can these performances help us understand victims' performances and bullying?

12 The stories told in this book matter as they are told, and we can and should learn about identity with them. However, we would be wise to further consider the *ongoing* and *processual* ways in which young communicators work to create and recreate themselves within the relational spaces of bullying. These identities are not static or stable, but multilayered and fluid. Some layers might not now (or ever) be visible to us and, like the communication in which these identities are constituted, are subject to change.

Also, while bullying creates the conditions that make possible and sometimes necessary the ways youth perform themselves, such aggression does not necessarily *cause* a certain mode of self-understanding. Youth are not sponges who automatically "soak up" and appropriate (i.e., interpret) all of the information they experience within bullying. They may appropriate some, but not necessarily all stimuli. Further, youth's ways of understanding themselves are not relegated only to the specific communicative contexts in which they are bullied. Youth relate across multiple contexts, many that may not involve bullying, but still inform who they understand themselves to be. Thus, youth's identity or subjectivity is multiple factored.

These phenomenological considerations suggest the need to always stay open to alternate ways of interpreting and understanding bullying, communication, and identity, and to remember that bullying is contingent on the contexts in which it is performed and made meaningful.

13 Berry and Adams, 2016; Monks and Coyne, 2011.

14 Foucault, 1994, p. 261.

15 While the point I am making here with the students relates to the affirming and welcomed identities cultivated within their storytelling process, I also wonder what other layers there are to their identities. Will they continue to understand themselves in positive ways, and continue to see the opening process made available from telling their stories as good parts of the process? Which students in the class are *not* so pleased with how storytelling has affected them, how the process opened them? Who remained more closed than open through the process? To be sure, not all "works of art" are or feel pretty.

16 Relational communication is conditioned by dialectical tensions (Baxter & Montgomery, 1996; Bochner, 1984; Cissna, Cox, & Bochner, 1990), or the routine and contradictory needs and interests persons bring to interaction and relationships. These tensions often make communication, the process whereby these tensions are reconciled, dynamic and messy. Future bullying research will have a field day in pursuing such a focus.

17 Rigby, Smith, and Pepler, 2004

18 Allison, 1996, p. 39.

19 Students included in the stories submitted for class reflections on their writing process. Their insights speak volumes to the ways in which such storytelling establishes the conditions that make the transformation of selves possible and necessary, and in good and bad ways. I do not include their prose here due to page constraints.

20 Autoethnography and personal narrative are communicative processes (Berry & Patti, 2015; Goodall, 2000). Thus, stories rely on and speak to others, including readers (see also Ellis, 2004; Ellis et al., 2011). Through reflexive and introspective immersion in bullying stories, readers also often understand themselves differently as a result of engaging with stories. Also, in Chapter 1 I discussed some of the ways in which the doing of autoethnography creates conditions that make possible and sometimes necessary a making and remaking of researchers' selves (see Berry (2013b) for a discussion on the *processual, contested, breaching, unapologetic,* and *hopeful selves* constituted in this inquiry).

21 Some readers might be wondering about how much significance to put on stories as an anti-bullying response. The book should show that I feel it would be a significant mistake to not try to use stories as a tool for accessing the often overlooked lived experience of youth who experience bullying. It would also be a terrible lapse in judgment to think that many (most?) youth, and for that matter the other constituencies the students and I discussed, don't have stories. At the same time, stories won't solve bullying. Stories can serve as invaluable step, perhaps one of the first couple steps, where adults are unable to understand how to respond. They serve as the invaluable building block to try to get thinking, feeling, and discussion started, and to establish the conditions for empathy, in particular, and understanding, in general, in response to youth ensnarled in the webs of bullying, especially victims. So, I ask readers: What's your story?

APPENDIX

In what follows I offer details on the teaching and research processes that inform this book. I also provide a list of organizations that offer anti-bullying resources.

Teaching

Syllabus

The course syllabus introduced the constitutive approach to interaction and relationships, which assumes that interaction and relationships are culturally situated and intertwined with identity, and informed by a range of influences, including perception, emotion, listening, messages, and conflict. I stress that the course offers a way to "better understand the good and harm that occurs through these ways of relating, and to reflect on and to practice ways of performing as engaged, empathetic, compassionate, and skillful communicators."

The syllabus also speaks to the class theme of bullying, youth, and identity. I described the semester as a way to "explore the ways interpersonal communication and relationships are connected to bullying, and how youth identities are formed through this troubling and intriguing way of relating." I described the "power of stories" to help us learn about bullying, and our lived experience with this societal problem. Also, I emphasized the concepts/practices of "reflexivity" and "mindfulness" as central to using stories in these ways.

Class Readings

I assigned students two books to read for the semester: *IPC* from West and Turner (2011) and *The Four Agreements: A Practical Guide to Personal Freedom* by

Ruiz (1997). We read West and Turner across the first three-quarters of the term and Ruiz during the last week of class. Ruiz offered students an additional way to think and feel about/with mindfulness.

We read additional articles or book passages that spoke to interpersonal communication and conflict, and provided exemplars of autoethnographic research: Adams (2006); Berry (2013a); Boylorn (2013a); Duke (2004); Epstein (2013); Frank (1995); Lamott (1995); Nadal (2013); Pelias (2007); and Ronai (1996). I also provided additional research articles that use autoethnography and personal narrative as optional reading.

The students participated in a "reading response" (discussion facilitation) assignment, which involved pairs of students facilitating group discussion in response to one of the articles about or that used autoethnography.

Films and Videos

We watched two films in full: the award-winning anti-bullying documentary *Bully* and the MTV film *Catfish*, which speaks to online technology, deceptive communication and relationships. Our *Catfish* viewing was meant to highlight interpersonal relationships, not anything related to bullying. We also viewed and discussed a number of short videos, including the YouTube clip of "Karen the Bus Monitor" (see Chapter 1).

Short Writings

Students wrote four "Reflexive Journal Entries." These writing assignments aimed to get them practicing writing and thinking about their personal relationship to bullying. Specific prompts guided their writings:

- *Entry #1*: What is your most powerful memory of bullying? What was the personal impact of that bullying on the person who was bullied? Why is it important to work toward alleviating the problem of bullying?
- *Entry #2*: What is the connection/s between bullying and interpersonal relationships shown in the documentary *Bully*? How does bullying shape relationships?
- *Entry #3*: How powerful is bullying to interpersonal communication? To identity?
- *Entry #4*: The *It Gets Better Project* is an international online organization in which people (e.g., everyday people, celebrities, politicians) make and share online video messages addressed to (largely) LGBTQ. The central message is for these youth to persevere in the face of bullying. Based on your experience, does life with bullying "get better" for youth after high school? Also, how can we *make* it better?

Students wrote fine responses to these writing prompts. I encouraged them to use Entry #1 as a way to experiment with a possible focus for their final class assignment. Many students did so.

Most impressive were many of the students' responses to Entry #4. Most students generally agreed that bullying does "get better" after high school, but not always, not without working on oneself and attending to the lessons they felt bullying teaches youth, especially victims, and it doesn't get completely better (i.e., scars and their impact on youth's well-being don't always fade). Page constraints in the book keep me from including these responses.

Writing

I emphasized for students writing as a multilayered process. I wanted them to practice writing, and to see their relationship to writing in more personal and invested ways. Thus, when discussing the authors we read, I asked them a range of questions: What do you think of the author's writing style? What did she/he, to you, do well? What troubled or confused you? Do you think this might be a style you can model in your bullying story? What style will *you* use?

Students were free to use a writing style of their choosing when writing their bullying stories. But they did need to choose a specific style, and to consistently use that style throughout the paper. I encouraged them consider using one of these writing organizations: *chronological* (temporal organization), *thematic* (conceptual organization); *layered approach* (a "messy text" comprised of diverse story fragments and other information or insights, "layered" into the account); and a *diary entry* approach (story comprising a number of entries written to oneself, as if in a personal diary).

Bullying Narratives: The Essentials

I stressed six aspects for the students about writing their stories:

1. This is a formal project. Spend a considerable amount of time working on your story. Try to write a little each day. Doing well on this project calls you to take the process seriously and put in hard work.
2. Crafting stories is a multilayered process that involves deep reflection, introspection, and working to remember the past. If possible, talk with others about your story, especially people who are familiar with bullying on which you are writing.
3. Write *openly* and *boldly*. Experiment with your "voice" on the page. It may be challenging and even painful to remember and possibly "relive" those experiences. So, be good to yourselves. Only write about issues, and use forms of writing, that allow you to feel safe.

4. Focus mainly on *significant* moments of lived experience with bullying, those that were/are meaningful to you and others. This will help in different ways, especially in terms of your being able to write with clarity and depth in detail.
5. "Show" what happened in your lived experience. In other words, instead of merely "telling" us what happened, creatively bring your lived experience to the page. Set the scene for readers—show what happened with heavy description and evocative detail, inviting readers "into" the bullying you experienced. Make us feel like we're experiencing it with you.
6. Ask yourself: "What lesson about bullying do I want to convey through my story?" Keep your answer in mind/heart as you move through the various stages of the assignment. Maybe even write your answer on a Post-It note that you stick on your computer screen.

Bullying Narratives: Feedback

All students were required to submit rough drafts of their full story to me for feedback. I used the "insert comments" function on Microsoft Word to be able to offer students individualized, descriptive feedback and to try to create a conversational tone in the review process. Most students completed this rough draft assignment. Many students greatly enjoyed being able to receive feedback and in this way.

My comments first and foremost took an encouraging tone about their writing, empathetically acknowledging difficult moments, applauding taken risks, and encouraging students to stay with and keep working on their story. My comments also indicated areas in which I felt the stories needed work. This most frequently related to their needing to write more descriptively and specifically about a given experience of bullying, the opportunity to enhance a moment with more evocative detail, and the need to address how emotions played a role in bullying.

Now that the class is a matter of the past and knowing what I know, I wish I would have assigned a "peer review" process. In this processes, which is similar to one I've used in other classes, especially classes that involve autoethnographic writing, each student selects a "writing partner." I encourage writing partners to get to know each other personally at the beginning of the semester. Writing partners later serve as peer reviewers for the rough draft and final version of the class assignment. I encourage students to use the "insert comments" function, and many have done so and liked that option. Also, I work significantly on what constitutes meaningful feedback.

I would assign peer review because it would give students a chance to receive feedback on their bullying stories from someone other than me, expanding the encouragement and ideas they receive and give. I also love how peer review provides students with a chance to practice leadership, and the giving and getting of direct, candid, and detailed feedback.

Research

The research presented here involved several components. These are some notable examples.

Launch of Project/IRB

In August 2013 I obtained approval (Pro00014179) from the Institutional Review Board (IRB) at the University of South Florida. My protocol called for the inclusion of bullying stories and the Reflexive Journal Entries from all students who agreed to participate in the study. It also included the chance to engage in follow-up conversations as needed.

I did not mention my plans to conduct a study on bullying, or share my hope to use their writings during the semester in which the course was taught. When completing my IRB application, I weighed the potential consequences of doing so, which included students feeling coerced into participating based on the possible belief that participation was a condition of earning a "good grade" in the course.

After posting final course grades, I solicited participation via email in December 2013 by sending each student an informed consent document, along with my request that they review it carefully and let me know at any time if they had questions or concerns. Twenty-two of the 52 students from the class agreed to participate.

Most students agreed with enthusiasm that I have never experienced with past research projects. Their responses mirrored the passion for the issue demonstrated during class discussions. They expressed that they were thrilled to participate, honored that I asked, and excited to do something good with their work. Their investment further fueled my excitement for doing the research and writing this book.

As I mentioned in Chapter 7, each participant in the study had an opportunity to revise and resubmit their stories, but no one chose to do so.

Examining Stories

Once I obtained persons' consent, I spent the next two months reviewing and becoming more familiar with their writing. I spent most of my time immersed in their bullying stories, deepening my consideration of their work. I looked closely at the communicative practices involved with the bullying conveyed in their stories, and the impact the bullying had on relational partners, especially concerning identity.

I moved through each account with a goal of getting to know the story, storyteller, and characters intimately. I decided a story was "grabbing" me if I began to care personally about what was going on in the account and bullying was influencing people's lives. I paid special attention to moments when I experienced strong thoughtful and emotional reactions, especially strong, empathetic responses to violence and pain. I used these ways of orienting to informally clue me in to a given story's promise. Once a story drew me in, I returned my focus to looking again at what the story said about bullying, communication, and identity.

Narrowing and Working with Stories

I selected five stories that make up the five main chapters in this book. A number of overarching questions guided my decision making in this phase: Was the story well written? Was it a "full" story that read in "complete" ways, rather than having a few strong parts and many other weak or missing parts? Did the story speak in compelling ways to identity, and were conceptual ideas conveyed in unique and interesting ways? I also made sure that each story spoke directly to bullying and identity issues and made a unique contribution in its own right.

A challenge when doing this type of a research study is that I could not predict or guarantee good quality writing, or stories that focused on specific concepts or backgrounds. Indeed, the approach required me to work with stories and writings the authors made available. Fortunately, I found an abundance of materials to explore, and even wished I could have included three or four other stories in this book.

However, prior to writing this book, I hoped to include stories from women *and* men. But only a few men agreed to participate in the study, and their stories were not written well enough to be included. In addition, I originally planned for this book to focus on LGBTQ bullying as it is experienced in high school. However, the women's stories didn't really engage such issues, and my stories focused more indirectly on my self-identification, or lack thereof, as a gay boy. I also wished the stories in the book engaged with additional dimensions of culture, exploring more about race, ethnicity, ability status, just for starters. Indeed, this is a different book than I had originally envisioned. Yet, I am also not surprised by the outcome. Research and writing are "methods of inquiry" (Richardson, 1994); the inquiry process itself takes us to unplanned places and teaches us unexpected lessons.

The participants' stories that comprise the first half of the five main chapters in this book come directly and extensively from the papers they submitted for my class. I have worked painstakingly to preserve their voice in telling their stories, working to adhere to the essence of their accounts in both content and style. In order to make them readable in the book, from time to time I needed to edit their stories. I did this mostly in situations of grammatical, punctuation, and spelling errors, and on a few occasions to help make their point clearer. As I describe, each of the women approved of the work I have done in telling their stories.

Continuing Bonds

I stayed in close contact with Iman, Jessi, Jezebel, Lauren, and Ena, for at least two reasons. First, the class experience and their interest in my research kept us in touch. I occasionally reached out to them, gave them updates on my research, and checked in to see how they were doing. In turn, each of these women occasionally wrote me to get a progress report on "the bullying book," and to let me know how happy they were I was writing the book. Other students who agreed to participate in the study but who do not appear in the book, and simply other students from the class, have also kept in touch. All of their investment has been a gift to my research and writing process. I feel grateful for their support.

Second, staying connected with the participants gave me the opportunity to have them review near final drafts of the chapters in which they are featured. We met over lunch or dinner. During our visit, each of the women and I quietly read through the story and my analysis. This approach gave me the chance to gauge their reactions, and to offer support as they returned to painful experiences. I also asked follow-up questions during these and other visits.

The women appeared to appreciate having the chance to read their chapter, and each told me they were excited that their story will appear in the book. Some offered brief clarifications, primarily in terms of names I had gotten wrong. Others wanted to offer more information on a given episode in their story. I made all of the changes to the manuscript prior to submitting the final version for production. Overall, their commentary was informative and supportive.

Resources

The following list offers some of the numerous organizations that provide anti-bullying resources:

- Born This Way Foundation
- Cyberbullying Research Center
- It Gets Better Project
- Mindfulness in Schools Project
- National Communication Association
- Point Foundation
- Stand for the Silent
- U.S. Department of Health & Human Services (StopBullying.gov)
- The Bully Project
- The Resilience Project (American Academy of Pediatrics)
- The Trevor Project

REFERENCES

Adams, T. E. (2006). Seeking father: Relationally reframing a troubled love story. *Qualitative Inquiry, 12*, 704–723.

Adams, T. E. (2011). *Narrating the closet: An autoethnography of same-sex attraction.* Walnut Creek, CA: Left Coast Press.

Adams, T. E., & Berry, K. (2013). "Size matters: Performing (il)logical male bodies on *FatClub.com. Text and Performance Quarterly, 38*, 308–325.

Adams, T. E., Holman Jones, S., & Ellis, C. (2015). *Autoethnography.* New York: Oxford University Press.

Allen, B. J. (2011). *Difference matters: Communicating social identity* (2nd ed.). Long Grove, IL: Waveland Press.

Allison, D. (1996). *Two or three things I know for sure.* New York: Plume.

Alsaker, F. D., & Gutzwiller-Helfenfinger, E. (2010). Social behavior and peer relationships of victims, bully-victims, and bullies in kindergarten. In S. R. Jimerson, S. M. Swearer, & D. L. Espelage (Eds.), *Handbook of bullying in schools: An International Perspective* (pp. 87–100). New York: Routledge.

Anderson, X. (2013). Masculinity and homophobia in high school and college sports: A personal journey from coach to research. In I. Rivers, & N. Duncan, N. (Eds.), *Bullying: Experiences and discourses of sexuality and gender* (pp. 120–131). New York: Routledge.

Arroyo, M. L., & Gomez, M. (Eds.). (2013). *Bullying: Replies, rebuttals, confessions, and catharsis.* New York: Skyhorse Publishing.

Bardhan, N., & Orbe, M. (Eds.). (2012). *Identity research in intercultural communication: Reflections and future directions.* Lanham, MD: Lexington Books.

Batchelor, S. (1997). *Buddhism without beliefs: A contemporary guide to awakening.* New York: Riverhead Books.

Baxter, L. A., & Montgomery, B. M. (1996). *Relating: Dialogues and dialectics.* New York: Guilford Press.

Berry, K. (2005). To the "speechies" themselves: An ethnographic and phenomenological account of emergent identity formation. *International Journal of Communication, 15*, 21–50.

Berry, K. (2006). Implicated audience member seeks understanding in autoethnography: Reexamining the "gift." *International Journal of Qualitative Methods, 15*, 1–12.

Berry, K. (2007). Embracing the catastrophe: Gay body seeks acceptance. *Qualitative Inquiry, 13*, 259–281.

Berry, K. (2012a). Reconciling the relational echoes of addiction: Holding on. *Qualitative Inquiry, 18*, 134–143.

Berry, K. (2012b) (Un)covering the Gay Interculturalist. In N. Bardhan, & M. P. Orbe (Eds.), *Identity research and communication: Intercultural reflections and future directions* (pp. 223–237). Lanham, MD: Lexington Books.

Berry, K. (2013a). Seeking care: Mindfulness, reflexive struggle, and puffy selves in bullying. *Liminalities, 9*, 14–27.

Berry, K. (2013b). Spinning autoethnographic reflexivity, cultural critique, and negotiating selves. In T. E. Adams, S. Holman Jones, & C. Ellis (Eds.), *The handbook of autoethnography* (pp. 209–227). Walnut Creek, CA: Left Coast Press.

Berry, K. (2013c). Storying mindfulness/(re)imagining relational burn. In S. Faulkner (Ed.), *Everyday relational challenges: Readings in relational communication* (pp. 86–96). Walnut Creek, CA: Left Coast Press.

Berry, K. (2014). Introduction: Queering family, home, love, & loss/relational troubling. *Cultural Studies <=> Critical Methodologies, 14*, 91–94.

Berry, K., & Adams, T. E. (2016). Family bullies. *Journal of Family Communication Research, 16*, 51–63.

Berry, K., & Clair, R. P. (2011). Contestation and opportunity in reflexivity: An introduction, *Cultural Studies <=> Critical Methodologies, 11*, 95–97.

Berry, K., & Patti, C. J. (2015). Lost in narration: Applying autoethnography. *Journal of Applied Communication Research, 43*, 263–268.

Bishop Mills, C., & Carwile, A. M. (2009). The good, the bad, and the borderline: Separating teasing from bullying. *Communication Education, 58*, 276–301.

Blumer, H. (1986). *Symbolic interactionism: Perspective and method.* Berkeley: University of California Press.

Bochner, A. P. (1984). The functions of human communication in interpersonal bonding. In C. C. Arnold, & J. W. Powers (Eds.), *Handbook of rhetorical and communication theory* (pp. 544–621). Boston: Allyn & Bacon.

Bochner, A. P. (2001). Narrative's virtues. *Qualitative Inquiry, 7*, 131–157.

Bochner, A. P. (2012). On first-person narrative scholarship: Autoethnography as acts of meaning. *Narrative Inquiry, 22*, 156–164.

Bochner, A. P. (2014). *Coming to narrative: A personal history of paradigm change in the human sciences.* Walnut Creek, CA: Left Coast Press.

Bochner, A.P., & Ellis, C. (2006). Communication as autoethnography. In G. J. Shepherd, J. St. John, & T. Striphas (Eds.), *Communication as ... Perspectives on theory* (pp. 110–122). Thousand Oaks, CA: Sage.

Bochner, A., & Ellis, C. (2016). *Evocative autoethnography: Writing lives and telling stories.* New York: Routledge.

Bond, L., Carlin, J. B., Thomas, L., Rubin, K., & Patton, G. (2001). Does bullying cause emotional problems? A prospective study of young teenagers. *BMJ, 323*, 480–484.

Bosacki, S. L., Marini, Z. A., & Dane, A. V. (2006). Voices from the classroom: Pictorial and narrative representations of children's bullying experiences. *Journal of Moral Education, 35*, 231–245.

Bowes, L., Wolke, D., Joinson, C., Tanya Lareya, S., & Lewis, G. (2014). Sibling bullying and risk of depression, anxiety, and self-harm: A prospective cohort study. *Pediatrics, 4,* 1032–1039.

Boylorn, R. M. (2013a). *Sweetwater: Black women and narratives of resistance.* New York: Peter Lang.

Boylorn, R. M. (2013b). *"Sit with your legs closed!" and other sayin's from my childhood.* In S. Holman-Jones, Tony E. Adams, & Carolyn Ellis (Eds.), *Handbook of Autoethnography* (pp. 173–185). Walnut Creek, CA: Left Coast Press.

Boylorn, R. M., & Orbe, M. P. (Eds.). (2013). *Critical autoethnography: Intersecting cultural identities in everyday life.* Walnut Creek, CA: Left Coast Press.

Brown, P., & Levinson, S.C. (1987). *Politeness: Some universals in language usage.* Cambridge: Cambridge University Press.

Brown, T. B., & Kimball, T. (2013). Cutting to live: A phenomenology of self-harm. *Journal of Marital and Family Therapy, 39,* 195–208.

The Bully Project. (2013). Resources for Educators. www.thebullyproject.com/ (accessed November 1, 2013).

The Bully Project. (2015). Resources for Educators. www.thebullyproject.com/ (accessed October 1, 2015).

Buber, M. (1970). *I and tho.* New York: Touchstone.

Burgoon, J. K., Berger, C. R., & Waldron, V. R. (2000). Mindfulness and interpersonal communication. *Journal of Social Issues, 56,* 105–127.

Canary, D. J., Lakey, S. G., & Sillars, A. L. (2013). Managing conflict in a competent manner: A mindful look at events that matter. In J. G. Oetzel, & S. Ting-Toomey (Eds.), *The SAGE handbook of conflict communication* (2nd ed.) (pp. 263–289). Thousand Oaks, CA: Sage.

Carbaugh, D. (1996). *Situating selves: The communication of social identities in American scenes.* Albany: State University of New York Press.

Carey, J. W. (1989). *Communication as culture: Essays on media and society.* Boston: Unwin Hyman.

Chödrön, P. (2002). *When things fall apart: Heart advice for difficult times.* Boston, MA: Shambhala Publications.

Cissna, K. N., Cox, D. E., & Bochner, A. P. (1990). The dialectic of marital and parental relationships within the stepfamily. *Communication Monographs, 57,* 44–61.

Cloud, J. (2012). The myths of bullying. *Time,* March 12.

Coie, J. D., & Dodge, K. A. (1998). Aggression and antisocial behavior. In W. Damon, & N. Eisenberg (Eds.), *Handbook of Child Psychology* (pp. 779–862). New York: Wiley.

Collins, L. (2008). Friend game: Behind the online hoax that led to a girl's suicide. *New Yorker,* January 21.

Cook, C. R., Williams, K. R., Guerra, N. G., Kim, T. E., & Sadek, S. (2010). Predictors of bullying and victimization in childhood and adolescence: A meta-analytic investigation. *School Psychology Quarterly, 25,* 65.

Cowie, H. (2013). The immediate and long-term effects of bullying. In I. Rivers, & N. Duncan (Eds.), *Bullying: Experiences and discourses of sexuality and gender* (pp. 10–18). New York: Routledge.

Cowie, H., & Jennifer, D. (2008). *New perspectives on bullying.* New York: McGraw-Hill International.

Crawford, L. (1996). Personal ethnography. *Communication Monographs, 63,* 158–170.

Crick, N. R., & Bigbee, M. A. (1998). Relational and overt forms of peer victimization: A multiinformant approach. *Journal of Consulting and Clinical Psychology, 66,* 337–347.

Davis, K., Randall, D. P., Ambrose, A., & Orand, M. (2015). "I was bullied too": Stories of bullying and coping in an online community. *Information, Communication & Society*, *18*, 357–375.

Denzin, N. K. (1988). *Interpretive biography*. Newbury Park, CA: Sage.

DeSalvo, L. (1999). *Writing as a way of healing: How telling our stories transforms our lives*. Boston: Beacon Press.

Duke, J. (2004). Bullies on the adult playground. In P. R. Backlund, & M. R. Williams (Eds.), *Readings in gender communication* (pp. 280–281). Belmont, CA: Thomson/Wadsworth.

Durham, A. (2014). *Hip hop feminism: Performances in communication and culture*. New York: Peter Lang International.

Ellis, C. (1991). Sociological introspection and emotional experience. *Symbolic Interaction*, *14*, 23–50.

Ellis, C. (2004). *The ethnographic I: A methodological novel about autoethnography*. Walnut Creek, CA: AltaMira Press.

Ellis, C. (2007). Telling secrets, revealing lives: Relational ethics in research with intimate others. *Qualitative inquiry*, *13*, 3–29.

Ellis, C. S. (2009). *Revision: Autoethnographic reflections on life and work*. Walnut Creek, CA: Left Coast Press.

Ellis, C., Adams, T. E., & Bochner, A. P. (2011). Autoethnography: An overview. *Forum Qualitative Sozialforschung/Forum: Qualitative Social Research*, *12*, http://nbn-resolving. de/urn:nbn:de:0114-fqs1101108.

Ellis, C., & Bochner, A. P. (2000). Autoethnography, personal narrative, reflexivity: Researcher as subject. In N. Denzin, & Y. Lincoln (Eds.), *The Handbook of Qualitative Research* (pp. 733–768). Thousand Oaks, CA: Sage.

Epstein, M. (2013). *The trauma of being alive*. New York: Penguin/Random House.

Espelage, D., & Low, S. M. (2013). Understanding and preventing adolescent bullying, sexual violence, and dating violence. In E. M. Vera (Ed.), *The Oxford handbook of prevention in counseling psychology* (pp. 163–183). New York: Oxford.

Farrington, D. P. (1993). Understanding and preventing bullying. *Crime and Justice*, *17*, 381–458.

Fassett, D. L., & Warren, J. T. (2007). *Critical communication pedagogy*. Thousand Oaks, CA: Sage.

Felix, E. D., & Green, J. G. (2010). Popular girls and brawny boys: The role of gender in bullying and victimization experiences. In S. R. Jimerson, S. M. Swearer, & D. L. Espelage (Eds.), *Handbook of bullying in schools: An international perspective* (pp. 173–185). New York: Routledge.

Forrow, K. (2012). When the strong grow weak. In K. Boykin (Ed.), *For color boys who have considered suicide when the rainbow is still not enough* (pp. 144–150). New York: Magnus Books.

Foucault, M. (1994). *Ethics: Subjectivity and truth*. In P. Rabinow (Ed.), *Essential works of Foucault, 1954–1984, Vol. I*. New York: New Press.

Fox, R. (2014). Autoarchaeology of homosexuality: A Foucaultian Reading of the Psychiatric-Industrial Complex. *Text and Performance Quarterly*, *34*, 230–250.

Frank, A. W. (1995). *The wounded storyteller: Body, illness, and ethics*. Chicago: University of Chicago Press.

Garfinkel, H. (1967). *Studies in Ethnomethodology*. Englewood Cliffs, NJ: Prentice-Hall.

Geertz, C. L. (1973). *The interpretation of cultures: Selected essays*. New York: Basic Books.

Gergen, K. (1991). *The saturated self: Dilemmas of identity in contemporary life*. New York: Basic Books.

Gergen, K. J. (2009). *Relational being: Beyond self and community*. New York: Oxford University Press.

Glover, D., Gough, G., Johnson, M., & Cartwright, N. (2010). Bullying in 25 secondary schools: Incidence, impact and intervention. *Educational research, 42*, 141–156.

Goffman, E. (1959). *The presentation of self in everyday life*. New York: Anchor Books.

Goffman, E. (1963). *Stigma: Notes on the management of spoiled identity*. Englewood Cliffs, NJ: Prentice Hall.

Goodall, H. L., Jr. (2000). *Writing the new ethnography*. Lanham, MA: AltaMira Press.

Grigg, D. W. (2010). Cyber-aggression: Definition and concept of cyberbullying. *Australian Journal of Guidance and Counselling, 20*, 143–156.

Hanh, T. N. (1975). *The miracle of mindfulness: An introduction to the practice of meditation*. Boston, MA: Beacon Press.

Harachi, T. W., Catalano, R. F., & Hawkins, J. D.(1999). United States. In P. K. Smith, Y. Morita, J. Junger-Tas, D. Olweus, R. Catalano, & P. Slee (Eds.), *The nature of school bullying: A cross-national perspective* (pp. 279–295). New York: Routledge.

Hawker, D. S., & Boulton, M. J. (2000). Twenty years' research on peer victimization and psychosocial maladjustment: A meta-analytic review of cross-sectional studies. *Journal of child psychology and psychiatry, 41*, 441–455.

Heidegger, M. (1996/1953). *Being and time,* trans. J. Stambaugh. Albany: State University of New York Press.

Heinemann, P. P. (1972). *Mobbning – gruppvåld bland barn och vuxna*. Stockholm: Natur och Kultur.

Hinduja, S., & Patchin, J. W. (2008). Cyberbullying: An exploratory analysis of factors related to offending and victimization. *Deviant Behavior, 29*, 129–156.

Hinduja, S., & Patchin, J. W. (2010). Bullying, cyberbullying, and suicide. *Archives of Suicide Research, 14*, 206–221.

Hoff, D. L., & Mitchell, S. N. (2009). Cyberbullying: Causes, effects, and remedies. *Journal of Educational Administration, 47*, 652–665.

Holman Jones, S., & Adams, T. E. (2010). Autoethnography and queer theory: Making possibilities. In N. K. Denzin, & M. G. Giardini (Eds.), *Qualitative inquiry and human rights* (pp. 136–157). Walnut Creek, CA: Left Coast Press.

Holman Jones, S., Adams, T. E., & Ellis, C. (2013). *Handbook of autoethnography*. Walnut Grove, CA: Left Coast Press.

Hymel, S., & Swearer, S. M. (2015). Four decades of research on school bullying: An introduction. *American Psychologist, 70*, 293–299.

Infante, D. A., Riddle, B. L., Horvath, & Tumlin, S. A. (1992). Verbal aggressiveness: Messages and reasons. *Communication Quarterly, 40*, 116–126.

Infante, D. A., & Wigley, C. J. Jr. (1986). Verbal aggressiveness: An interpersonal model and measure. *Communication Monographs, 53*, 61–69.

Jackson II, R. L. (2002). Introduction: Theorizing and analyzing the nexus between cultural and gendered identities and the body. *Communication Quarterly, 50*, 242–250.

Jeffrey, L. R., Miller, D., & Linn, M. (2001). Middle school bullying as a context for the development of passive observers to the victimization of others. *Journal of Emotional Abuse, 2*, 143–156.

Jimerson, S. R., Swearer, S. M., & Espelage, D. L. (2010). *Handbook of bullying in schools: An International Perspective*. New York: Routledge.

Juvonen, J., Graham, S., & Schuster, M. A. (2003). Bullying among young adolescents: The strong, the weak, and the troubled. *Pediatrics, 112*, 1231–1237.

Kilpatrick, H. (2012). *The drama years: Real girls talk about surviving middle school—bullies, brands, body image, and more.* New York: Free Press.

Kimmel, M. S., & Mahler, M. (2003). Adolescent masculinity, homophobia, and violence: Random school shootings, 1982–2001. *American Behavioral Scientist, 46,* 1439–1458.

Kosciw, J. G., Greytak, E. A., Palmer, N. A., & Boesen, M. J. (2014). *The 2013 National School Climate Survey: The experiences of lesbian, gay, bisexual and transgender youth in our nation's schools.* New York: GLSEN.

Kowalski, R. M. (2011). Teasing and bullying. In B. H. Spitzberg, & W. R. Cupach (Eds.), *The darkside of interpersonal communication* (2nd ed.) (pp. 169–197). New York: Routledge.

Kowalski, R. M., & Limber, S. P. (2007). Electronic bullying among middle school students. *Journal of Adolescent Health, 41,* S22–S30.

Kumpulainen, K., & Räsänen, E. (2000). Children involved in bullying at elementary school age: Their psychiatric symptoms and deviance in adolescence: An epidemiological sample. *Child abuse & neglect, 24,* 1567–1577.

Kurzweil, A. (2015). *The forty-year search for my twelve-year-old bully.* New York: Harper.

Laing, R. D. (1967). *The politics of experience.* New York: Pantheon.

Lamott, A. (1995). *Bird by bird: Some instructions on writing and life.* New York: Anchor Books.

Langer, E. L. (1989). *Mindfulness.* New York: Addison-Wesley.

Langsdorf, L. (2002). In defense of poiesis: The performance of self in communicative praxis. In W. McBride and M. B. Matustik (Eds.), *Calvin O. Schrag and the task of philosophy after postmodernity* (pp. 281–296). Evanston, IL: Northwestern University Press.

Leavy, P. (2015). *Method meets art: Arts-based research practice* (2nd ed.). New York: Guilford Press.

Laye-Gindhu, A., & Schonert-Reichl, K. (2005). Nonsuicidal self-harm among community adolescents: Understanding the "whats" and "whys" of self-harm. *Journal of Youth and Adolescence, 34,* 447–457.

Leder, D. (1990). *The absent body.* Chicago, IL: University of Chicago Press.

Li, Q. (2007). Bullying in the new playground: Research into cyberbullying and cyber victimisation. *Australasian Journal of Educational Technology, 23,* 435–454.

Lines, D. (2007). *The bullies: Understanding bullies and bullying.* London: Jessica Kingsley Publishers.

Littlejohn, S. W., & Domenici, K. (2007). *Communication, conflict, and the management of difference.* Long Grove, IL: Waveland Press.

Lutgen-Sandvik, P., Tracy, S. J., & Alberts, J. K. (2007). Burned by bullying in the American workplace: Prevalence, perception, degree and impact. *Journal of Management Studies, 44,* 837–862.

Madison, D. S. (2005). *Critical ethnography: Methods, ethics, and performance* (2nd ed.). Thousand Oaks, CA: Sage.

Martin, J. N., & Nakayama, T. K. (2004). *Intercultural communication in contexts* (3rd ed.). Boston: McGraw Hill.

McRae, C. (2015a). Compassionate critical listening. In J. T. Warren, & D. L. Fassett (Eds.), *Communication: A critical/cultural introduction* (2nd ed.) (pp. 63–78). Thousand Oaks, CA: Sage.

McRae, C. (2015b). *Performative listening: Hearing others in qualitative research.* New York: Peter Laing.

Mead, G. H. (1934). *Mind, self, and society: From the standpoint of a social behaviorist* (Vol. 1). Chicago: University of Chicago Press.

Monks, C. P., & Coyne, I. (Eds.) (2011). *Bullying in different contexts*. Cambridge: Cambridge University Press.

Muehlenkamp, J., & Gutierrez, P. (2004). An investigation of differences between self-injurious behavior and suicide attempts in a sample of adolescents. *Suicide and Life Threatening Behavior, 34*, 12–23.

Muehlenkamp, J., & Gutierrez, P. (2007). Risk for suicide attempts among adolescents who engage in non-suicidal self-injury. *Archives of Suicide Research, 11*, 69–82.

Nadal, K. L. (2013). *That's so gay! Microaggressions and the lesbian, gay, bisexual, and transgender community*. Washington, DC: American Psychological Association.

Nakayama, T. K., & Krizek, R. L. (1995). Whiteness: A strategic rhetoric. *Qualitative Journal of Speech, 81*, 291–309.

Nansel, T. R., Overpeck, M., Pilla, R. S., Ruan, W. J., Simons-Morton, B., & Scheidt, P. (2001). Bullying behaviors among US youth: Prevalence and association with psychosocial adjustment. *Jama, 285*, 2094–2100.

Neiman, S., & Hill, M. R. (2011). Crime, violence, discipline, and safety in U.S. public schools: findings from the school survey on crime and safety: 2009–10 (NCES 2011–320). U.S. Department of Education, National Center for Education Statistics. Washington, DC: U.S. Government Printing Office.

O'Connell, P., Pepler, D., & Craig, W. (1999). Peer involvement in bullying: Insights and challenges for intervention. *Journal of Adolescence, 22*, 437–452.

Olweus, D. (1973). *Hackkycklingar och oversittare: Forskning om skolmobbning*. Stockholm: Almqvist och Wicksell.

Olweus, D. (1993). *Bullying at school: What we know and what we can do*. Oxford: Blackwell.

Olweus, D. (2010). Understanding and researching bullying: Some critical issues. In S. R. Jimerson, S. M. Swearer, & D. L. Espelage (Eds.), *Handbook of bullying in schools: An International Perspective* (pp. 9–33). New York: Routledge.

Olweus, D. (2012). Cyberbullying: An overrated phenomenon?. *European Journal of Developmental Psychology, 9*, 520–538.

Ong, W. J. (1982). *Orality and literacy: The technologizing of the word*. London: Methuen.

Orpinas, P., & Horne, A. M. (2006). *Bullying prevention: Creating a positive school climate and developing social competence*. Washington, DC: American Psychological Association.

Pascoe, C. J. (2007). *Dude you're a fag: Masculinity and sexuality in high school*. Berkeley: University of California Press.

Patchin, J. W., & Hinduja, S. (2013). Resources. The Cyberbullying Research Center. http:// cyberbullying.us/cyberbullying-research-2013-update/ (accessed November 1, 2013).

Patchin, J. W., & Hinduja, S. (Eds.). (2012). *Cyberbullying prevention and response: Expert perspectives*. New York: Routledge.

Pelias, R. J. (2000). The critical life. *Communication Education, 49*, 220–228.

Pelias, R. J. (2004). *A methodology of the heart: Evoking academic and daily life*. Walnut Creek, CA: AltaMira.

Pelias, R. J. (2007). Jarheads, girly men, and the pleasures of violence. *Qualitative Inquiry, 13*, 945–959.

Pelias, R. J. (2015). Moving forward, looking back: A momentary pause. Paper presented at the the Eleventh International Congress of Qualitative Inquiry, Champaign, IL.

Pörhöla, M., Karhunen, S., & Rainivaara, S. (2006). Bullying at school and in the workplace: A challenge for communication research. *Communication Yearbook, 30*, 249.

Rawlins, W. K. (2009). *The compass of friendship: Narratives, identities, and dialogues*. Thousand Oaks, CA: Sage.

Richardson, L. (1994). Writing: A method of inquiry. In N. K. Denzin, & Y. S. Lincoln (Eds.), *Handbook of Qualitative Research* (pp. 516–529). Thousand Oaks, CA: Sage.

Rigby, K. (2001). Health consequences of bullying and its prevention in schools. Doctoral dissertation, Guilford Press.

Rigby, K., & Slee, P. (1999). Suicidal ideation among adolescent school children, involvement in bully—victim problems, and perceived social support. *Suicide and Life-Threatening Behavior, 29,* 119–130.

Rigby, K., Smith, P., & Pepler, D. (2004). Working to prevent school bullying: Key issues. In P. K. Smith, & D. Pepler (Eds.), *Bullying in schools: How successful can interventions be?* (pp. 1–12). New York: Cambridge University Press.

Rivers, I. (2011). *Homophobic bullying: Research and theoretical perspectives.* New York: Oxford University Press.

Rivers, I., & Duncan, N. (Eds.). (2013). *Bullying: Experiences and discourses of sexuality and gender.* New York: Routledge.

Rivers, I., Poteat, V. P., Noret, N., & Ashurst, N. (2009). Observing bullying at school: The mental health implications of witness status. *School Psychology Quarterly, 24,* 211–223.

Ronai, C. R. (1996). My mother is mentally retarded. In C. Ellis, & A. P. Bochner (Eds.), *Composing ethnography: Alternative forms of qualitative writing,* (pp. 109–131).

Ruiz, D. M. (1997). *The four agreements: A practical guide to personal freedom.* San Rafael, CA: Amber-Allen Publishing.

Salas, J. (2005). Using theater to address bullying. *Educational Leadership, 63,* 78–82.

Salmivalli, C. (1999). Participant role approach to school bullying: Implications for interventions. *Journal of adolescence, 22,* 453–459.

Salmivalli, C., Lagerspetz, K., Björkqvist, K., Österman, K., & Kaukiainen, A. (1996). Bullying as a group process: Participant roles and their relations to social status within the group. *Aggressive behavior, 22,* 1–15.

Savage, D., & Miller, T. (Eds.). (2011). *It gets better: Coming out, overcoming bullying, and creating a life worth living.* New York: Penguin/Random House.

Schatzki, T. R., Knorr-Cetina, K., & Von Savigny, E. (2001). *The practice turn in contemporary theory.* New York: Psychology Press.

Schrag, C. O. (1994). *Philosophical papers: Betwixt and between.* Albany, NY: State University of New York.

Schrag, C. O. (1997). *The Self after postmodernity.* New Haven, CT: Yale University Press.

Schrag, C. O. (2003). *Communicative practice and the space of subjectivity.* West Lafayette, IN: Purdue University Press.

Schultze-Krumbholz, A., & Scheithauer, H. (2015). Cyberbullying. In T. P. Gullotta, R. W. Plant., & M. Evans (Eds.), *Handbook of adolescent behavioral problems: Evidence-based approaches to prevention and treatment* (2nd ed.) (pp. 415–428). New York: Springer.

Shotter, J. (1993). *Conversational realities: Constructing life through language.* London: Sage.

Sisaye, S. (2015). Bullying rates drop. Data.Gov. www.data.gov/education/bullying-rates-drop/ (accessed on November 1, 2015).

Slonje, R., & Smith, P. K. (2008). Cyberbullying: Another main type of bullying? *Scandinavian Journal of Psychology, 49,* 147–154.

Slonje, R., Smith, P. K., & Frisén, A. (2012). Processes of cyberbullying, and feelings of remorse by bullies: A pilot study. *European Journal of Developmental Psychology, 9,* 244–259.

Smith, P. (2011). Bullying in schools: Thirty years of research. In C. P. Monks, & I. Coyne, (Eds.), *Bullying in Different Contexts* (pp. 38–60). Cambridge: Cambridge University Press.

Smith, P. K., Mahdavi, J., Carvalho, M., Fisher, S., Russell, S., & Tippett, N. (2008). Cyberbullying: Its nature and impact in secondary school pupils. *Journal of child Psychology and Psychiatry, 49*, 376–385.

Smith, P. K., Morita, Y., Junger-Tas, J., Olweus, D., Catalano, R., & Slee, P. (1999). *The nature of school bullying: A cross-national perspective*. New York: Routledge.

Smorti, A., Menesini, E., & Smith, P. K. (2003). Parents' definitions of children's bullying in a five-country comparison. *Journal of Cross-cultural Psychology, 34*, 417–432.

Solomon, A. (2012). *Far from the tree: Parents, children, and the search for identity*. New York: Scribner.

Stewart, J. (1995). *Language as articulate contact: Toward a post-semiotic philosophy of communication*. New York: State University of New York Press.

Teglasi, H., & Rothman, L. (2001). STORIES: A classroom-based program to reduce aggressive behavior. *Journal of School Psychology, 39*, 71–94.

Thornberg, R., & Knutsen, S. (2011). Teenagers' explanations of bullying. *Child & Youth Care Forum, 40*, 177–192.

Tillmann-Healy, L. M. (2003). Friendship as method. *Qualitative Inquiry, 9*, 729–749.

Turkle, S. (2011). *Alone together: Why we expect more from technology and less from each other*. New York: Basic Books.

Turner, V. (2002). *Secret scars: Uncovering and understanding the addiction of self-injury*. Center City, MN: Hazelden.

Vangelisti, A. L. (1994). Messages that hurt. In W. R. Cupach and B. H. Spitzberg (Eds.), *The darkside of interpersonal communication* (pp. 53–82). Hillsdale, NJ: Erlbaum.

Vogl-Bauer, S. (2014). When disgruntled students go to extremes: The cyberbullying of instructors. *Communication Education, 63*, 429–448.

Warren, J. T. (2001). Absence for whom? An autoethnography of White subjectivity. *Cultural Studies <=> Critical Methodologies, 1*, 36–49.

Watzlawick, P., Bavelas, J. B., & Jackson, D. D. (1967). *Pragmatics of human communication: A study of interactional patterns, pathologies, and paradoxes*. New York: W. W. Norton.

West, R., & Turner, L. H. (2011). *IPC*. Boston: Wadsworth.

Wilmot, W., & Hocker, J. (2011). *Interpersonal Conflict* (8th ed.). New York: McGraw Hill.

Wiseman, R. L. (2002). Intercultural communication competence. In W. B. Gudykunst, & B. Mody (Eds.), *Handbook of international and intercultural communication* (pp. 207–204). Thousand Oaks, CA: Sage.

Wood, J. T. (2015). *Interpersonal communication: Everyday encounters* (8th ed.). Independence, KY: Cengage.

Yep, G. A., Lovaas, K. E., & Elia, J. P. (2003). Introduction: Queering communication: Starting the conversation. In G. A. Yep, K. E. Lovaas, & J. P. Elia (Eds.), *Queer theory and communication: From disciplining queers to queering the discipline(s)* (pp. 1–10). Binghamton, NY: Harrington Park Press.

Yoshino, K. (2007). *Covering: The hidden assault on our civil rights*. New York: Random House.

INDEX

Information in chapter notes denoted by *italicized n*